CHRISTIAN
FIGHTER PILOT
is not an oxymoron

Jonathan C. Dowty

"Christian Fighter Pilot" is not an Oxymoron
By Jonathan C. Dowty

ISBN: 978-0-6151-4453-5

www.ChristianFighterPilot.com

The views expressed in this book are solely those of the author and do not necessar-ily represent the policies or positions of the United States Air Force, Department of Defense, or any other governmental or non-governmental organization.

Oxymoron definition (p.iii) is from Webster's New World College Dictionary, Fourth Edition, MacMillan, USA, 1999.

oxymoron *(äk'si môr'an') n. a figure of speech in which opposite or con-tradictory ideas or terms are combined*

CONTENTS

ACKNOWLEDGEMENTS

THIS BOOK would never have been completed, never mind put into print, without the substantial help of dear friends and family. Each of them had an incalculable impact on my life and this book.

Lt Col Terry Stokka and his wife Artha acted as my family and mentors as I grew as a Christian and Air Force officer. Their example provided the foundation for my life as a Christian officer, and thus they are the proximate source of this entire work. The Stokkas have provided me with invaluable insight, guidance, and advice for living for Christ. I owe them much.

Rick Bereit (Colonel, USAF Retired), author of *In His Service* (Dawson Media, 2002), selflessly volunteered an immense amount of professional editing and insightful experience in communicating the military Christian lifestyle. His critiques were indispensable.

MSgt Billy Bailey, a Christian brother and role model, reviewed the manuscript in its early and difficult stages. His editing was instrumental to this book, and my family has been blessed with the friendship of his family.

Finally, my wife Beth has been a patient, loving, and encouraging soulmate since the day we were married. While I was writing, she weathered the days that the computer seemed to get more attention than she did, and her English expertise provided invaluable guidance to the sometimes interloping project. This book would not have been completed without her encouragement and support, and my life is complete only with her.

Without God, the builder labors in vain. He has brought me thus far. May it all be for His glory.

INTRODUCTION

SOMEONE ONCE SAID that being a fighter pilot is like being in a motorcycle gang, except that your mother is still proud of you. I now understand how true that statement really is. This book focuses on the spiritual challenges that confront the Christian fighter pilot. The broader lessons will certainly apply outside the world of the fighter pilot, but the day-to-day specifics may be foreign even to pilots of other kinds of aircraft.

I don't mean to imply that only fighter pilots face spiritual challenges; *any* Christian in the world faces the potential of ridicule and scorn for living out his faith. The reason I direct this book to fighter pilots is because of the degree of antagonism in the fighter pilot world. Fighter pilots have worked hard to develop a reputation for being exceptionally worldly. I'd be pleased if others find application for Christian living in their world outside of the military. This book, however, is written primarily for those who are heading into the fighter pilot community. It is meant neither to encourage people to become fighter pilots nor to discourage them from doing so. The intent is to give Christians information to prepare them for the fighter pilot life, if that's what they choose. My hope is that those who are heading down the same path I did will have a bit more light to guide their way.

The inspiration for this book came first through the instruction of God in my own life. Though I became a Christian at a fairly young age, I have struggled to live an *active* Christian life. I sought God's counsel many times and had many internal arguments about what I should and should not do as a fighter pilot and as a Christian; much of this book is the verbalization of those debates. Then, I was surprised when I noticed younger Christians entering the fighter pilot world—they were challenged with many of the same issues I had faced, and many were completely unprepared to make Biblically-based decisions about those challenges, just as I had been. I was unable to provide them as much help as I wanted; I found myself unable to sufficiently articulate the secular and spiritual reasons for the decisions I had made in the face of the pressures they, too, were experiencing. I began writing the early pages of this book to capture my ideas so I could better support my fighter pilot brothers in Christ.

Finally, I was disheartened by the examples of military leaders I saw who claimed to be Christians but lived no differently than non-Christians. I've met few good examples of Christian fighter pilots in the higher ranks of the military, and I wanted to prove that a Christian could indeed be a fighter pilot and still be a Godly person. Many people in this world—and many fighter pilots themselves—assume that being a Christian and a fighter pilot are mutually exclusive. Many fighter pilots who may be Christians today reinforce that assumption when they live in a way that is inconsistent with Christianity in order to be successful. My objective is to demonstrate the fallacy of that inconsistent lifestyle, to persuade fighter pilots—those that are and those that would be—that "Christian Fighter Pilot" is not an oxymoron.

PART 1:
FIGHTER PILOT FOUNDATIONS

Chapter 1:
Operation IRAQI FREEDOM

FLYING FASTER THAN THE SPEED OF SOUND, pouncing on enemy aircraft, swirling—outnumbered—in an aerial dogfight, landing to the cheers of a crowd after saving the day—glorious are the visions that most people have of the typical American Fighter Pilot. Robert Duvall (*The Great Santini*), Tom Cruise (*Top Gun*), and even Will Smith (*Independence Day*) have portrayed the cigar-smoking, beer-drinking, hard-nosed, arrogant fighter pilot who pushes the limits, beats the bad guys, and comes home victorious. Obviously, there is significantly more to the story. Few people know or understand the years of training a fighter pilot endures or the impact the demanding life has on his family. Rarer still are depictions of fighter pilots who have an active and evident faith in God. This is caused in part by cliché—most stereotypical fighter pilot traits are inconsistent with what even non-Christians understand to be a Christian lifestyle. Another cause is fact—there are few examples of Christian fighter pilots. I am one of them.

I became a fighter pilot in the fall of 2001. I arrived at my first operational assignment in the F-16 in October 2001, nearly 2 years after I had initially soloed in pilot training. I was assigned to the 23rd Fighter Squadron at Spangdahlem Air Base, Germany. The 23rd flew the Block 50 F-16CJ, a version whose specialty was SEAD—Suppression of Enemy Air Defenses. SEAD was the premier mission for helping other aircraft achieve their objectives. It was born in Vietnam, when aircraft would bait surface-to-air missile (SAM) sites to get them to activate their radars; they would then attempt to shoot the SAM site with radar-seeking missiles before the SAM site shot them. It was a dangerous game of cat and mouse but honorable—and prestigious. Men would risk their lives to protect others so that they could accomplish their missions. It was a mission that meant something. The primary weapon of an F-16CJ was the AGM-88 HARM (High-speed

Anti-Radiation Missile), a 13-foot 1,000 pound missile that homed on SAM sites and destroyed their radars. Other versions of the F-16 dropped bombs using a targeting pod; the TV-like video from the pod gave immediate feedback of the attack and also looked splendid on the TV news. With no targeting pod, there was no such feedback for a HARM shot.[1] F-16s also carried four air-to-air missiles: 3 radar-guided AIM-120s and one heat-seeking AIM-9. Our Gatling gun could be used for air or ground targets and held 510 rounds of ammunition—enough for a mere 5 second trigger squeeze. The F-16 also carried a jamming pod and 12,000 pounds of fuel, which was enough for about a 2-hour sortie. This was the first version of the F-16 I flew, and the first I would fly into combat.

Because of the nature of the modern political world, some fighter pilots may go their entire careers without fighting a war. It is as much a result of timing and world events as anything else. I had the unique opportunity to "do my job" as a lowly lieutenant during my first assignment. In February of 2003 I joined a large group of servicemen sent to the Persian Gulf in support of Operation IRAQI FREEDOM (OIF). During the build-up, troops were readied and stood down alternately for weeks on end. I found out that I was leaving for the Middle East less than two days before I got on the plane. In a peculiar turn of events, we traveled from Europe to the Middle East on Miami Air, part of the Civil Air Fleet the President had recently activated. We had a short stopover for fuel in Sicily and then finished our flight to Al Udeid Air Base, located in the Persian Gulf nation of Qatar.

Qatar's support of our operations in Iraq was discrete but not secret. International news briefings occurred in the gulf's primary command and control center in the country, but the amount and type of combat firepower located in the small Arabic country was downplayed. We lived in Camp Andy, a tent city that housed the entire base population. The tents varied in size, but most were 12 men to a tent and some larger tents held nearly 75 people. We erected shower curtain walls to separate us from the snoring of the person sleeping in the cot bumped up against ours. As had happened in the previous gulf war, 24 hour operations became the rule, and we altered everyone's schedule so that a new shift started every 6 hours. This meant that a large group of people had to get used to being awake at night, rather than the normal day shifts we'd been on since arriving. The swing from day to night had to come relatively quickly for pilots, because being unable to fly because of fatigue, or becoming dysfunctional during the sortie for the same reason, were not options. We capitalized on a rare day off just before the war started, but some people opted to get help from the flight surgeons, who provided sleeping pills (also called *no-go* pills). The medication enabled us to sleep through a day and thus stay up all night; once on the new schedule, the pills were no longer necessary.

The doctors also occasionally provided what were popularly dubbed *go pills*, which gave tired pilots alertness without the diuretic or jittery side

---

[1]Recent upgrades have given even the Block 50 F-16s the ability to carry targeting pods.

effects of caffeine. Go pills had been associated with a fratricide incident in Afghanistan when an American F-16 dropped a bomb on members of the Canadian army. While the connection between the pills and the pilot's actions was based more in the news media than reality, the incident made them politically unpalatable. Flight doctors still issued the go pills when combat missions dictated their necessity, but they also started offering super-caffeinated tubes of pudding as an alternative. The pudding essentially did the same job but had all the side effects of caffeine that the pills had avoided. I never had cause to use the go pills; I took off and landed during hours of darkness, which kept my body from being significantly affected by the environment. The pilots that had the greatest challenge were those who were on their way home from their tiring mission just as the sun started rising. The combined effects of the fatiguing sortie, the "relaxing" hour and a half flight home, and the rising sun provided a significant challenge to pilots who still had to navigate and land their aircraft. Anecdotally, the group of pilots who flew in that shift relied most heavily on medication, primarily near the end of their sortie to increase their alertness prior to landing.

In the combat environment there was the potential risk that the enemy would attempt to attack our aircraft and bases even outside the borders of Iraq. While our airfield was well outside of the main battle area, in the modern era of unconventional warfare and terrorist attacks the threat was still quite real. To mitigate the risk against departing aircraft we conducted *combat departures*. During such a take off, my flight lead would take the runway, turn off his lights, and immediately plug his engine into afterburner. I followed suit 20 seconds later. As soon as we reached take off speed we rotated, got airborne, and raised the landing gear. We leveled off 50 to 100 feet above the runway. In maximum afterburner, even with a full combat load of fuel and weapons, we could accelerate to almost 500 knots by the time we reached the end of the runway. As we passed the end of the runway at low altitude, we pulled the nose up to nearly 90° high, enabling us to climb at an exceptionally fast rate within the confines of the base perimeter, which was patrolled and secured. Passing through 10,000 feet a few seconds later we would let the nose fall off to one side or simply lay the jet over on its back and head north.

While there was little for us to see from the air at night, particularly in our desert environment, the combat departures were impressive to watch from the ground. The afterburners shook the ground even in Camp Andy some distance from the runway. As we stood on the homemade porch outside our tents we could hear the aircraft accelerate down the runway. As the sound dissipated slightly we peered at where we knew the end of the runway was; a few seconds later we would see a small, bright light—the plume of the afterburner—suddenly appear and rapidly shoot up into the sky. It had the eerie appearance of a SAM launch or a reverse shooting star. Once at altitude my flight lead would turn his lights back on and we would rejoin for the hour and a half flight up to the combat area.

In February 2003 I went on my first combat sortie. It was "combat time" only in the academic sense of the term. The US and Britain had been enforcing the southern and northern no-fly zones over Iraq for over 12 years, and my first combat time was a brief sortie in support of Operation SOUTHERN WATCH (OSW), before it became OIF a month later. Our callsign was Pistol 25; we took off out of Al Udeid long after sunset, tasked to provide SEAD protection for the many coalition aircraft that would be flying over Iraq. The weather was poor, but we completed the first hour and a half of the sortie uneventfully as we flew up the gulf, talking primarily to the US Navy air traffic controllers who filled the water below us. The flight up the gulf was one of the more boring parts of the sortie. A few pilots had even confessed to nearly falling asleep in the cockpit when they turned on their autopilot and automatically navigated the route to the tanker tracks.

We received gas in the chaotic air-to-air refueling tracks that lined the border between Iraq, Kuwait, and Saudi Arabia. Though the Air Force has made significant advances in aerial refueling over the past 50 years, it is still a test of a pilot's skills. More than 20 tankers were in the refueling tracks, making tanker rendezvous one of the more dangerous parts of the sortie. The tracks were crowded with aircraft going to and from the tankers from all directions. On at least one occasion in the refueling tracks my lead and I passed another flight of aircraft going the opposite direction—it was at night and in the weather, so we only saw a quick flash, but we passed close enough to hear their engines and feel their jet wash. Flight leads faced the challenge of finding the correct tanker, completing a rendezvous while not running into any of the other tankers or fighters, and then receiving gas.

To aerial refuel, a fighter matches the tanker's altitude, attitude, and airspeed to pull to within 20 feet of an aircraft the size of an airliner. He then maintains that precise position while the boom operator moves the probe and connects with the air-to-air refueling port; on an F-16, the port is behind the cockpit on the spine of the jet. The pilot flies in tight formation on the tanker—within a window of only a few feet—for 5 to 15 minutes, depending on how much fuel he needs. It is not an easy thing to do, but it is one of many things fighter pilots pride themselves on doing well. Occasionally fighter pilots charge each other "fines" (like a case of beer) for tanker "buffoonery," such as falling off the boom (sliding so far aft that the probe disconnects) or, worse yet, causing the tanker to *breakaway*, in which the tanker and receiver do an emergency separation because the fighter has gotten too close to the tanker. Proficient pilots are able to effect rapid rejoins and get a four-ship across the boom in short order.

After leaving the tanker we checked in with the airborne controller and found that we were one of the first flights to arrive. Weather along the northern coast of the gulf had kept most of the other aircraft on the ground. As we crossed into Iraqi airspace my flight lead told me to *fence in*, meaning set my switches for combat operations, and we prepared for the actual combat portion of our sortie. A few calls from the controller soon made us realize that we were the first to enter the airspace and the furthest north

6

when the entire OSW package was cancelled. We turned south and exited the airspace, as did the few aircraft that had entered behind us. We still had plenty of fuel and so turned directly back over the gulf and made our way back to Qatar. We had been in Iraqi airspace for only a few minutes, with a thick undercast below us obscuring our view of the land (and preventing the hostile forces below from seeing us). Still, in accordance with Air Force regulations, by virtue of having entered hostile airspace we had flown a "combat" sortie, and all our flight time, from take off to landing, counted as combat time. For having touched the airspace of Iraq I logged over 3 hours of combat flight time. We landed uneventfully well into the night.

Our reunions with the KC-135 and KC-10 tankers were unfortunately frequent. Our fuel load enabled us to fly about an hour and fifteen minutes between each refueling. That gave us enough extra gas to land at a friendly airbase if for some reason we were unable to refuel. On average we refueled 3 to 6 times a night, with sortie lengths of 4 to 8 hours. The duration of our sorties was fatiguing, particularly given our cramped cockpits. We were unable to stretch, much less get up and walk around as some could in other aircraft. Many pilots developed body sores from less than perfect-fitting equipment; some night pilots were distinguishable by red marks on the bridges of their noses, which carried the weight of their night vision goggles (NVGs) for the duration of the sortie.

Our F-16CJs would often be assigned to protect a specific strike package or asset, which could be anything from slow moving A-10s to the silent, swooping B-2s. Early in the conflict some flights, like the A-10s and the British Tornadoes, specifically requested SEAD before they entered their target area. Others, like B-1s and B-2s, would often "accept" the SEAD coverage but would generally plan on entering their strike zone even if the F-16CJs could not provide protection, relying on their self-protection systems or stealth as their primary means of defense. A few days into the war it became evident that the SAMs would be a little menace. Years of sanctions and the effectiveness of our anti-radar weapons had made most of their defense systems and operators work with limited efficacy. Our primary threat was unguided anti-aircraft artillery (AAA, or "triple A") and ballistic (unguided) SAMs, which were really no threat at all given the low probability that an aircraft and the missile would coincidentally end up in the same piece of sky.

This is the same belief from previous wars that an aircraft would be downed not by a dramatic surface-to-air intercept but by a "golden BB." The AAA was only effective at lower altitude and the Iraqi gunners had demonstrated no ability to down any coalition aircraft. I had seen my first AAA barrage while flying an OSW sortie; while impressive as a glowing fireworks display, it was obviously being randomly sprayed into the air by gunners hoping to get lucky. A few pot shots were taken at various aircraft but no missiles had even been guided through an engagement; since the radars were staying off, they were little threat, and the radar-killing SEAD platforms had little at which to shoot. The surface threat was so low, in fact, that SEAD squadrons soon stopped outfitting their flights solely with HARMs. Our role of suppressing SAMs was being so underutilized that we began to fly mixed elements, with one aircraft carrying HARMs and the other bombs. It was only the necessary reassurance of the presence of SEAD support to the coalition packages that prevented us from totally switching from HARMs to bombs.

Unlike other aircraft, the Block 50 F-16s did not launch with assigned targets; this meant that to expend our bombs we had to find someone who would assign us a target and give us permission to drop. At any one time my flight lead and I might have been on four different frequencies on each of our two radios, each trying to find a controller who wanted us to strike a target. There were two primary sources of target information. The first was AWACS (Airborne Warning and Control System), one of the multiple E-3 Sentry aircraft controlling the airspace and battle area. They often passed information from the command and control cell, callsign *K-Mart*, if the cell had received information on a target of opportunity. These targets varied greatly but generally had some strategic purpose and were often based on sensitive, perishable intelligence.

When an intelligence source revealed, for example, that the Iraqi leadership was at a known location, or if a targeting system had found one of the elusive mobile Scud launchers, K-Mart would pass the coordinates of the high-priority target through AWACS to us or one of the other aircraft that had available bombs. We would then enter the data into our systems and proceed to attack the target. In some other instances we simply monitored other flights' target data and then provided them SEAD coverage while they attacked. The second source of targeting information was a Forward Air Controller (FAC) assigned to either the Army or Marines. These targets were primarily military vehicles or occasionally a bridge or other structure that was tactically important to the ground unit. After a flight from our squadron successfully found a "lucrative" frequency they would pass that information on to new flights as they checked in, so new flights could go directly to that radio channel. While our more interesting targets were assigned by AWACS, our greatest number of successes came with the FACs, particularly with the Marines on the eastern front.

My flight lead generally carried our flight's bombs while I carried the HARMs. Since there were few opportunities to fire a HARM, in all my combat sorties I hit the pickle button (fired a weapon) on only one occasion. One other squadron pilot who flew as many sorties as I did never expended ordnance. The sole time I pickled was during an attack on an Iraqi SA-2 site. My flight lead was directed by AWACS to drop his bombs on the SAM site's missile launcher. As we attacked the SAM, he directed me to fire a preemptive HARM, which would guide on the radar if it turned on as we approached; this was a standard practice that we trained to nearly every day at home. When I fired the HARM it left my right wing like a bottle rocket; I tried to follow its plume with my NVGs as it arced into the distance but it quickly disappeared. The radar site never turned on, and I never saw any indication of the impact of my missile. I later realized that on our way to the target we had passed another two-ship from our squadron that had been tasked against the site's radar—the radar hadn't threatened us because it had almost certainly been destroyed. I hit the pickle button one time during the entire conflict, and I was somewhat disappointed that I had expended a missile on what was probably a dead radar site, though it was not a risk we could afford to take. Prowling for SAM sites that never turned on didn't seem prestigious, but it was the very threat of an inbound HARM—demonstrated time and again in the first gulf war—that had convinced the SAM operators not to turn on their radars in the first place. No aircraft were lost due to Iraqi radar guided ground threats, so the SAM-suppressing F-16CJs were doing their job well.

Though surface threats were rare, there were occasions when we were endangered. During a daylight sortie another flight from my squadron was targeted by an SA-2 as they headed back to the tanker; two missiles streaked off the launcher as the flight lead maneuvered and the wingman fired a HARM back at the site. The SAM operator had left his radar off as long as possible so as to conceal their position from our sensors. As soon as they realized they had been targeted by a HARM they shut down their guidance radar, causing their missiles to miss.

On one of my night sorties my flight flew north of Baghdad and I was "lit up" by (targeted by the radar of) an SA-2. I quickly keyed the radio and called out, "Wicked 19, mud 2 south, defending 090"—everyone now knew that I was being illuminated by an SA-2 and that I was defending. I maneuvered my jet to defeat the SAM threat and looked through my NVGs in the direction of the radar site to search for inbound missiles. I did not expect to see any, as there had been few SA-2 launches and many false radar locks. I heard another SEAD flight call *empty*, meaning they were searching for the SA-2 that was targeting me but were unable to see it. After a few defensive maneuvers the SA-2 radar went back off air. After we returned to base my flight lead asked me why I had expended flares during my defensive maneuvers, and I told him that I hadn't. It was only then that we realized that the SA-2 radar had been used to cue AAA; the flashes he thought were flares were actually AAA bursts following my aircraft as the ground gunners used the SA-2 radar to track me. It was an innovative, though ineffective, tactic.

Nearly a week after full-blown hostilities had started my flight lead and I were targeted against what we would later affectionately refer to as the Baghdad "Blue Room." Baghdad had been the former home of what was called the "Super MEZ," a name for the multiple overlapping missile engagement zones (MEZ) from all the SAMs that were in the city. However, the complete lack of missile launches from the area in the previous week had caused some to ridicule the dramatic moniker by renaming it the "Mini MEZ." Regardless, attacks by a variety of aircraft had occurred in Baghdad over the preceding week with no significant Iraqi response. On this particular occasion, AWACS tasked us to destroy a target in Baghdad; it was a unique opportunity to "go downtown" and employ ordnance on what sounded like a high-value target.

My flight lead turned us north and we headed to the well-lit city of Baghdad. I was carrying two HARMs, but, again, there had been few radar sites on air up to that point in the war. We made sure our cameras were on and we "armed hot" so that we could employ ordnance quickly when required. My systems indicated no radar threats on air as we ingressed. It soon became evident, though, that the defenders on the ground could hear our jets approaching. In my NVGs I could see low caliber AAA well below us. I was flying in a tactical formation about a mile and half from my flight lead. As we neared the target I transitioned from looking at my systems to primarily looking outside and scanning for surface threats below us, since we were now directly overhead the Iraqi capital city.

I looked behind my flight lead to check for threats, and as I brought my head back forward I saw a flash and burst between our aircraft. A large AAA gun had managed to either track our sound or get lucky and explode a single round directly between our aircraft, exactly equal to our altitude. I moved my formation wider. A few moments later my flight lead dropped his bombs, and we egressed the target area to the south and east, leaving Baghdad's airspace. We were able to see the impact of my flight lead's bombs, but since we didn't have any kind of targeting pod we could not judge whether or not a target had actually been destroyed. We passed this information to the controllers, checked out, and then hit the tanker on the way home. The Blue Room event was one of perhaps two when I actually thought that I was at risk; even then it was but for a minute, and it was the result of a single, lucky AAA shot.

Though I was occasionally reminded of the risk, during my entire stay I never experienced fear for my life, either in the air or on the ground. Our base was on a peninsula in the Persian Gulf, relatively distant from the fighting in Iraq and low even in potential terrorist threat. Prior to the outbreak of hostilities, a small civilian aircraft had approached the airfield undetected, much to the chagrin of the Patriot batteries ringing the base. During the war, the presence of a light aircraft near the base was the cause of the only increased threat condition during our stay. The base rapidly went from MOPP 0, a protective posture where no chemical protection gear is worn, to MOPP 4, where full gear—heavy overgarments, boots, gas masks, and gloves—is required. This occurred during the night while I was airborne, so I knew of it only second-hand. Whatever it was that approached the base turned out to be no threat, and there were no further reactions while we were there. In fact, a few days before I returned home they brought the base out of lock-down and allowed us to leave the base to see the local area.

Our home was a fairly safe one, particularly when compared to the airbases further north that came under fire from Scuds and other missiles and were in a MOPP 4 fairly frequently. Our route to and from the combat area was also safe. While we flew along the gulf we were in range of several neutral countries, but we could virtually walk along the US Navy sea craft up the gulf to Iraq. The true threat only began once in Iraq, and even then the threat was minimal. With AAA such a minor threat, no enemy air force, and SAMs virtually unused, our combat flights took on the tone of training sorties with the caveat that the remote golden BB—which we could do nothing about—might find us. Some pilots even considered the American defenses a higher threat than the Iraqi ones; due to failures on many levels, the "friendly fire" of US Patriots had downed twice as many coalition aircraft as had the Iraqis.

Occasionally, events reminded us of the risk we faced. While headed into the tanker track on one sortie I observed two bright explosions just north of us near our altitude: Patriots had intercepted a missile inbound to a Kuwaiti base. The sorties also took on a more serious tone when aircraft went down; the coalition lost aircraft to mechanical malfunctions, pilot error, and US Army Patriots. In late March a British Tornado was shot down by a Patriot while on approach to land. In early April an F-18 was shot down, again by a Patriot. An F-15E was also lost in April. When emergency events occurred, pilots did go above and beyond to attempt to rescue and protect those on the ground. We also attempted to provide as much assistance as possible to the other coalition members and services. My flight was tasked during one sortie to provide SEAD coverage to a US Army deep helicopter strike. We covered our assigned period and then continued to monitor the general area. Though we never observed any radar sites on air, the Army experienced tremendous ground fire and severely damaged several helicopters that night. When one helicopter made frantic emergency radio calls, my flight and virtually every other one on frequency offered assistance through AWACS. The next day we saw two captured helicopter crewmen on TV. With those few exceptions, the vast majority of our sorties were routine, and hardly more dangerous than those we practiced in the skies over our home base.

While routine, our missions were still highly visible, given the immediate and worldwide news coverage of every event. When a missile exploded in a downtown Iraqi market, all our pilots had to review their tapes and collect data on the precise locations of their HARM shots to preclude the possibility it had been one of our missiles. In the end, not only was the explosion not caused by our squadron, it was determined to have not been caused by any US weapon. It was likely the result of an Iraqi SAM that, like everything fired into the air, must eventually come down.

The majority of our sorties carried a similar threat to the training sorties we accomplished on a nearly daily basis. While the low level of risk may have made our families feel better, the lack of real danger actually had a restraining affect on a Christian's ability to talk about God. In the military there is the oft-quoted phrase that "there are no atheists in a foxhole" because the mortal threat forces even the most unbelieving men to acknowledge a Supreme Power. The majority of fighter pilots, though, did not experience any mortal threat, but felt as though they were at the "big show" and therefore accomplishing the "fighter pilot dream." This had the regrettable effect of reinforcing the godless lifestyles and attitudes of the pilots, rather than drawing men to God as they faced their own mortality. I made no secret of my Christianity; still, combat did not present any direct witness opportunities. In fact, my flight lead throughout the majority of the conflict was a self-described atheist. He joked that we'd know it "got bad" when I started drinking and he started believing in God. On a spiritual level, it may be unfortunate that it never did.

Another unfortunate consequence of the lack of a true threat was the apparent willingness of some pilots to put *themselves* in danger. With our sorties increasingly feeling like training flights, a few pilots overcame airborne boredom with less than respectable choices. Some pilots maneuvered their flights into scenarios that made them more exciting, often inviting a response from the Iraqi surface gunners. One example was the "hard deck" established for most aircraft at about 10,000 feet. Above that altitude the unguided AAA was virtually worthless, but below it the potential for a golden BB strike increased dramatically. While I know of no pilot who actually violated that rule, I do know one flight lead who positioned his formation at exactly 10,000 ft—well below our normal tactical altitude—directly over the outskirts of Baghdad. It is true he was there for a reason: he had been tasked to protect aircraft striking targets in the city and he effectively did so. But in choosing to fly low over a high threat area he attracted the attention of the Iraqi gunners and exposed his flight to ground fire.

When he landed he proudly related how his flight had come under enemy fire as they bravely protected the high value assets striking priority targets in the heart of the Iraqi capital—on the surface an amazing and heroic event. In fact, he had taken a routine mission and needlessly endangered his flight for no other purpose than to have a story to tell. Though his choices were not representative of the majority of the squadron, he was not the only one to have participated in marginally motivated actions in the air. In other cases, pilots expended flares at night to highlight their positions, flew below their required minimum fuels, and orbited over or near known anti-aircraft positions, all without any imperative mission requirement to do so. Each time, the increased threat of the sortie led them to recount their tales bravely to the rest of us on their return, and the glory of the sortie, as well as the "heroism and imminent danger," would no doubt make its way into a recommendation for a medal.

Fighter pilots are natural storytellers; with the need to communicate threat, target, and intelligence data from every sortie, most pilots were aware of each other's actions. The stories that circulated the squadron led to a series of one-upmanship. I once flew in a mixed element with my flight lead carrying the bombs and myself the HARMs. On this particular night, we dropped one bomb in Baghdad and one in the southern part of Iraq on a target designated by the Marines. After he had dropped his two bombs, my lead reported to the Marine FAC that we were *winchester*, or out of ammunition, and we headed home. After landing I half-jokingly reminded him that while he was out of bombs, we hadn't been out of ordnance: between us we still had 1,000 rounds of 20mm bullets in our guns. The next night I was assigned to the planning cell, and my flight lead went out with another wingman—he dropped both bombs and both pilots made several strafing passes with the gun. After he had opened the door, several other pilots started strafing with their flights. From high altitude, though, where we were required to remain, the 20mm rounds were ineffective; the potential that pilots would bend the rules to do more with the gun, along with several other factors, resulted in the order that strafing only be accomplished to support troops in desperate need.

The invasion was completed in relatively short order, though combat would continue for some time in the form of an insurgency. Since the Iraqi military no longer posed a SAM threat to coalition aircraft, our unit was one of the first to go home. Though not pristine, our unit had done its job and done it well. I felt I made a positive contribution to the Air Force and my country. I wondered, though, if I could have done something better as a *Christian* fighter pilot.

Chapter 2:
The Making of a Fighter Pilot

IT TOOK TWO YEARS OF FLIGHT TRAINING before I officially became a fighter pilot. I graduated from the United States Air Force Academy (USAFA) in 1999.[1] I had chosen USAFA because of its academic degrees, closeness with flying, and the fortuitous lack of tuition. In my graduating class there were more pilot slots available than pilot-qualified cadets to fill them, so all medically-qualified cadets were guaranteed a pilot training job if they wanted one; this was an impressive opportunity since pilots are an elite group that make up less than 4% of the total Air Force population.[2] I started my year-long Undergraduate Pilot Training (UPT) in August of 1999 at Laughlin Air Force Base in Del Rio, Texas.

After a month of classes learning the academic concepts of flight and navigation, we started learning basic flight in the T-37, a twin engine jet trainer with the instructor pilot (IP) and student sitting side-by-side. The 1950s era plane had an agonizing high-pitched engine sound and was nick-named the *Tweet*.[3] It was in this aircraft that we were taught the fundamentals of take off, landing, and instrument flight. The first flight in UPT is traditionally called a *dollar ride*, a term which is sometimes applied to the

---

[1] Air Force fighter pilots must be commissioned officers. They can be commissioned through the US Air Force Academy (USAFA), Officer Training School (OTS), or the Reserve Officer Training Corps (ROTC) college program. The Army and Navy have similar programs, including the US Military Academy at West Point and the US Naval Academy at Annapolis. Each of the Academies also allows *cross-commissioning*, meaning a graduate of any Academy can be commissioned in any one of the services.

[2] "Service Demographics Offer Snapshot of Force," 10/13/2005, Air Force News, http://www.af.mil/news/story.asp?storyID=123012106. Viewed 9 March 2007.

[3] Not long after my class graduated, the Air Force began phasing the aging T-37s out of service and replacing them with the single-engine T-6A Texan II, a tandem-seat turboprop that vastly outperformed the Tweet.

first flight in any flying training program in a new aircraft. The student is so clueless and the IP has to demonstrate (and thus fly) so much that the student is essentially a passenger. Traditionally, the student gives the IP of his first sortie a dollar bill as a "tip" for the ride. The dollars are often decorated with magazine clippings (some more risqué than others), phrases, or other details that might characterize the flight, the student, or the IP. Many UPT instructors' desks were littered with laminated, vandalized dollar bills.

The journey from dollar ride to first solo is amazingly short. In October 1999, only one month after my first flight, I soloed for the first time in an Air Force jet. I took off with an IP first; after he was confident I could fly without killing myself (or getting him in trouble), we landed and shut down one engine. He climbed out, I restarted the engine, and I launched again with an empty seat next to me. Flying alone for the first time inspired confidence, though it was somewhat unnerving—it was well-known that solo student pilots would hear noises and feel things in the jet that they never experienced before. There wasn't anything wrong with the jet; the solo pilots were simply more aware of every creak and groan of the aircraft. After I landed from my first solo flight I was dunked by my fellow classmates in the solo pool, a small swimming pool where all the student pilots who had successfully soloed were soaked. Thus began my military flying career.

A few pilots were eliminated (washed out) early in the program, and one quit (self-initiated elimination, or SIE) when he decided that flying just wasn't for him. Pilot training was challenging, and many people got discouraged when "mean" instructors were hard on them or when they hooked (failed) rides. Still, a few IPs took time to encourage the students. One of our IPs had a particularly harsh reputation. While flying with one of my fellow students he said, "I have the aircraft," and took control away from the student. "Take a look at yourself in the mirror," he said. T-37s had adjustable rearview mirrors on both sides of the cockpit. His student shifted the mirror to look at himself, expecting to see something wrong with his helmet or mask. To the student's surprise, the IP said, "Now isn't that one of the coolest things you've ever seen? You're a pilot, flying a jet. You are getting paid to do what others would pay money to do. Now you *are* that pilot that you always thought was so cool." He gave his student a moment to admire the profile of his face in the helmet, with the aircraft just behind him and the Texas landscape far below; then he said, "You have the aircraft. Now stop screwing up."

Though they had varied personalities, most of the T-37 instructors had come from heavy airframes, and many were on their last assignment before they separated and became civilians. They were enjoying their time and building flight hours; often they would take leave to go to job interviews or complete their airline check-outs. They headed home early every Friday to spend time with their families or travel somewhere for the weekend. In February of 2000 I flew my last ride in a T-37 and moved to the next phase— flying T-38s—where the instructor pilots were dramatically different.

With the exception of one former B-1 pilot, the T-38 instructors were all fighter pilots, and they were only instructing UPT because the Air Force required it. All were itching to return to their fighters, and while they were waiting they brought their aggressive attitudes to their instruction. These instructors took flying seriously and modeled the classic characteristics of the fighter pilot personality. They were aggressive, terse, and blunt. Here I first learned that fighter pilots need to have a thick skin, because criticisms were not couched in pleasant words but were delivered with severity. It was not meanness for meanness' sake; but they were critical and demanding in a harsh way, at least from the viewpoint of a young student pilot. The criticism did have a purpose: the second track of pilot training was not to teach the basics but the foundations of flying a tactical aircraft. We flew more solo sorties, learned formation flying, and executed *fluid maneuvering*, basically an elementary precursor to dogfighting.

Besides the flying, we were taught to frame our thought processes in the same terms as a fighter pilot. Most US Air Force fighters are single-seat aircraft, which means most fighter pilots spend their time as solo aircraft commanders flying in formation with another solo pilot. (The two-seat F-15E is an obvious exception. The Navy also has several multi-seat fighter aircraft.) Previously, the side-by-side seating of the T-37 had made several of the controls, particularly the radio, a stretch for the left seat (student) pilot. It was not uncommon for a student pilot to ask the IP to make a radio channel change for him. Most instructors were open to this and even encouraged it as a crew concept. In the tandem seating of the T-38, all the controls were within easy reach. Besides that, the T-38 IPs emphasized the need for the fighter pilot-to-be to execute the complete mission without assistance. Some IPs would sit quietly in the back and not say a word during the entire flight. We quickly learned to be the masters of our own domain, and gradually learned the beginnings of what it took to be a fighter pilot.

After graduating pilot training we accomplished several more training courses. The Air Force sent its new pilots to training tailored to their specific airframe. For example, fighter pilots went through a slightly different water survival than heavy pilots; most fighter pilots would probably eject and be alone, while heavies might ditch and have a crew. In the case of resistance training, which was training for conduct if we became a prisoner of war (POW), there were "special" courses for pilots assigned to aircraft with intelligence missions. Older Academy graduates had completed the forest survival portion of SERE (Survival, Evasion, Resistance, and Escape) while we were cadets; the resistance portion of the course had been removed from the cadet syllabus after a scandal occurred and was broadcast on national TV. I completed the resistance training at Fairchild Air Force Base, Washington. After a week at Fairchild I went to water survival at Pensacola Naval Air Station, Florida, which houses a little-known unit of US Air Force boats. We had also accomplished part of the water survival training as cadets; we completed the top-off parachuting course in the Gulf of Mexico.

A more significant milestone specific to the fighter pilot is attending the centrifuge, a dastardly little machine made famous by its amusement park portrayals in various movies. The centrifuge was not nearly as fun to actually experience. Future F-16 pilots were required to withstand a force of 9 Gs for 10 seconds. A person sitting or standing experiences 1 G, or a force equal to gravity. At 9 Gs, a 200 pound person feels as though they weigh 1,800 pounds. Though significant, the increased "weight" is bearable. The more challenging aspect of Gs is that the outward force causes a pilot's blood to pool in his legs and feet. The potential result is a lack of sufficient blood to the brain which causes a blackout under G, called a "G-induced Loss of Consciousness," or G-LOC (pronounced Gee-Lock). A G-LOC that occurs while airborne is often fatal, as the plane may fly itself into the ground while the pilot is regaining consciousness.

The specialists did a good job of teaching us the proper techniques and gave us equipment to wear in the form of a chap-like g-suit. Much as the movies showed, we were seat-belted into a cubicle that simulated a cockpit. The cockpit was on the end of a long arm that spun at amazing speeds, compressing us under increased gravity forces. I failed the first time I attempted; I was able to maintain 8.5 Gs but G-LOC'd at 9 Gs. I returned to the centrifuge again and finally passed by successfully staying conscious during the 9 G profile. Sustaining Gs in the centrifuge is significantly more difficult than in the actual aircraft and is extremely physically demanding. Fortunately, so long as fighter pilots stay current in their airframe they are not required to return to the centrifuge. It is a rite of passage that I would not want to repeat.

Once I had completed those courses I attended Introduction to Fighter Fundamentals (IFF) at Moody Air Force Base, Georgia. There we flew AT-38Bs, a slightly modified version of the T-38 we'd flown in pilot training, and learned the basic fighter pilot tactical concepts of dogfighting and bomb dropping. The emphasis was formation flying, basic fighter maneuvers, and ground attack. The IFF squadron was the first one I was in that was composed exclusively of fighter pilots. From Moody I was assigned to Luke Air Force Base, Arizona, for the F-16 basic course (B-course). It was a six-month class that started with the fundamentals of taking off and landing in the F-16 and finished with learning to use the F-16 as a weapon. The B-course involved many long days; it was intense in a different way than pilot training because the F-16 was vastly more complex than our trainer aircraft. It had significantly more systems which required greater systems knowledge. By this time, though, I was used to the rigor and the schedule of the training. What was new was the fighter pilot persona that was finally displayed in full force.

Chapter 3:
What is a Fighter Pilot?

"What's the difference between God and a fighter pilot? God doesn't think he's a fighter pilot." – Unknown

SOME PEOPLE HAVE COMPARED FIGHTER PILOTS with the knights of old; chosen because of their superior skills and courage, they charge into battle with little or no support at great personal risk to further the greater good. Though modern training and equipment have taken many of the uncertainties away, flying can still be dangerous, and flying in combat is more dangerous still. Being a fighter pilot does have the qualities of a noble profession. Men and women sometimes become fighter pilots because of the impact they can have for the good of their country.

While some want to nobly fly and fight for their country, many want to be fighter pilots just because it looks fun. Who isn't impressed by the amazing acts they see at airshows, from the performance demonstrations of an F-15 climbing straight up into the sky or a formation of F-16s with their wingtips within inches of each other? Like race car drivers or firefighters, fighter pilots are a group who live their lives on the edge, are the best at what they do, and do what few other people in the world can. Flying is undoubtedly fun, and flying a fighter puts a pilot on top of the world. Fighters are the sports cars of the aircraft world. Civil and heavy pilots concentrate on quality take offs and landings; in between, the autopilot flies. Fighter pilots *fly*; take offs and landings are just a means to that end. They can fly higher than 40,000 feet or down on the deck at 500. They may slow to less than 100 knots as they fight an adversary or fly more than twice the speed of sound in an intercept. They roll upside down, zoom, bank, and pull Gs. An individual fighter pilot is trusted with the keys to a multi-million dollar aircraft with unbelievable performance and combat capabilities. Getting that chance requires skill and hard work; those who are ultimately allowed to fly fighters are the best of the best. Fighter pilots *do* nobly fight for their country; they *are* the best at what they do; and it *is* fun.

The stereotypical and popular fighter pilot is a lethal extension of the military's most advanced weapons systems. Enduring unceasing and arduous training, they rise when ordered by their country to fly into enemy territory to execute with lethal force the directives of the government. They most often fly alone, with a single wingman in another aircraft. They can use their skills to down enemy fighters beyond visual range, destroy a single building on a single block in a densely populated city, lay waste to massed enemy troops, and provide vital air support within yards of friendly troops on the ground—all on the same mission. They must combine their expert knowledge of their aircraft with the dynamics of the changing battle scenario to defend themselves and their fellow servicemen, take the battle to the enemy, and win in accordance with the stated objectives. One fighter pilot can cause an international incident—or end one. With a single button, a pilot can take countless lives of those he will never see. A fighter pilot is trained to kill people and break things; controlled violence is his profession. No fighter pilot truly hopes for war, but if one comes he wants desperately to be there to use his training and bring the combat to a victorious end. Until that time comes, he will train to fight the enemy and be ready to fight when called upon. In the words of the Air Force cliché, his job is to fly, fight, and win.

Fighter pilots tend to be Type A personalities, intensely controlling, and obsessively organized. They demand perfection from themselves and from those around them. Their relationships are often based on criticism, cynicism, sarcasm, and mutual degradation. Because they are often successful in driving toward perfection they are extremely proud, which is often perceived as arrogance. They compartmentalize extraordinarily well: there is no need for them to "talk it out" prior to a complex mission or a dangerous combat sortie. They can leave the emotions and conflict on the ground while they fully concentrate on their mission in the air. What fighter pilots do is fly, and that they love; they have little time or tolerance for *queep*, a term for all paperwork and related jobs that keep a pilot out of the cockpit. They train hard; planning, briefing, flying, and debriefing a single sortie may take as long as 16 hours, and they may do that anywhere from 2 to 10 times a week. Missions, even training ones, are intense. A pilot must at all times know his position in a four-dimensional world of latitude, longitude, altitude, and time. He must fly his own aircraft, monitor those of his flight, and scan for those of the enemy. The hundreds of switches in his cockpit must be in the correct position at every moment for every phase of flight; a single switch error can result in mission failure.

Fighter pilots train hard because the risk is high; they play just as hard. The same pilot who used his skills and training to execute a difficult mission flawlessly on Tuesday may wake up hung over on Saturday afternoon and not even remember the previous night. Self-confidence, intensity, and aggression run through all aspects of their lives. A fighter pilot's favorite vocabulary words are profanities; *God* is just another expletive, and sex is their favorite subject.

Chapter 4:
Fighter Pilot Traditions

G IVEN THE NATURE AND DANGER of the fighter pilot profession, comradery is strong. Fighter pilot traditions are a means of sharing, strengthening, and celebrating the common bonds of combat pilots. The pilot profession is relatively young—the Wrights first flew in 1903—so the traditions of the Air Force are not nearly as ingrained as those of the centuries-old Army, Marines, and Navy. While some fighter pilot traditions pass on the history of flying and fighting, some are rooted merely in fraternity and revel in the exclusivity of the fighter pilot culture. Some fighter pilot traditions have taken on the air of reindeer games—they are nothing more than something one has to be a fighter pilot to understand.

Pilots are exposed to traditions from the very beginning of their training. At our graduation from pilot training we paraded across the stage in our service dress uniforms and received a brand new set of wings. The tradition of the wings that a pilot pinned on at his graduation was that he never wore them again; to do so is considered bad luck. Instead, the wings were to be broken in half; many pilots had their wings cut in half and framed one part with a certificate listing the date and the text of the tradition. The second piece of the wings was given to a significant other. The two pieces were not supposed to be joined again until the pilot's funeral.

Another tradition that had somehow surfaced was that of *blood wings*. I had first heard the term as an Academy cadet. When freshman cadets completed *Recognition*—the rite of passage trial that enabled them to be full-fledged cadets—they earned their "Prop and Wings," a pin that was modeled after the early Army Air Corps flying badge that was worn by upper class cadets. The wings were pinned on by an upperclassman; in the case of blood wings, the upper class cadet would pin the wings to the cadet's shirt without the protective backing and drive them into his chest with his fist, usually drawing blood...hence the name. Officially, this cadet tradition was forbidden, though I know some who participated in it. At the end of pilot training the tradition was essentially the same, and it was probably the source of the cadet one. I know a few who actually wanted to participate in that tradition. In my pilot training class it was neither encouraged nor pro-hibited.

Once a pilot arrives in an operational fighter squadron one of the first traditions to which he is exposed is the squadron welcome. At the first official meeting of all the unit pilots, the new guys receive a ritual greeting that was also shown in the movie *Flight of the Intruder*. In the movie, much as in many fighter squadrons, the new pilots were told to "stand up and tell us about yourselves." As soon as they opened their mouths, they were cut off by the expected outburst from the crowd of pilots: "Sit down, (*expletive*)!", which is followed by jovial murmurings of "It never gets old," and "They never learn...."

Some traditions are merely lighthearted attempts at doing something different or unique. In Mustache March, normally clean shaven pilots grow mustaches—but only for the month. A corollary applies to deployments— fighter pilots traditionally grow mustaches while deployed and some also shave their heads. While I was deployed for OIF the latter was more for hygienic reasons than fashion. Due to the limited number of barbers for the huge number of deployed servicemen, soldiers took to cutting each other's hair. No skill was required to close-cut a head of hair. While I passed on the head shave (the desert sun would burn me red in a short time if I did), I did grow a mustache, more for the novelty than anything else. Along the same lines, fighter pilots often participate in the calendar traditions of flat-top February and side-burn September. These pseudo-traditions are followed in varying degrees in different fighter squadrons. It's more an opportunity to see what everybody looks like in a mustache or with a different hairstyle than anything else. The beginning of March, though, when flat-tops are growing out and mustaches are growing in, does tend to be a time when fighter pilots look a little odd.

Consuming alcohol in excessive amounts is, in many respects, a virtual fighter pilot tradition in its own right. Stereotypically, fighter pilots are known as much for their drunkenness as they are for their skill in the air. Flight debriefs are often conducted with beer in hand. Buying a round or a case is a typical punishment for rule infractions. (It is worth noting that many units will enforce the spirit of the tradition on non-drinkers by asking them to provide equivalent quantities of non-alcoholic beverages.) If a pilot breaks an aircraft through his own buffoonery and causes the maintenance personnel more work, he is traditionally obligated to provide them with beer. During major training exercises, when a fighter pilot shoots a simu-lated missile at a friendly aircraft or drops a simulated bomb on a friendly ground position, he is required to buy a keg as punishment for the fratricide or *frat*. (This is in addition to the humiliation of the debrief, as fighter pilots consider frat the gravest of sins.)

Since drinking alcohol is an integral part of a fighter pilot's life, it is logical that a fighter squadron have its own bar, which has its own traditional rules. (The rules are sometimes also applied to the bar at the Officers' Club, or whatever bar a group of fighter pilots has overrun.) The rules of the bar are generally posted on a wooden or engraved plaque in grandiose language. Infractions are self-policed; if someone observes a rule being broken, they "ring the bell," which is generally hanging near the bar, and point out the infraction. Most penalties associated with rule violations require purchasing a round for the room or, in some cases, a hefty monetary fine. The penalty is levied on the one who rang the bell if he was mistaken about the violation. Examples of rule violations include wearing a hat into the bar, placing your hat on the bar, receiving a phone call from your wife while at the bar (amended to spouse, in most places), drinking with your right hand, or pointing at another pilot with anything other than your elbow. Often there are additional local rules, such as not saying a number associated with a rival unit. Finally, a common rule is that you can't read the rules, though sometimes a waiver is granted for the initial visit. There are often off-the-wall bar traditions; one unit was famous for burning a piano every year.

Another fighter pilot tradition that is little more than a drinking game is that of *Deceased Insect*. Deceased insect is the proper name for "dead bug." At the phrase "dead bug," everyone is supposed to fall on the ground and put their hands and feet in the air, imitating the look of a dead bug. The initiator remains standing to catch the slowest person to assume the position. That person is then liable for whatever the bad deal is for the moment, whether drinking from a grog bowl or buying the next round.

The squadron Doofer Book is another fighter pilot ritual (which has spread to other services and career fields in one form or another). It is generally a running compilation of the missteps of the various members of the squadron that may be updated daily, or at weekly or monthly pilot events. While entertaining as a day-to-day squadron chronicle, they are most interesting when kept during deployments—they serve as a unique collection of history (and often humor) for a unit. Generally, there are few rules, either about content or language—the only criterion is that the story must be at least 10% true. Doofer books have fallen out of favor because they have been made public and have had their seedier details published in the national news; several ranking officers have lost their jobs over the books' illicit content. Versions that are predominantly politically correct still exist, and true doofer books—complete with racier entries—nevertheless continue to survive.

Another tradition that has found a place in virtually every military branch is that of the unit coin. Nearly every military unit has designed a coin that reflects its personality and history. In the strictest tradition, a fighter pilot earns the right to carry his unit coin when he becomes mission ready (MR), meaning he is a true "go to war" member of the squadron. The internet is rife with stories that credit every branch of the military with creating the tradition of the coin. The Army and Special Forces claim to have initiated the coin tradition in Vietnam or the Philippines, and another tradition credits the Army Air Force (AAF).[1]

In the AAF version, a rich young pilot in World War I purchased medallions for each member of his squadron. A member of the squadron was subsequently shot down over enemy territory, and his captors took all his belongings except the coin he carried around his neck. He made an escape and was able to rejoin friendly forces by using the coin to prove he was an Allied soldier. The tradition then became to ensure that all pilots carried their coin at all times, which was ensured by issuing a challenge. A challenge occurs when a pilot says the word "coin" or when a pilot presents his coin, generally by slamming it on a wooden bar or table or by clinking it against metal or glass. In the fighter pilot ritual of using unusual words for normal things, to prevent issuing a challenge when talking about the coin they refer to it as a *round metal object*, or RMO. Anything that generates the *clink* of the RMO is considered a challenge, even accidentally dropping it. When challenged, all pilots are required to present their coins, ensuring that the correct face of the coin is up. If a pilot is found without his coin, he buys the next round for everyone present. If everyone presents their coin, then the challenger buys the round.

Fighter pilot songs probably do have enough history to be justifiably called a tradition. The concept of such songs is not new—think of them as combinations of Irish bar tunes and military anthems. The danger of combat and thrill of aviation led many to pen songs about flying, patriotism, missed loves, and the more humorous topics of broken equipment, bad food, clueless superiors, the faults of the enemy, and the virtues of the allies. Fighter pilot songs aren't just tales of those who have gone before, though. During brutal wars and unpopular conflicts, the songs began to reflect the cynicism of the times, and they did so using the basest of terms. Popular fighter pilot songs glorify sex, death, prostitution, and adultery, are laced with profanity, and chorus on virtually every natural and unnatural sexual organ and function. True, some songs deal with the talents of flying and fighting and occasionally reference Air Force history, and some songs are actually decent—but those are not the popular ones. Sometimes even the seemingly innocent songs are allegories referring to the previous vices.

The historied songs have been made famous in today's fighter pilot community by Dick Jonas, a retired Air Force Lieutenant Colonel and former F-4 pilot who runs his own record label to produce albums of the songs. While most CDs that included those vulgarities would require a parental advisory label even in today's culture, Dick Jonas puts a simple caution on the back of his distributions: the lyrics on the CD use what he calls "the warrior's vernacular" and might be offensive. Today, many of the songs

---

[1] The unit coin tradition is listed on virtually every coin vendor website in identical form, though there is not a documented source. The Air Force published a version in a news article entitled "Challenge coins a trademark tradition for American military," A1C Jonathan Snyder, 5 March 2007. Online at http://www.pacaf.af.mil/news/story.asp?id=123043494. Viewed 18 March 2007.

sung in fighter pilot bars are still from the era of Vietnam. A couple of fighter pilots set out to correct that oversight and formed a duet called *Dos Gringos*. The two pilots—one of whom went through the F-16 B-course with me—have produced CDs of modern fighter pilot songs with the assistance of Mr. Jonas. These songs don't stray far from the convention of the older songs.

Another fighter pilot tradition is the Friday night event, which goes by various names depending on the squadron. Generically, they are often called "Roll Calls." At Luke Air Force Base, the squadron emblem was the Emerald Knight, so Friday afternoons were called the "Crusades." At Spangdahlem Air Base, they were called "Hawk Buds," and an Aviano Air Base squadron called theirs "the Merge." The general theme was the same; it was a time to hang around the bar and tell funny stories about what other pilots had messed up during the week.

The Friday night gathering is essentially a peacetime continuation of a wartime ritual. After combat sorties were complete for the day, pilots would gather in the bar to talk about their comrades who hadn't made it back and regale each other with stories (some solemn and true, others humorous and almost purely fictional). The congregation was a way to fellowship with fellow warriors, relieve stress, and deal with the various internal struggles brought on by combat operations. In the modern convention, there are generally rules of order about who can tell stories and how they are to be introduced. (The Knights started each story with a toast, while at Spangdahlem pilots opened with the melodramatic phrase "*So there I was...*") Fighter pilot songs are often sung and several serious as well as ludicrous toasts are made. At the end of the event a poll is taken through some form of vocal feedback to determine the best story. The pilot that inspired that story (the one who had committed the act that others had mocked) then "won." At Luke he was passed a plastic sword; at Spangdahlem, it was a hat-sized baby bottle top that looked like a nipple. In both cases, the winner was responsible for being the master of ceremonies for the next Friday's event.

Fridays are also the source of other minor fighter pilot traditions. Many squadrons wear unit colored t-shirts under their flight suits on Fridays, though major Air Force commands have varied in recent years about whether such uniform choices are regulation. There are often "Friday nametags," which contain not the pilot's name but only his given callsign. Friday nametags generate another tradition, which is "First Name Friday," a day in which you are not allowed to call a pilot by his callsign but only by his real first name. It is not unusual for a group of pilots to have no idea what each others' first names are; with fines of $1 per violation, such events are often used as fundraisers for squadron social events.

Namings

Probably the most well-known fighter pilot tradition is assigning a fighter pilot a *handle* or *callsign*. Virtually all aviators (and many who want to be) have tactical nicknames, similar to "Maverick" and "Goose" of *Top Gun* fame. Historically, tactical callsigns arose from a combination of necessity—the ability to talk to or about a person without the enemy knowing who he was—and personality—fighter pilots with big egos and dramatic storytelling abilities love to give their comrades "affectionate" appellations. Sometimes callsigns were given merely to give fighter pilots something else (more aggressive or apropos) to call a person with a less-than-desirable name.

Pilots who have not yet been named in a squadron are referred to as FNGs, where *NG* is "new guy" and the *F* is a profanity. In a naming ceremony that may be called anything or simply referred to as a *Naming*, new pilots are given their name (thus, *named*) by the older pilots of the squadron. (In the Air Force, every pilot new to a unit is expected to go through the Naming, even if they were already named by a previous unit.) The new guys are often expected to bring a bribe to persuade the older pilots to give a quality name rather than an acronym of the worst construction. These bribes range from games and equipment for the squadron to alcohol and pornography.

The basis of the new pilot's name could be a stand-out event in the pilot's flying experience, a play on his real name, a reference to a person to which the pilot bears a physical resemblance, or the name could be formed from an acronym that refers to nearly anything. Examples that I have heard are "Deuce," for a pilot who had ejected twice in his short career (few pilots even do that once), "Reverend," for a pilot whose name was the same as the cult leader who murdered his followers with poisoned Kool-Aid, and "Duke," for a pilot who walked like John Wayne. Examples of acronym names were *STOGI*, for a pilot who "Stole the OG's Indian," and *STUFR*, for "Stop Talking U Retard," with the *F* added for profane emphasis. The result of the Naming could be random; any new guy could be named anything, with one caveat: if a pilot had previously dropped in anger (that is, been in combat) with a given name, then he could keep that name at his option. Namings themselves varied in style and content from one unit to another; some units are famous for their Namings, while others keep their ceremonies a virtual secret. Most include alcohol, games, unit history, and aspects of an initiation.

PART 2:
BEING
A CHRISTIAN
AND
A FIGHTER PILOT

Chapter 5:
Christian Fighter Pilot Living

IN A BASIC SENSE, a Christian in the fighter pilot world lives a "ministry of presence." Living among those to whom a Christian hopes to minister opens a door that the TV evangelist, street corner Bible thumper, and pulpit preacher will never have. Few fighter pilots would give those people the time of day—they'll simply change the channel, cross the street, or watch football on Sunday. The Christian fighter pilot, on the other hand, they know and work with. When a Christian lives a wise and successful professional life, they will respect and trust him. If he lives a Christ-centered life, they will see Jesus in him. That is the essence of a Christian fighter pilot's ministry.

Importantly, though, just as being a Christian in a foreign land does not inherently make a man a missionary, simply being a Christian in an un-Christian fighter pilot world does not mean he's a ministering pilot. While a Godly presence is one of a Christian's strongest ministry tools, to impact the fighter pilot world he needs *more* than presence—he must live an *active* Christian life. Living active Christianity doesn't mean delivering sermons at work, but living a Christ-like life and making God-honoring choices that are consistent with Biblical commands.

Without taking up the space of 66 books on the topic, suffice it to say that a Christian life is moral, honorable, edifying, and glorifying to God. Succinctly, it is one characterized by "love, joy, peace, patience, kindness, goodness, faithfulness, gentleness, and self-control" (Galatians 5:22-23). The life of a Christian must reflect Christ; John said that those who claim to know God but do not live a God-honoring life are liars (1 John 1:6, 2:4). In deliberately living an active Christ-centered life a Christian should let others hear him give God credit for all the things that happen in his life, rather than attributing them to fate, luck, or his own skill. He must let people see that he glorifies God when he has good times, and that he continues to de-

31

pend on Him when he has bad times. Such a God-honoring life—which is a stark contrast in lifestyle and principles to most other fighter pilots—will differentiate a Christian from his peers.

Contrast is important. Christians are supposed to be *different*, not conformed to the world. Other pilots will see that difference; some won't care about it, some will be curious of it, and others may even be hostile toward it. It is distinctly possible that other pilots may avoid a Christian because of his faith. They may view him as a *Holy Joe*, a term that is old military slang for chaplains but can also mean a "sanctimonious or overly pious person."[1] Regardless of perception, if a Christian leads an active life of faith his fellow fighter pilots will know who he is, what he believes, and for what he stands. My wife, a former Air Force officer herself, related a story of talking to another officer on the topic of religion. The officer mentioned that he was a Christian, to which my wife reacted with surprise, saying, "I never would have guessed you were a Christian." Her reason was simple: he behaved the same as every other non-Christian officer. The self-professed Christian took offense, but my wife's point was valid—if his life was no different, how could she have known?

In It, But Not of It

A Christian must have a life ministry and proactive faith to positively influence the world. There is a subtle underlying presumption to that truth, however: to effectively influence the world, a Christian has to be *in* it. By choosing to become a fighter pilot a Christian has elected to be deeply *in* the world, a choice that results in immense tension, a literal struggle between good and evil. A Christian in the fighter pilot world faces immeasurable pressure to compromise his convictions to conform, and he confronts the struggle of trying to be an effective Christian witness to the fighter pilots around him.

A Christian's eternal battle is how to be "in it but not of it"—to be *different* without necessarily being *separate*. God has called the Christian to be salt *in* the world. Christians cannot separate themselves so far from their peers in the world that their salt isn't even in the same restaurant. Nowhere in the Bible does God command Christians to segregate themselves from sinners—quite the contrary: the Corinthian church once thought Paul had told them to do just that; he wrote to them and explained that the only way they could disassociate themselves from every sinner would be to "leave this world" (1 Corinthians 5:9-10). Still, there are many aspects of the fighter pilot world from which Christians *must* shelter themselves to prevent becoming *of* the world. The choices that a Christian makes in his life— choices between how he will separate or differentiate himself—will form the basis of his ministry and the framework of his "in but not of" life.

---

[1] *Random House Unabridged Dictionary*, Random House, Inc, 1997.

Chapter 5: Christian Fighter Pilot Living

Beginning early in pilot training a Christian will gradually enter the fighter pilot world. I received my introduction to extracurricular fighter pilot activities while flying T-38s during pilot training. Some student pilots would stay after work on Friday nights to drink alcohol and gamble in a game called "4/5/6." After pilot training, each new assignment moves the fighter pilot progressively deeper into the fighter community, and he learns not only tactical skills but also how the fighter pilot life is supposed to be lived. More than once I have had fighter pilots tell me that it's not about the flying, as much fun as that is; they told me it was about the comradery, the drinking, and the traditions.

I stayed away from much of the drinking and morally questionable traditions. This led some pilots to take me aside and give me guidance to nudge me to the correct fighter pilot lifestyle. I received similar counseling at each new place along the way, through T-38s, IFF, the B-course at Luke, and each of my operational assignments. The speech basically went like this:

> Your failure to participate in event 'x' has been noticed.
> You have to realize that these are the guys you're going to
> train/go to war with. Now, while we can't make you go,
> we highly encourage you to attend the event next Friday.

Each time I was told that my failure to participate in what I considered morally questionable events was going to detract from my professional advancement; at one point I was even encouraged to reconsider my fighter pilot career. Some fighter pilots seemed convinced that I would be an unsuccessful pilot if I didn't participate in the basest detail of the fighter pilot social life. Part of their desire to set me straight was based on their assessment of my attitude; when a person does not attend the social events of the squadron and appears to claim the moral high ground, he can develop the perception that he is "holier than thou" and thinks he is "too good" to be around everyone else. Once begun, the opinion that a person is snobbish and aloof is difficult to overcome. While it was not fact, the mere perception was enough to make the early days of each of my assignments uncomfortable. While I didn't want to yield in the places I felt I had a moral obligation, I also didn't want to be perceived as standoffish merely because of my personality.

At one base I received the same speech, but it was somewhat unique. I was told without hesitation that my work had been exceptional and my flying was above average. I was also bluntly told that my failure to participate in certain unofficial squadron events would result in me not being placed in the position of flight commander, which was advertised as a coveted position. It irritated me to be told that I was, for all intents and purposes, professionally doing everything right, but that I would be denied a job based on something outside of my profession. While I bristled at the fact that an official job had an unofficial requisite, it was not a completely unexpected turn of events. I was finally confronted with the important question: if my principles were in conflict with career progression, would I compromise them? As far as some non-Christian pilots were concerned, I was on track to retire as a Major (rather than, perhaps, two ranks higher as a Colonel), because in their view I would never get promoted with the principles I was displaying.

The crux of the issue was my refusal to bend to the morals of the squadron. I had made a conscious decision to do what I believed to be right and in God's will, regardless of how the squadron, my leadership, and the military viewed it. I decided that I would perform my duty to the best of my ability and be the greatest asset I could to my profession and my country, but I would not compromise my principles. Since I strived to make sure that my life choices were consistent with God's will, if that meant that I retired at a less prestigious rank—or didn't get to become a flight commander— then I believed that must be the result that God intended. (I really hoped that I'd be promoted to four-star general so that I could prove that God's way was the better way, but I was willing to accept the more realistic outcome.)

Though I frequently received the *this-is-how-it-is* lecture near the beginning of my assignments, by the end of my tours I still had some successes even without changing my attitude or boundaries. I left one assignment as the air-to-ground top gun, meaning that my bombs had been more accurate than others'; at another base, I left as one of the top flight leads. I *did* eventually become a flight commander, even without attending the events I was told were a requirement. Many of the pilots came to respect my abilities, decisions, and even the strength of my convictions. Though it wasn't always easy, as the days passed at each of my assignments the squadron eventually realized that while I was *different*, I wasn't "that bad," and they saw that I could be a good pilot and personable peer without participating in *every* fighter pilot event.

While I have not always received the accolades or opportunities that others have, my experiences to this point have been generally positive. Such is not always the case for those who make a stand for God. Daniel was tossed into the lion's den when he made his stand on his knees (Daniel 6). His friends Hananiah, Mishael, and Azariah (better known as Shadrach, Meshach, and Abednego) were thrown into the furnace for their faith (Daniel 3). All four faced the choice of worldly acceptance or death. God did not prevent them from seeing the 'negative' consequences of their righteous choice. He allowed them to be taken to the point where they should have died; only His direct intervention altered the outcome. There are worldly consequences for following Christ, and God will not necessarily shield Christians from them. Some good Christian officers *do* retire as Majors (and I may yet). Making the 'right' choice doesn't necessarily mean we will be rewarded, at least not in this world.

My experience with lectures and misperceptions is not entirely uncommon for a military Christian; the counseling I received and "holier than thou" perception I developed are two obstacles that many have had to overcome. Whether by his own actions or by simple misunderstandings, a Chris-

34

tian is often in a position where he feels he must excel above his peers to simply prove himself an equal. I know that I have made correct decisions based on my Christianity that made me lose value in the sight of my peers, the very people to whom I wished to witness. I knew then that I had to be exceptional professionally to overcome that deficit and earn their respect. Anything less and I would be but another mediocre Christian to the men around me. A Christian who is mediocre in his profession weakens his witness because he doesn't have a credible leg on which to stand. Fighter pilots don't respect—or follow—mediocre men. A Christian is not disadvantaged by his faith because God is not an impediment; however, he must prove to the non-Christian pilots not only that he can be a good pilot, but also that he can do so without lowering himself to the their worldly devices—that his faith is not an impediment, but an advantage.

The prophet Daniel is a sterling example of such a scenario. Carried away in exile by Nebuchadnezzar, he resolved not to defile himself by eating the royal Babylonian food and wine (Daniel 1:8). After a ten day test, he was able to prove that "God's way" made him healthier than the other officials (Daniel 1:12-15). With God's blessing, Daniel would so distinguish himself as an advisor that the king planned to put him in charge of the entire kingdom (6:3). Even though he was a Godly man in a pagan court, he excelled without compromising God's Word—though at times he had to "prove" his value. Without lowering himself to their devices, Daniel was able to demonstrate that he could be "just as good" as—or better than—they.

Christian Choices in the Fighter Pilot World

Making choices to live a Christian life in an unChristian world is not easy. I once heard a preacher say that in some ways the martyrs of old actually had an easier spiritual life. Faced with the choice to deny God or die, they did not back down from their faith. If asked what they would do in the same circumstances, many Christians today would probably say that they, too, would be willing to die for their faith. But, as the preacher pointed out, it's *living* for the faith that is often harder. Explicit Biblical commands and moral absolutes are easy to understand; it's the gray areas of life that are more difficult. Even devout Christians—who claim they would die for the faith—have been known to set their cruise control 5 mph above the speed limit or watch a movie that, when pressed, they would confess was probably not appropriate.

So how does a Christian bring focus to the blur of gray? The starting place has already been mentioned; to live a Christian life the fighter pilot should strive for the fruit of the spirit, as quoted from Galatians above. In the same letter Paul also listed what a Christian should *avoid*: "The acts of the sinful nature are *obvious*: sexual immorality, impurity and debauchery; idolatry and witchcraft; hatred, discord, jealousy, fits of rage, selfish ambition, dissensions, factions and envy; drunkenness, orgies, and the like"

(5:19-21, emphasis added). The Biblical commands are clear; the spiritual goals (and their opposites) are evident. A Christian must live his life and make his choices within these criteria. Some aspects of the fighter pilot life will obviously be inconsistent with Christian living, and the correct choice will be clear even if the decision isn't any easier to make. Others may present a much more difficult choice, and a Christian must be spiritually prepared to make the correct decision.

Profanity

One of the more clear-cut examples is profanity—including the use of God's name in vain—which is gradually becoming more socially acceptable and is rampant in the fighter pilot community. Profanity punctuates the hyperbolic bravado of nearly every fighter pilot's speech. Some consider it a requisite to being a fighter pilot, much like the Navy cliché of "cursing like a sailor." Fighter pilots who do not curse do exist, though they are rare. In several cases I even knew fighter pilots who attended church regularly with their families but still used vulgar language. The temptation for any fighter pilot to use profanity will be strong, particularly if he used it in his past. Also, refusing to use profanity is difficult even for a strong Christian for one significant reason: constant exposure. Regardless of a Christian's personal actions, the fighter pilots around him will still use profanity in their language and casual conversation. The continuous, daily bombardment of profanity leads to the greatest threat to modern Christianity: desensitization. When the words cease to be shocking it is only a short time before they don't even seem to be wrong—when they no longer seem wrong, it is easy to accept and then start using those words.

One key way to prevent desensitization is to not be silent while others curse up a storm. Remaining silent conditions a Christian: The first time he hears profanity, he wants to say something but doesn't. The second time he notices but doesn't feel the need to say anything. The third time, he doesn't even notice. Desensitization to a point that he no longer feels offense or embarrassment at sin is not a good thing; this same lack of shock and shame was listed by God as a reason for His punishment of the nation of Israel (Jeremiah 3:3, 6:15). Silence condones the actions of others, but worse, a Christian may inadvertently learn to accept the language he hears. Sometimes it takes a new Christian showing up and expressing shock to make an accepting Christian realize he has become desensitized to sin.

While not all situations will be appropriate for a response, a quick reproach is a good way to communicate displeasure with profanity and prick the conscience of those who use it. For non-Christians, a brief and witty conversation that critiques profanity may establish the foundation of a relationship. When done in a light-hearted and non-accusing manner, it can even cause fighter pilots to become self-conscious about their own language, even if it's only while the Christian is present. For Christians, the response can be more direct. Modern movements in Christianity have occasionally tried to de-emphasize the sinful characteristics of profanity. Some have implied that by focusing on a minor behavioral issue that is a virtual social norm a Christian is stiff and legalistic. Christian-themed movies have included profanities because it made them "more real." Some have even gone so far as to imply that Christians should use profanity as a veritable outreach tool to fit in. I do not believe such assertions are scriptural. I've liked the pithy quote that "profanity is the sign of a weak vocabulary," but the Biblical ordinance that praise and cursing should not come out of the same mouth is supreme. James says,

> With the tongue we praise our Lord and Father, and with it we curse men, who have been made in God's likeness. Out of the same mouth come praise and cursing. My brothers, this should not be. Can both fresh water and salt water flow from the same spring? My brothers, can a fig tree bear olives, or a grapevine bear figs? Neither can a salt spring produce fresh water. (James 3:9-12)

James points out that profanity and vulgarity are inherently inconsistent with a Christian character. Profanity from a Christian is inexcusable. Under no circumstances should a Christian allow himself to use profane language or make excuses when he does. As James said, Christians should refrain from profanity because they praise their God and "kiss their mother" with the same mouth. More importantly, they *should* refrain from profanity because it's incompatible with their Christian nature; profanity should be no more a fruit of a Christian's life than olives the fruit of a fig tree. A Christian's lack of profanity is often the single greatest distinguishing factor between him and other pilots—and it is frequently the first doorway to the opportunity to witness.

Fighter Pilot Songs

While I have never been in a position where fellow pilots have demanded profanity in my speech (some have even complimented my ability to form a grammatically correct sentence without it), I *have* been placed in positions where fellow pilots have insisted that I participate in singing fighter pilot songs. Unfortunately, the decisions surrounding pilot songs are more difficult to make. At Luke, the F-16 B-course students were responsible for providing entertainment for the instructors at pilot meetings. This entertainment necessitated a pilot song or two. At Spangdahlem, every fighter pilot event ended with stirring renditions of traditional fighter pilot songs. In each case, there was tremendous pressure to join in on the singing to support my wingmen and squadron mates. Regardless of the strength of tradition in fighter pilot songs, the profanity, vulgarity, and glorification of evil in fighter pilot songs makes them an anathema to the Christian spirit.

Because of their content, I believe that a Christian should not participate in singing vulgar fighter pilot songs. The question, then, is how much
he allows himself to be around *other* pilots who are singing those songs.
Their vulgar lyrics are set to familiar and catchy tunes; what goes in, even if
only passively, will invariably attempt to come out. If a Christian attends
events in which fighter pilot songs are sung, he will likely find himself
whistling their tune even if he did not participate in the singing. On the
other hand, if he decides to avoid all fighter pilot events in which songs are
sung he may not be able to attend any events at all. When routine and structure allow, he may be able to walk out of the room as the songs are sung,
but even that may have a negative impact on the other pilots.

There is a delicate balance between exposure to immoral songs and a
Christian segregating himself from other pilots to avoid them. The balance
is made more difficult by the recent increase in popularity of fighter pilot
songs. *Dos Gringos* have revived the genre beyond the Air Force fighter
pilot community. Intelligence officers, air traffic controllers, Navy crews,
foreign pilots, and many others have posted their signs of support on the
duo's website. In an unfortunate development, crew chiefs—young airmen
and sergeants who crew the maintenance on fighter jets—have also acquired
a taste for this fighter pilot vice.

If the right situation presents itself, there may be a place that a Christian can meet the other pilots: there are a few—just a few—little known
fighter pilot songs that contain no profanity, no sexual references, and do
not glorify that which God hates.[2] If a Christian pilot can get his fellow
fighter pilots to join him in a rousing performance of such a fighter pilot
song, one that calls on history and tradition without stooping to worldly
vices, then he may be able to demonstrate that he doesn't object to the tradition, just the means in which the tradition is communicated. Just as *Dos
Gringos* have reinvigorated the genre of fighter pilot songs, I once thought
of trying to do the same with clean songs; unfortunately, I have no talent
when it comes to writing witty and catchy songs, never mind trying to find
clean fighter pilot topics. While I was stationed at Spangdahlem, our squadron commander asked a musically-inclined pilot to write a clean version of
our squadron song; commonly referred to as the unclassified version, it was

---

[2] There are several collections of fighter pilot songs, though most are out of print and difficult
to obtain. Two are available through Dick Jonas' website, and because of my lack of desire to
patronize his site I have not attempted to order one from him. Otherwise, I have been unable to
find and review any collection of fighter pilot songs. The likely candidates for those who
would like to learn "clean" fighter pilot songs would be to find *Wild Blue Yonder: Songs of the
Air Force (Volume 1)* by C. W. Getz (Editor), Redwood Press (June 1, 1981), or *Army Air
Force Lyrics: A Collection of WW II U.S. Army Air Force Marching Songs, Poems, and Paro-
dies to Popular Songs of the Period and the Past* by J. K. Havener, Aero Pub Inc (June 1,
1985). *Wild Blue Yonder Volume 2* claims to have bawdy pilot songs, which at least implies
that *Volume 1*, which claims to have lyrics to some 600 songs, may be cleaner. *Army Air Force
Lyrics* simply sounds as though it may have songs of a more historical nature, though there are
probably less than desirable lyrics in there as well. I have reviewed neither, and neither is readily available due to limited publication.

family friendly in verbiage and topic. Some pilots objected—it was too clean to be a real fighter pilot song—but as a whole it was accepted as the unit anthem, in an unclassified environment.

Fighter Pilot Innuendo, so to speak

Unfortunately, profanity is not the only vice to which a Christian fighter pilot will be exposed. Standard fighter pilot lingo is laced with various forms of sexual innuendo, most through the use of linguistic games. The most frequently used fighter pilot linguistic skill is the phrase "so to speak" (often written as "sts"). The phrase follows any sentence that can in any way, shape, or form be construed as a double entendre; the frequency of the phrase in a fighter pilot's speech indicates how often he can come up with a sexual reference in virtually any combination of words in the English language. If a pilot uses a phrase that is worthy of a "so to speak" because of its potential double meaning, other pilots in the room will generally say "so to speak" and cajole those who do not.

A less vulgar use of the "so to speak" phrase is in reference to the misuse of a pilot's name. For example, in the movie *Top Gun*, Tom Cruise's weapons system officer had the nickname *Goose*. If another pilot said that he had to "goose the power," a fighter pilot would suffix the phrase with "so to speak" to acknowledge the use of Goose's callsign.

Another fighter pilot linguistic skill is replacing certain words that have a possible sexual connotation with their generic or scientific equivalent. This is not to avoid the words but rather highlight them. Without stooping to an illicit explanation, a generic example would be a fighter pilot using *cranium* in place of the word *head*; instead of saying someone fell and hit their *head*, a fighter pilot would say someone fell and hit their *cranium*, since *head* could have a possible sexual connotation.

I believe there is the potential for significant negative impact on a Christian's life should he participate in fighter pilot linguistic games. I recommend strongly against "so to speak" and word replacement because participating in these fighter pilot games requires constantly thinking in sexual undertones. Every phrase a pilot utters is first filtered against sexual connotation. This thought process becomes part of the subconscious, and a pilot will soon find himself analyzing his pastor's sermon for potential sexual innuendo, or saying "so to speak" in the presence of his wife, children, and mother. A Christian should not put himself in the position of explaining to his family that he said "so to speak" because of the sexual innuendo he just perceived. How would he explain to his child that he uses an unusual word for something because of its potential sexual connotation?

I have known Christian fighter pilots who allowed themselves to use "so to speak" in reference to the misuse of other pilots' names but not in the sexual way. This is an example of where I and another Christian differed in what we would and would not participate. I personally believed that if I allowed myself to use that phrase in some circumstances and not in others, I would run the risk of failing in my mental gymnastics and using it when I should not. I understand that there is no true harm in saying "so to speak" to acknowledge the use of another pilot's name; but it draws me dangerously close to a phraseology and habit pattern in which I think there *is* true harm. For me, refusing to use "so to speak" or replace words with their scientific equivalent means that I fail to acknowledge any potential innuendo in my language; this keeps my own mind out of the gutter—which benefits my spiritual well-being—and it is another way that I distinguish my speech from the non-Christian, in much the same way I do by not using profanity.

The use of "so to speak" or singing songs laced with innuendo is obviously not specifically addressed in the "Thou shalt nots" of the Bible. The most explicit instruction comes from Ephesians, where Paul instructs the church of Ephesus in aspects of Christian living:

> But among you there must not be even a hint of sexual immorality, or of any kind of impurity, or of greed, because these are improper for God's holy people. Nor should there be obscenity, foolish talk or coarse joking, which are out of place, but rather thanksgiving. (Ephesians 5:3-4)

In his instructions, Paul's reference to coarse joking does not imply a lack of humor but is a reference to what Christians know are dirty jokes— nowhere in the Bible does it say Christians can't be funny. Paul says to the Ephesians—and the lesson can apply to Christians today, too—that there must not even be an intimation, not even a *perception*, of sexual immorality or impurity in their lives; Paul's reason is that such behavior is *unfitting for God's people*. Because He is holy, His followers should strive to be holy (Leviticus 11:44, quoted in 1 Peter 1:16). God has called Christians to be holy, and Paul's list of vices is certainly not a pattern of sacred behavior.

If Paul says that sexual immorality, impurity, obscenity, and coarse joking are unfit for the people of God, what does that say for a fighter pilot who thinks through a sexual "so to speak" filter and sings songs that cover the gamut of those very vices? By participating in such behavior Christians are not acting as God's people should; this is not only an affront to God, but it is a contradiction that will potentially undermine a Christian's witness. Non-Christians will seize on the inconsistency of an unholy Christian to criticize the hypocrisy of his life.

The Biblical instructions for a Christian's speech are actually one step more directive. In Ephesians Paul also says, "Do not let any unwholesome talk come out of your mouths, but only what is helpful for building others up according to their needs, that it may benefit those who listen" (4:29). While the previous instructions have been what a Christian should *not* do, the second half of this verse describes what his speech *should* do: it *should* be *only that which builds up and benefits* those who listen. His speech should be limited to that which improves, enlightens, and uplifts morally and spiritually. The simple filter that a Christian *should* use for his speech must be, "Is it edifying?" A Christian that uses a different filter—because of a different worldview—will distinguish himself without separating himself from non-Christians.

While the public perception of a Christian's speech is important, there is another reason for him to control his thoughts and words: "For out of the overflow of the heart, the mouth speaks" (Matthew 12:34). That which men speak on the outside is a reflection of who they are on the inside. Fighter pilot songs focus a pilot's thoughts on carnal things; the use of "so to speak" and word replacement forces his every thought to be filtered through a sexual paradigm. This focus on base thoughts is injurious to a Christian's internal spiritual life and will be reflected on his external. A person cannot help but become what he is thinking, which is why Paul wrote to the Philippians: "Finally, brothers, whatever is true, whatever is noble, whatever is right, whatever is pure, whatever is lovely, whatever is admirable—if anything is excellent or praiseworthy—think about such things" (4:8). The content of the heart dictates the words of the mouth, so a Christian should think about praiseworthy things not only because of the people around him but also because of the impact it has within himself.

Jesus also spoke about the reflection on the outside of an internal spiritual state when He said, "the good man brings good things out of the good stored up in him, and the evil man brings evil things out of the evil stored up in him" (Matthew 12:35). People store up the things to which they are exposed—things they read, watch on TV, study for school, and hear on the radio. Often they do so subconsciously; ever wonder why people suddenly find themselves whistling the songs they heard on the radio hours ago? In the same way, if a Christian does not actively work against it, he stores up inside his heart the profane phrases, sexual innuendo, and vulgar songs to which he is exposed in his life as a fighter pilot. Unless he actively works against it, from this internal storage comes his external action. Jesus continued to warn "that men will have to give account on the day of judgment for every careless word they have spoken" (v36).

Ultimately, when men stand before God they will be held accountable for every word—however casual or thoughtless—they have said. When it comes to the fighter pilot world of profanity and sexual innuendo, a Christian has been called to Christ and must live a life worthy of his Savior. Would Jesus approve of the way he thinks and speaks in his fighter pilot life?

Christian Fighter Pilot Participation

The degree to which a Christian chooses to participate in traditional fighter pilot activities must be based on several things. A Christian must consider God's commands, his own character, his objectives, and the potential impact on his witness.

Consider God

First, a Christian must consider God. This is essentially the "big brother" question that is asked every day in the military. During a fighter pilot's combat or training sorties he will be forced to consider what his leadership will think of his decisions and their potential outcomes. If he feels that his leadership would support him, perhaps even if he fails, then he'll probably execute his decision. If he decides that he may not be able to answer the mail about his judgment, then he'll probably forego it or choose to accept the potential negative consequences. A Christian's leader is God. Would God be pleased by the actions that a fighter pilot takes and the activities in which he participates? Do they glorify God? Are they edifying? In the now famous words of the Christian youth movement, what would Jesus do?

While this sounds like a canned Sunday School question that may prohibit virtually any fighter pilot activity, remember the New Testament: Jesus ate with prostitutes, traveled with fisherman, and contended with the religious elite—all things that the religious authorities of the time (mistaken though they were) considered inconsistent with the character of God. Matthew, chosen by Jesus to be His disciple, was a tax collector, a profession of outcasts and sinners that worked for the occupying Romans and extorted money from fellow Israelites (Luke 19:2, 7). When Jesus called Matthew to follow Him, He went to his house and ate; many of those that were with Him were Matthew's peer tax collectors and others who are described as sinners. In the Jewish culture, eating with sinners violated both Jewish tradition and law.[3] The Pharisees saw this and criticized Jesus for associating with sinners; in their eyes, Jesus' own credibility, reputation, and "witness" were weakened by His associations. His response, though, was simple:

> It is not the healthy who need a doctor, but the sick. But go and learn what this means: 'I desire mercy, not sacrifice.' For I have not come to call the righteous, but sinners. (Matthew 9:9-13)

Jesus said that He had come for the sinners; they were His objective. While the Pharisees were hardly a righteous audience, there was still the perception that Jesus was participating in an unholy activity. Jesus was willing to do this because by associating with the outcasts He reached the lost He hoped to save.

Therefore, the question "Would God be pleased with my actions?" does not imply that Christians cannot attend *any* fighter pilot related activity, because it is not God's desire that Christians refuse to associate with sinners. It is those very sinners to whom they are called; Christians cannot separate themselves so far from the fallen that they can't even reach to help them up. To witness to the world Christians must often meet them on their

---

[3] Church, Leslie F., ed. *Matthew Henry's Commentary*. Zondervan, Michigan, 1961.

turf. The question is *participation*. God may approve of attending an event, just as Jesus attended socially with sinners—it may present the opportunity to interact and be a witness to others—but would He necessarily approve of participation? While Jesus' example shows that Christians can justifiably associate with "sinners," it does not give them carte blanche approval to participate in immoral events—Jesus ate with sinners, He didn't join them in their sin. He spoke with prostitutes, but He didn't patronize brothels. When choosing how much to participate in fighter pilot traditions, Christians must consider God. They must ask themselves if God would be pleased by their actions and the activities in which they participate.

Consider Self

Second, a Christian must consider himself when determining his participation. Each individual best knows his own character; by this I mean a person's physical, emotional, and spiritual strengths and weaknesses. A Christian with a weakness for alcohol will have different criteria than one who can't stand the thought of drinking. One who gets TV commercial jingles stuck in his head easily will need to decide if he wants to expose himself to pilot songs, while another may have the mental discipline and spiritual strength to withstand such an onslaught. A Christian who is influenced or succumbs to pressure easily may need to be careful in calling his fellow fighter pilots friends—harking back to every mother's warning to "choose your friends wisely"—while another may be equally sociable with fighter pilots and church friends without concern.

This self-assessment is not unlike the decision process that a fighter pilot goes through on a mission. Fighter aircraft aren't the simple engine, wings, and gun that they used to be. There are hundreds of integrated systems that must work together to create an effective weapons platform. It is not unusual to have minor malfunctions that degrade the capability of an individual system. Ultimately, the pilot must make a decision to accept or reject the aircraft for his mission. Depending on the level of the threat and the mutual support he can call on, a pilot may determine that it is unsafe to fly into combat, or he may decide that the degraded system is not all that important. During OIF I once rejected a jet with a munitions problem because it would have prevented me from expending ordnance even to defend myself. On the other hand, I also took a jet into combat that had an inoperable gun because recent sorties had demonstrated that there was little chance I would use the gun anyway. The choices were made based on the capabilities of the aircraft and the anticipated environment.

Fighter pilots must also assess the acceptable level of risk (ALR) associated with a mission. Sorties with a high ALR may demand that the target be destroyed—even if there are significant friendly losses in the process. A mission with a low ALR may dictate that no friendly losses are acceptable, even if it means the target is not attacked. Similarly, there are levels of risk associated with a Christian exposing himself to his non-Christian environment.

The level of risk that a Christian is willing to accept should be proportional to his capabilities; that is, his personal strengths and weaknesses. He must make decisions consistent with his level of spiritual growth and personal maturity. If he exceeds his limits, he risks not only his witness but also the strength of his convictions. The temptations of the world can be overwhelming. In the New Testament, Demas and Paul were "fellow workers," but Demas "loved this world" and was lost (Philemon 24, 2 Timothy 4:10). While the exact details aren't clear, Demas—at one point teamed with one of Christianity's greatest evangelists—chose the world over Christ. It is wise for a fighter pilot to step out where he can reach the lost; it is unwise to expose himself unnecessarily to an area in which he knows he has a spiritual weakness. Thus a Christian needs to assess himself when determining his level of participation in fighter pilot events.

The Objective

Third, when deciding how much to participate in fighter pilot activities, a Christian needs to consider his objective. The objective has two parts: motivation and target. First, what is the desired outcome of participating? Is the objective to build relationships with other pilots? Is the goal to appease the peer pressure to participate in the event? Is there a spiritual objective to reach a particular person or group? A Christian's primary objective should be to spiritually impact the pilots around him. As already mentioned, Jesus' actions while He was on this earth were consistent with His objective—He came to save the lost, which is why He associated with sinners to the chagrin of the religious leaders. The second objective is the target audience: to whom does the Christian want to be a witness? Who is it he'd like to influence? If his objective is to convert crusty old Colonels then his actions may be different than if his objective is to be a supportive mentor to young Lieutenants barely out of pilot training.

Knowing his objective is important. If a Christian cannot answer to whom he is witnessing, then he is probably a witness to no one. No combat mission can be successful without clear objectives, and the same is true for the mission of representing Christ to the world. A Christian's motivation for his participation decision must be consistent with his spiritual goals, and he must know his target audience. With a clearly defined objective, he will be able to view his degrees of participation and attendance with the proper perspective and be assured that they are correctly motivated.

The Impact on the Christian Witness

Fourth, a Christian must assess whether his witness is helped or hindered by participation in a fighter pilot activity. Participation may present or prevent an opportunity to witness to non-Christians. Importantly, however, his witness is not *only* to non-Christians; he also has a significant impact on other Christians. If a Christian chooses not to participate in morally questionable events, he risks distancing himself from the very pilots he hopes to evangelize, but he may lend significant spiritual support to his Christian audience, particularly those who are younger in their faith or who still hold tightly to a conservative and traditional faith lifestyle.

If he participates he may endear himself to non-Christian pilots and open doors for witness opportunities. Conversely, the most significant impact that a Christian pilot could have on a *Christian* audience would occur should he decide to participate in a questionable event. By participating in such an event, a fighter pilot may communicate to fellow believers that there is nothing wrong with doing so, or even that they *need* to participate in those events to be successful as a pilot and military officer. If he doesn't also convey the limitations he places on his participation, he may inadvertently lead other Christians into sin if they subsequently choose to participate and don't adhere to his boundaries. This could lead to considerable confusion in a young Christian pilot who still sees the inherent inconsistency in a moral Christian attending an event laced with immorality.

This is one case where I believe that Christians may not have the freedom to participate even if they feel there is benefit from doing so. If a Christian's actions could be misperceived by another, then it is important to talk to that Christian before he falters because of the example he sees. If a person's actions cause a Christian brother or sister to stumble, then he needs to prayerfully consider whether it is the right time and place to be engaging in those activities. It may not be appropriate for another Christian to participate in the same events that he does, even if what he is doing isn't inherently wrong. The fourteenth chapter of Romans goes into great detail in describing how the relative strengths of faith can affect what Christians should allow themselves to do. In the end, Paul says that so long as it is not a question of sin, one person may be able to rightfully do what another cannot. The caveat is emphasized, though, in verses 20 and 21, when Paul says that it *is wrong* for someone to do something if it causes his brother to stumble or fall—even if the act is not wrong itself.

Finally, a decision to participate could potentially weaken another Christian's moral argument. In one squadron, I chose not to participate in certain events and based my decision on moral grounds; my actions in the squadron evidenced that and I was known as a moral pilot. An unfortunate detractor for me, though, was the activities of other pilots who were perceived as moral. Several fighter pilots in my squadron were members of the Church of Latter-Day Saints, and to the rest of the squadron the Mormons were moral. They didn't use profanity or drink alcohol, and they went to religious services on Sunday. However, the Mormon pilots *did* participate in many of the squadron activities that I did not; their ability to claim a moral high ground while still attending questionably moral events weakened my argument in the eyes of other fighter pilots.

The non-Christian pilots couldn't see any difference between Mormons and me; as far as they were concerned, if other religious pilots could attend and still be moral, then I should be able to as well. Therefore, there was no moral reason for me not to attend those events. Even if the spoilers had been Catholic or Baptist, the observations of the non-Christian pilots were unfortunately logical. A Christian pilot's actions can positively or negatively impact the witness of another Christian. In situations of opposing choices, both should understand (even if they do not agree with) the other's position so they can support each other to non-Christians.

Consider Perception

When assessing the impact on a Christian witness to the various audiences, it's worth noting the importance of perception. When I was a cadet I struggled with people thinking things about me that I did not think were true. Over the course of my freshman year someone talked to me about it and I put a summary of their words on my bulletin board: "Perception equals reality." People instantly generate opinions of a person regardless (or in spite) of actual events, in the great tradition of not letting facts get in the way of a good story. Two people may draw completely different conclusions from the same situation. If non-Christians develop a perception that a Christian is "holier than thou," or if Christian pilots develop the perception that another "Christian fighter pilot" is just a Sunday Christian, then the potential witness to those groups could be seriously harmed, regardless of whether or not the perceptions were accurate. The participation decision, therefore, needs to consider not only the factual aspects of the actions, but also the potential perceptions that the decision will generate.

Christian Agitation – Rocking the Boat

A Christian is to be *different* to prick the consciences of the non-Christians around him—not to be a thorn in their sides. A Christian needs to make moral choices, but he does not need to be contrary, disloyal, or argumentative because of his faith. Some decisions may have little to do with morality; they may relate to opinions, preferences, or personality but not an absolute right or wrong. A Christian should never compromise his faith, but when his values allow choices that are amenable to a greater number of people there is nothing wrong with making a less contentious decision. If a Christian insists on making divisive morally-neutral decisions then he may only increase the discord he has with non-Christians. One who makes a choice that is unpleasant but unrelated to a moral right or wrong will cause the least friction with his peers. The correct decision in some situations may be wholly dependent on interpretation, which may vary from one person to another.

For example, Daniel is repeatedly used as an example of moral forti-tude because he refused to defile himself with the king's food, and he was ultimately thrown into the lion's den for defying the king's order by praying to God (Daniel 1:8, 6:16). But there were other circumstances of arguable moral bearing that the Bible does *not* say Daniel resisted:

- Though he was kidnapped by a pagan king from his God-given land he did not physically rebel against his exile or attempt to run away (Daniel 1:1-6).
- He not only learned the language and literature of his hea-then captors but also excelled in them (1:4, 17, 19-20).
- He accepted being addressed by a Babylonian name, *Belteshazzar*, that replaced the *God* of his Israelite name (*God's Judge*) with an idol (*may Bel protect his life*) (1:7, 2:26, 4:19, 5:12, etc.).[4]

In none of those situations does the Bible say that Daniel—the same man who was willing to lose his life in obedience to God—resisted or challenged his captors. In comparable modern situations many Christians might feel the desire to "take a stand" for God against the perceived immoral demands of the heathen leadership. Did Daniel not protest those instances because they were not moral absolutes? Was he merely choosing his battles?

Daniel's acceptance of his Babylonian name may have a unique appli-cation for fighter pilots, a community in which pilots are "assigned" new names. When fighter pilots wear callsign nametags on Fridays, new pilots who have not yet been given a name are sometimes expected to wear name-tags with *FNG*. In places with multiple new pilots they may even have *FNG 1*, *FNG 2*, etc. When I was a new fighter pilot I refused to wear that name-tag because the acronym represented a profanity. Surely, though, a profanity is less severe than trading *God* for *Bel*, as Daniel did. It is worth noting, however, that while Daniel responded to those who called him Belteshaz-zar, throughout his book he refers to himself only as *Daniel*. Was my re-fusal of a profane nametag an incorrect choice? Would I have been less argumentative if I had worn the nametag, or might it have compromised my faith? Did I gain anything spiritually or in my witness by refusing to wear the abbreviated profanity?

Another example of a Godly man taking a less controversial path is Naaman, a new convert so excited and motivated for God that he wanted to take Israelite dirt with him to build an altar (2 Kings 5). After being cured of his leprosy by Elisha, Naaman says

> But may the Lord forgive your servant this one thing:
> When my master enters the temple of Rimmon to bow

---

[4] Douglas, J.D. and Merril C. Tenney, eds. *The New International Dictionary of the Bible.* Zondervan, Grand Rapids, Michigan, 1987.

> down and he is leaning on my arm and I bow there also—
> when I bow down in the temple of Rimmon, may the Lord
> forgive your servant for this. (2 Kings 5:18)

A zealous man of God could have simply returned to his ruler (who, incidentally, had given him permission to go and be cured (5:5)) and refused to let his master lean on his arm because it resulted in him committing an immoral act: bowing to an idol. Instead, he chose the more harmonious option and asked God's forgiveness for any perceived unrighteousness. If other righteous people knew of Naaman's conversion they might question his sincerity or his moral choices if they saw him "bowing" in the pagan temple. Did Naaman compromise his morals, or was he merely choosing the less controversial path? Did Naaman increase his chance of making an impact for God in his governmental position by not protesting? Did he threaten his witness and credibility with other potential converts? God's judgment of the situation is in Elisha's reply: "Go in peace" (v19).[5]

By choosing not to rock the boat unnecessarily a Christian can minimize the secular strife he experiences. Such decisions will lay the foundation for an amiable relationship that will aid his ability to be a strong witness. Avoiding being constantly contrary also strengthens his credibility when his morals *do* dictate that he go against the flow. I will return to the example of drinking alcohol. Aside from those that believe associating with alcohol in any form is forbidden, most Christians would be open to discussion on what is permissible. If a Christian was inclined to shun drinking alcohol in any form and avoided all functions at which it was present, he might risk "persecution" because alcohol permeates so much of the fighter pilot world—he would probably never socially associate with his peers and be criticized as a result. On the other hand, if he at least allowed himself to attend events where alcohol was present—arguably no less moral of a decision—then he might gain favor with his comrades. Making a less contentious—but no less moral—choice can prevent unnecessary conflict. A Christian living in an unChristian world will have enough conflict without adding to it on his own.

Obviously, this logic can be misconstrued: if going to events with alcohol is permissible, will reduce persecution, and improves relationships with non-Christian pilots, then surely having a drink with the other pilots is even better—so getting drunk with them must be the *best* thing to do. The ability to have an acceptable range of decisions must be restricted to the bounds of absolute Christian values.

Another example is the prevalence of gambling in the fighter pilot community. The dice game 4/5/6 has already been mentioned, and fighter pilots often place bets on the "sport of kings," or Basic Surface Attack

---

[5] Nelson, Tommy. *God and the Military.* (Video Series) Hudson & Nelson, Dallas, TX, 1997. The importance of Daniel and Naaman making difficult Godly decisions in ungodly environments was Pastor Nelson's concept as taught in his video series.

(BSA). During BSA a pilot drops practice (non-explosive) bombs onto a ground target painted to resemble a bull's-eye. The standard bet is a quarter per bomb. Whoever hits closest to the bull's-eye wins the other pilots' quarters for that bomb, assuming he met the stringent parameters for the perfect release of the bomb. The total pot of such a sortie is generally around $6 based on the number of training bombs an F-16 normally carries. The bet often serves as motivation for perfection and critique, as each pilot strives to have the best passes and will critically analyze the other pilots' in order to find the errors in their passes and secure a victory for himself. Occasionally it simply adds a bit of excitement to an otherwise mundane sortie. But what should a Christian do? Should a Christian who believes gambling to be a sin abstain from the bet, or would risking 25 cents per pass and not rocking the boat be worth the comradery? (Better still, what if the Christian fighter pilot won all the quarters?)

Making proper Christian choices in these situations is difficult. One could easily argue that by not resisting being called *Belteshazzar* Daniel "condoned" the apparent protection of Bel his name recalled. Others might argue that by not causing discord in "less important" situations he preserved his life and positioned himself to prosper and gain the favor of the king. Though in this case we know the outcome (Daniel's divinely engineered success made him one of the most powerful men in the Babylonian government), in our personal lives we rarely have such foresight. Christians could successfully argue both sides of most issues like Daniel's name or a fighter pilot's FNG nametag. Truthfully, Christians can *what if* any potential decision in the fighter pilot world to make it impossible to solve. *What if* I offend a non-Christian who rejects Christ as a result? *What if* another Christian is confused by what he perceives as moral inconsistency? There is no repeatable formula or easy answer.

The Christian Fighter Pilot's *Fight Floor*

The boundaries that a Christian sets help him figure out where his "line in the sand" or "fight floor" will be.

When fighter aircraft prepare for mock combat, they brief a *floor*. The floor is the altitude that simulates the ground. It is the altitude that must not be crossed for any reason; to do so results in immediate 'simulated death.' Depending on the weather, terrain, aircraft, and pilots, the floor may be only a few hundred feet, or it may be thousands of feet above the ground. The fight floor teaches fighter pilots to keep track of their altitude even during the most intense maneuvers so that one day—in combat—when the 'fight floor' really *is* the ground, they won't fly into it while engaging the enemy.

In the same way, a Christian making a participation decision must determine his *floor*—the limit or boundary he will work to and no further. Every situation will be different—even among Christians—because people are different. One Christian may see a wrong where another is indifferent (Romans 14-15). Also, choices among Christians may vary because we have freedom in Christ, as Paul noted in 1 Corinthians 6:12: "Everything is permissible for me, but not everything is beneficial..." We *can*, but *should* we? (It is important to remember, however, that there *is* right and there *is* wrong; there *are* moral absolutes.) There are Christians with the spiritual strength to be deeply in the world and yet not be phased by it; there are also Christians *in* the world who struggle to keep themselves from becoming part *of* the world. There are Christians that are called to be a light to non-Christians, and there are those that are called to disciple younger Christians.

There are a multitude of degrees of attendance and participation when it comes to the events and occasions of a fighter pilot life. Fighter pilot events themselves range from the harmless and fun to the vulgar and evil. There is no single cookie-cutter answer that will fit every person, personality, place, and party. Each Christian must make his decision based on prayer, discernment, discretion, prudence, common sense, and wisdom. Is it likely that a Christian pilot will be criticized by other fighter pilots for not participating in certain fighter pilot traditions? Definitely. On the other extreme, is it possible that some religious and moral people may furrow their brows at a Christian's actions as a fighter pilot, just as the Pharisees did at Jesus? Most certainly. The concerns of non-Christians have already been addressed. With respect to religious criticisms, if a Christian is right with God in all he chooses to do—which includes the perceptions that younger Christians may develop because of his actions—then their discontent may not be his concern.

Even though a Christian's floor may be situation dependent, he still needs to decide what it is ahead of time, be prepared to defend it (in theological or secular terms, as appropriate), and stick by it. The reason is simple. Beyond the cosmic struggle of good and evil, a Christian faces a more basic challenge to making the right choice: peer pressure. The stereotypical fighter pilot is the break-all-the-rules maverick who pushes the boundaries, goes it alone, and uses his "I know better than they do" attitude to win the war (and the girl). Reality is a slightly different story. Air Force fighter pilots have a host of regulations they are required to follow both in flight and in their professional lives. As a whole, the Air Force prefers to err on the conservative side, so a saying has developed that "if the regs don't say you can do it, then you can't." (The Navy, which has a slightly more liberal reputation, has the saying that "if the regs don't say you *can't* do it....")

Where the rules stop, the pressure of fellow fighter pilots steps in. For better or worse, fighter pilots face pressure from their peers to act a certain way. The result is that a fighter pilot isn't the stereotypical individualist or nonconformist—rules, regulations, and ridicule cause him to act in a manner that is consistent with the rest of the group. Whether it is "safety in numbers" or "mob mentality" (either of which could accurately convey a fighter pilot perspective), fighter pilots tend to act like a herd. When one fighter pilot is different, he sticks out from the pack, and the pressure to conform is immense. The best way a Christian can make Godly choices in the face of this pressure is to have made up his mind ahead of time. In that sense, participating in fighter pilot events is much like dating: a person must decide ahead of time how he will conduct himself, because once he's out there he will face immense pressure and temptation. The strength of his Christ-centered convictions—firmly decided ahead of time—will be his guide.

The location of a Christian's fight floor should be governed by a balance of himself, his fellow Christians, and his non-Christian peers. Some floors may be necessary to protect himself: "I can't cross this line because I'll sin or dishonor God." Some may be decided with other Christians in mind: "I know I can go further than this, but if that young pilot sees me, he may not understand and may stumble as a result." Other floors may be chosen with the objective of reaching the lost: "This floor is a little out of my comfort zone, but it's not wrong, and I'll be able to reach that non-Christian pilot." Whatever the logic and reason, a Christian must define the limits of what he is and is not willing to do in the fighter pilot world.

For example, I have come to the personal conclusion that while I do not believe drinking alcohol is morally wrong, I have never seen any good come out of it. In the fighter pilot culture, there is rarely such a thing as *a* drink. When the social opportunity presents itself, many fighter pilots imbibe until they are literally falling down drunk. In my opinion, such excess, which occurs because drinking alcohol is essentially *on* or *off*, is a definitive example of immaturity—and a dangerous example at that, given the liberating effects of alcohol. I once heard a successful general officer give a speech in which he said he had never done anything of which he was ashamed; nothing he wouldn't tell his wife, his boss, or his pastor—except, that is, when he had been drunk. When filled with liquid courage he had broken things, stolen things, and done things of which he *was* ashamed— and would never relate to those important to him. Unfortunately, I don't believe his speech had the sobering effect he intended on the audience. In the adult fighter pilot world, getting drunk is just not that big of a deal, and the buffoonery that goes on while drunk is often seen as part of the game.

For those reasons and others, I do not drink. That "fight floor" is easy, but the execution is always more complex. Many people—both Christian and non-Christian—think that non-drinking is religiously related, and I must consider how my choice impacts my relationships with them. Will I go to social events at which alcohol is served? Yes, I will; I feel that the chance of a negative perception from non-drinking Christians is minimal, and the chance of a positive impact in my interaction with those around me is greater. However, in that same social event I would not hold someone's drink, nor would I purchase alcohol for someone else. In my opinion, the potential damage to my witness because of a negative perception outweighs any possible benefit. By deciding the fight floor ahead of time, I'm not forced to spontaneously generate and defend an answer; I'm equipped to communicate my spiritual and secular reasons to those who ask, and it may even present a witness opportunity.

The Naming of a Christian Fighter Pilot

A fight floor that was more difficult for me to draw was at my Naming. One of the first and more dramatic examples of the fighter pilot culture that a new pilot will face is that of the traditional Naming. Done professionally and respectfully, a traditional rite of passage Naming could be considered a source of comradery and esprit d'corps. Unfortunately, the Namings in which I have participated have been more akin to fraternity initiations than events that call on the history and pride of a unit, the Air Force, or the country. My Naming at Luke Air Force Base began with mandatory drinking (they respected my desire not to drink, but those who did were frequently ordered to do so), moved into the singing of fighter pilot songs, and finally ended in a scripted "knighting" ceremony (because the squadron was the Emerald Knights) at which we were given our names. By the time we were done, several of the new pilots were vomiting and falling over themselves. One pilot ended up standing on the bar in his underwear. Another had inebriated courage and wrestled one of the instructor pilots until he took a face plant and broke a tooth. As the sole sober member of our class I had the pleasure of driving him to the emergency room, but he refused to go in for fear that he'd get in trouble for hurting himself while drunk. Fortunately (for me), his wife (not fortunate for her) met us there and took care of him.

I'd long been told I was more mature than my peers, but among adult military officers I had only recently thought it might still apply. I once thought to myself that if I really wanted to participate in such events, I'd resign from the military, go back to college, and join a fraternity. Even if I could accept the immaturity, it was tedious and conscience-strickening to be one of the only sober people around. When groups of drunken pilots start tossing tables out of windows, the only ones concerned about safety and the police are the owners and the sober ones in the room. Also, once committed to a group of drunken pilots, it's difficult to leave them; if a sober person leaves and something happens, the next day someone will question why he left his inebriated friends to fend for themselves. The repercussions can actually be one step more serious. I know a sober fighter pilot who received disciplinary paperwork for failing to prevent his drunken friends from causing damage during a night of partying. The fact that the drunkards are grown adults responsible for their own actions may not prevent a sober officer from bearing some responsibility for them.

While I did not have any positive feelings about the Naming experience I had at Luke, I thought I would see if the one held at my first assignment was any different. My first operational assignment was to the 23rd "Fightin' Hawks" of Spangdahlem Air Base. The more experienced 23rd pilots had convinced me that the Hawk Naming was a tradition that would foster a mutual respect among those with whom I would go into combat. Even so, I made known my desire not to participate in some questionably moral aspects of the event. While officially no one would talk about what occurred during the Naming (to maintain its mystique), I found out that at some point the new guys were required to sing the "Hawk song," which was rife with foul language and sexuality. When I mentioned that I would not sing it, the Ancient Hawk (the pilot who had been in the squadron the longest and ran the Naming) was livid. When he realized that I wasn't going to change my mind, he allowed me to participate and substituted *Happy Birthday* instead.

The Hawk Naming began with an immense amount of drinking and a round of golf. To make up for the lack of inebriation in those who did not drink, teetotalers were required to drink disgusting concoctions of various drinks or imbibe immense amounts of highly caffeinated beverages. After each hole of golf we were required to yell a phrase that was related to the score. The only clean example is what happened if we birdied a hole; since our mascot was a Hawk, and our squadron phrase was "Hawks Rule!," whenever we birdied the new guys were supposed to yell "Hawks Rule!" The phrases for other scores are unacceptable for repetition, and I refused to say them at the time as well. After the golf game we ate and then moved through an obstacle course that was part of the base. There were various trivia questions to be answered along the way, and various drinking penalties associated both with the obstacles and the trivia. The final portion of the ceremony involved eating a concoction of various foods that under normal circumstances would be unpalatable, but when mixed together was revolting.

Finally, the new guys were corralled off by themselves and then called one by one to kneel before the Ancient Hawk, who asked a list of scripted questions: why are you here, why do you want to be a Fightin' Hawk, what were you before you were a part of this squadron, and things of that nature. We were challenged to present our coin, which we had to do in the correct "manly fashion." The next step was to drink from the chalice, which was yet another excuse to consume immense amounts of alcohol. The new guy was ordered to sing the squadron song, and finally, the new pilot had to "consume the ovum," or eat a whole, raw egg. I have no idea what the source of that tradition is, though many unit Namings include it. What I do know is that at a previous Naming a pilot had contracted salmonella; as a protective measure, at future Namings the flight surgeon gave the new guys an antibiotic at the beginning of the Naming. After that last step, we were told our new "Hawk name," everyone cheered and shook our hand. If at any point we answered a question to the dissatisfaction of the crowd, we could be sent back to the group of new guys only to have to repeat the same events again. While waiting, the group of new guys was egged on to sing fighter pilot songs. By the time all the new guys were done, the Naming had lasted nearly an entire day.

The Naming I went through in the 23rd Fighter Squadron was so demeaning, degrading, and immature that I swore I would never go through another. While new guys were always coming into the squadron, I avoided their Namings. On one occasion I met the group at the end of their Naming ceremony; I wanted to check on the status of a fellow Christian (also a non-drinker) who had been in that group. The pressure to attend an initial Naming was intense, and I did not actively discourage him from attending (though he told me he considered it), as even I had attended my initial Naming. To skip one's initial naming was unheard of.

My next operational assignment was to the 36th Fighter Squadron at Osan Air Base, Korea. The "Flying Fiends" flew the Block 40 version of the Viper, or the F-16CG, which specialized in dropping laser guided bombs (LGBs). The fighter pilot mentality was significantly more pronounced at Osan than at Spangdahlem, primarily because the majority of the pilots were on an unaccompanied remote tour. This meant that they were without their families, were only at Osan for a year, and their lives revolved around the squadron. I was torn on how much to participate in the raucous revelry at the squadron. It wasn't good to totally separate myself from the other pilots: those among whom I worked were the same with whom I would fly into combat. On one hand, I feared I might alienate those to whom I might witness because I didn't want to participate in foolishness; conversely, I might estrange younger Christians looking for a mentor in the struggle against the evils of the fighter pilot life.

The tradition of the 36th combined the characteristics of Friday night events and Namings. These events were called the Fiend "Show of Colors." The fighter squadron put on one of its shows just a week after I arrived. I was unsure if I should attend; I didn't really know what the content of the show would be, but experience told me it would involve alcohol, profanity, and movies and songs that were hardly edifying. The pressure to attend was significant, particularly since it would be my first show—my attendance was essentially required. Virtually every day I was asked if I was attending and was forced to justify my vague replies. Ultimately I skipped the show. I avoided subsequent shows as well, and since the show doubled as a Naming, I became the oldest (and only) unnamed Fiend.

I knew that many disliked my avoidance of the shows. Since I sidestepped the Naming at Osan, though, my perspective broadened from my previous experience at Spangdahlem, where I had attended the Naming and not discouraged others from attending. I had now done the unprecedented by not becoming a Named fighter pilot, and felt added assurance to support those who were struggling with the peer pressure to participate in those kinds of events; I could speak experientially about Namings but could also discourage Christians from participating if it was appropriate.

Not all units have Namings as "bad" as the ones I went through. Some may be immature but not necessarily immoral. Some may actually be fun. For some fighter units the Naming may be the basis for many of the relationships a Christian has in his squadron. As discussed earlier, choosing to attend a Naming will almost certainly be the less controversial decision. While I believe my decision not to attend the initial show at Osan was correct, avoiding a Naming may not be the correct choice for every fighter pilot and could *potentially* be detrimental to a Christian's witness to his fellow fighter pilots. At least one Christian fighter pilot who did attend the shows was able to talk to other Christians who also went because they had a common frame of reference. Conversely, I shared something with those who *didn't* go to the shows. My choice doesn't represent *the* answer but *an* answer, and perhaps not even the best one. I do not believe that either I or the show-attending Christian fighter pilot was necessarily wrong. It is entirely possible that God was using each of us exactly where He wanted us.

An event similar to fighter pilot namings occurs on a much smaller scale during the Friday night roll call. I saw the beginnings of this when the members of my pilot training class gambled and drank in the flight rooms on Friday after work. At IFF, the members of my class *pushed it up* every Friday night. In aviation, *pushing it up* refers to increasing the throttle setting; e.g., pushing the throttle up, or forward. In the fighter pilot culture, the phrase refers to a night of partying and heavy drinking. Because I knew vaguely what the group was doing I abstained from their escapades and the peer pressure to attend was light. Early the next week I would hear portions of their Friday night exploits as they recounted their legends at work; they often involved a great deal of inebriation, someone vomiting on the hood of a car, and escapades with the employees of the local strip clubs. Because of their unique training environment, the pilot training and IFF events were somewhat different than those of the operational fighter community. In an operational squadron on a Friday night, the pilots gather at the squadron bar to tell funny stories about each other and regale others with tales of other pilots' missteps throughout the week. Some of the more experienced pilots will relate their war stories and argue tactics. There will be a significant amount of drinking, profanity, and the singing of fighter pilot songs.

So, what should a Christian's criteria be on whether or not he will attend? What is his fight floor? There may be some positive aspects to the event: in sharing in the story telling and listening to the tactical arguments, he'll build comradery with the squadron pilots and perhaps even increase his tactical knowledge of his aircraft. If he attends but chooses not to participate in the singing of the fighter pilot songs, he could be a potential witness to those that do sing, particularly if they claim to be Christians; if they're not Christians but notice his silence, it could be a door to a witnessing opportunity. On the other hand, there are significant negative aspects to the evening. The evening will be laced with profanity: becoming desensitized to profanity is one of the greatest threats a Christian faces. Even if he doesn't participate in the entire event, he risks his silent presence being perceived as approval. Other Christians may be confused by his presence.

What should a Christian do? Would God be glorified by his attendance? Is the event edifying? Is he strong enough to attend without being spiritually harmed? Would going to the event appease the peer pressure, or would it serve a spiritual objective? Who does he hope to influence by going? What will other Christians think? Will his witness be helped or harmed by going?

There is no single correct answer. Each Christian must make his decision and rely on God's power for the wisdom to make the correct choice. God does not toss us into the lion's den, but helps and upholds us:

So do not fear, for I am with you; do not be dismayed, for I am your God. *I will strengthen you and help you*; I will uphold you with my righteous right hand. (Isaiah 41:10, emphasis added)

Ultimately, whatever decision a Christian makes, God will be his witness.

Chapter 6:
Priorities

T HE AMERICAN MILITARY is faced with tremendous operational demands, or what is often called a high *ops tempo*. This refers to the constant demands placed on a unit in the form of frequent deployments, exercises, and inspections. While the nation has virtually always had immense global obligations, in the modern military era a significant emphasis has been placed on "doing more with less." Since the early 1990s the US military has actually decreased in size while the number of worldwide contingencies has increased. This has increased the workload of the individual Airmen, Soldier, Marine, and Sailor. High ops tempos mean different things in different units and at different times. A few years ago, fighters tended to go on fewer deployments but for longer periods, up to 90 days or more at a time. This was primarily due to the great number of operations they were supporting: NORTHERN WATCH, SOUTHERN WATCH, and the operations in Bosnia were just a few. Heavy airframes tended to go on shorter deployments, perhaps only a few days or a week, but at a rate of nearly one or two a month.

Since the end of Operation IRAQI FREEDOM, the true ops tempo for the fighter bases has actually declined. There is still the occasional deployment to Iraq or protective patrols over US cities, but overall the demand for fighters has decreased significantly. On the opposite end of the spectrum, the US Global War on Terror has been largely accomplished by Army and Marine forces. These widely scattered forces have been deployed, transported, and continuously resupplied by the heavy airlift side of the Air Force; so, over the past several years, the true ops tempo of the heavy community has significantly increased. These changing ops tempos are merely an example of the various sinusoidal phases that everything goes through in the Air Force (and the military as a whole). Military history reveals the peaks where recruiting was at its highest, followed by the troughs where committed servicemen were forced out of the military due to cut-backs. There were highs in spending and acquisition, and lows where equipment was used well beyond its intended life. Those same peaks and troughs characterize ops tempo, military expansion and reduction, budget-ary allotments, training emphasis, and every other aspect of the American military.

A Christian needs to understand how the ops tempo affects him. The ops tempo in some ways defines how busy the pilot will be, regardless of the overall mission of his unit. In a unit with a high ops tempo, flying will be frequent, urgent non-flying duties will be constant, and days will be long. It is often difficult in this environment to commit to activities outside of the squadron, particularly during the week, because the demands of the job may keep a pilot at work at unusual hours, or he may return home and feel so physically or emotionally exhausted that he just wants to collapse on his couch and rest. Currently, it seems that every Air Force fighter unit is ex-periencing a high ops tempo. With these challenges, a Christian must de-termine his priorities, continually reevaluate them, and make decisions in his life in accordance with them. In the constant high ops tempo of the mili-tary life, there is often the joke that there are countless #1 priorities—if one thing isn't a crisis, another is. Whether true or not, deadlines, squadron leadership, and personal organizational skills will all combine to create a list of important, urgent, and "hot" things to accomplish. A Christian has additional priorities, including spiritual growth, fellowship, contribution to the body of Christ, and family.

A Christian's priorities should serve as a guide rather than a list of rules engraved in stone. Even if he has his priorities set, there are times that sacri-fices must be made, and situations in life may require temporary adjust-ments to priorities to achieve a required goal or fulfill obligations. With that in mind, I suggest the following thoughts when setting personal priorities:

God First

God is always first. When a Christian tries to make Him anything but that, his entire life suffers as a result. The application of this God priority is largely in the personal, because regardless of the demands of duties a Chris-tian must still choose to make God his priority in his personal life. What-ever his spiritual habits, he must allow himself time for prayer, personal Bible reading, spiritual stretching that will result in growth, and communion with a church body. The God priority means that instead of hanging out at a squadron party late on Saturday night and being unable to get up the next morning, the Christian goes home and goes to bed so that he'll be coherent at church. It may mean that in his packed schedule he gives up a precious TV sitcom to have a few minutes of Bible reading. Ultimately, the God pri-ority means that when ideas, goals, and activities conflict, he values God above men—and himself.

In the professional application, the God priority doesn't mean that a Christian should refuse to accomplish his duty—if the orders are legal and moral, he has little reason to contest them. Obedience to God is required above obedience to men, but there may still be times when legal, official duties conflict with desired spiritual activities (Acts 4:19; 5:29). In those cases a Christian may need to make a change in his personal life to ensure the preeminence of the God priority. If he's required to accomplish an official duty on Sunday morning, he may need to alter his normal schedule and go to a Sunday evening service; though it consumes precious free time, he makes the extra effort because of the priority of God in his life. In the case of a regular interruption that he cannot make up in his personal life, it is not unreasonable to ask for occasional time from a supervisor to attend to spiritual needs. For example, if a Christian is required to work every Sunday morning and could not somehow attend an evening or Saturday service in lieu of Sunday morning worship, he should feel free to ask his supervisor for time to attend a service; depending on the circumstances, the supervisor may even be required to allow him time to do so.[1]

Family Second

A Christian's second priority should be family, and it is high priority for good reason. I knew a pilot who had a young wife and a daughter who was less than a year old. During a lull in a base exercise his wife thought it would be nice to try to bring him lunch at the planning cell, where he was hard at work behind a desk instead of flying. She strapped their baby into the car and deftly navigated around the concertina wire and concrete barricades. She arrived at his work just in time to get caught in the middle of a mock ground battle. A young airman from the security forces unexpectedly lay across her hood and let loose hundreds of blank rounds from an M-60 machine gun. Fortunately, she had some experience with the military and knew it was part of the exercise; she managed not to panic as brass rounds bounced off her windshield. She was concerned for their daughter, but she needn't have been: the kid slept soundly through the entire firefight.

While her situation was somewhat unique, her circumstances were not unusual; the family is just as much *in* the military as is the fighter pilot. The military life is challenging not only for the service member, but also for the

---

[1] Air Force Instruction 36-2706, *Military Equal Opportunity (MEO) Program*, 29 July 2004. Paragraph 8.1.2 states that "commanders will approve requests for accommodation of religious practices when accommodation will not have an adverse impact on military readiness, unit cohesion, standards or discipline." This does not mean that a commander is required to let a person do a specific thing at a specific time. Paragraph 8.2.1 states that "these guidelines do not require a specific form of religious accommodation." 8.2.4 says "commanders and supervisors cannot guarantee accommodation of religious practices. Accommodations are subject to change if circumstances warrant." According to 8.3.1, the member's responsibility is to "initiate the request for accommodation at the lowest level," meaning he starts with his supervisor, not his congressman, when he desires to make such a request.

spouse and children. An oft quoted phrase regarding the military/family relationship is that "you'll retire from the military in 20 years, but your family will be around for your lifetime." If a Christian wants his family to be there when he separates or retires, he needs to give them the attention that they need *now*.

God has given specific commands for husbands, wives, and parents to be responsible for their families (through Paul, for example, in Ephesians and Colossians); additionally, the Air Force, which has generally been regarded as the more "family friendly" of the armed services, continues to recognize that a military member's family life directly influences the performance of his duties. The family priority means that after the Christian assesses his actions in relation to his God priority, he determines what the impact will be on his family. He may be offered a duty assignment that would be beneficial for his career but would consume so much of his life that it would detract from his support of his family. He may be faced with the prospect of a remote assignment that will separate him from his family for a year or more. In the case of an involuntary remote assignment, the family priority may mean investing in cameras, internet connections, large phone bills, and an immense amount of personal time to maintaining the integrity of his family.

Again, the family priority does not mean that because he has a family a Christian will refuse to accomplish his duty. It is important to note that legal, required, and moral duties can still be "harmful" to the family: one obvious example is the deployment of troops to war. Wars are not fought only by single, childless men. The separation that occurs and the stress that it places on the family are unfavorable, but this is one case where I believe the commitment to country rises above the needs of the family. Outside of responding to the nation's call to war, though, there will be many times when a Christian will need to carefully assess the requests of his professional career with the needs of his family.

As a general rule, fighter pilots work long days. In many cases the long days are separated by short nights; it is often tempting to come home, fall asleep, wake up, and go back into work. While that is easy and maybe occasionally desirable for a single pilot, the families of others will not appreciate it. In a perfect world, a pilot's spouse will understand that the military will sometimes make those requirements of him and will honor his fatigue. However, his family still needs his presence, time, and effort. Most honest time stealers are temporary in nature: combat, preparing for combat, exercises, and inspections all demand extra time but also have limited durations. Even during those times, a Christian may need to make up lost time and attention by making special efforts on the weekend.

I personally believe that a fighter pilot should try to keep his weekends sacred to relax and be with his family—if he is not required to work on the weekend, he should make every effort not to. When life is harder—when it's toughest to spend time with family—family time is more important, not less so. Even those who are single need to consider the family priority. Single fighter pilots still have parents and siblings, and at some point they may eventually desire to have a family of their own. Considering the impact of decisions on a family life—even while single—will make a Christian habitually consider his family priority after he is married and has children.

A Christian must also carefully consider perceived conflicts between his God and family priorities. There is no Biblical example of God demanding (or allowing) the break-up of a family to accomplish His will; on the contrary, the Old and New Testaments place priority on the marriage and family relationship, which are to be *followed* by Godly service. In the Old Testament, newly married men were not sent to war until a year after their wedding (Deuteronomy 24:5). In the New Testament, God commanded that men be in control over their own houses before they started working for Him (1 Timothy 3).

Unfortunately, there are countless examples in the Christian community of those who have had the foundations of their faith questioned by the break-up of their family. Sandi Patty was one of the leading figures in the contemporary Christian music movement; her positive contributions were virtually forgotten when she committed adultery with a band member, then divorced her husband and married her newly divorced lover.[2] Amy Grant, a popular Christian singer, practically fell out of the Christian music industry when she divorced her husband and married country music artist Vince Gill (also recently divorced) less than a year later.[3] Dr. Charles Stanley, pastor of the First Baptist Church of Atlanta and the personality of the television ministry *In Touch*, divorced his wife of 44 years in 2000.[4] Dr. Stanley's case gained particular notoriety because of his celebrity status and because in 1995 he had promised to step down as pastor if his then-separation became divorce. When he did not do so, he was supported by his church and widely criticized outside of it for leading a life that was inconsistent with God's commands; in 1 Timothy 3:4-5, Paul said that someone who wanted to be a church leader had to have his family in order, because, Paul asked, if he could not manage his family, how could he take care of God's church?

Besides such infamous stories of spiritual shortcomings, there are also many anecdotes about missionaries' marriages failing due to the unique challenges of the mission field. One couple rationalized their failed marriage by saying that they were "serving God so faithfully" they had neglected their own relationship; I don't believe such an attitude is scriptural. God repeatedly emphasized the marriage relationship throughout the Bible—from the union of Adam and Eve "as one" in Genesis, to Jesus' "let man not separate" directive and the description of the church as Christ's bride in the New Testament (Genesis 2:24, Matthew 19:5-6). Ultimately, *obedience* to God is the highest priority, but a Christian must not take on the

---

[2] Morgan, Timothy E. "Sandi Patty Stages Comeback." *Christianity Today,* January 1998.

[3] Moring, Mark. "Simply Complicated." *Christianity Today,* August 2003.

[4] Colson, Charles W. "A High Profile Divorce: The Cost of Biblical Faithfulness." Breakpoint, Prison Fellowship Ministries, June 2000.

attitude that what he perceives as *service* to God is worth the loss of his family. This is similar to what Samuel was trying to explain to Saul when he told him that "to obey is better than sacrifice" (1 Samuel 15:22). To obey God, including His commands that families are appropriately tended to, is better than any act of service.

Third: The Job

A Christian's third priority should be his job. The job priority means assessing how decisions and actions will impact his work, professional advancement, and career. I emphasize the word *job* and place this priority here for a specific reason: being a fighter pilot is a job, it is not a life. I have chosen a job that I enjoy and one I think I'm good at. In the end, though, it is still just a job. If I woke up tomorrow and could not be a fighter pilot, I wouldn't go out and commit suicide. I wouldn't wallow in self-pity or be unable to see my existence outside of a jet. There is more to this life. While I would be disappointed, I would still stand up straight and ask God, "What would You have me do now?" My job as a fighter pilot is not the definition of who I am; it is but a fraction of what I am. It is also not a Christian's *duty* to be a fighter pilot. A military job is often confused with duty. By virtue of choosing a military fighter pilot *job*, I have volunteered and vowed to accomplish my *duty*. There are times when a Christian may need to make sacrifices in other areas of his life to accomplish his military duties. I believe that a Christian should freely, even joyfully, sacrifice to accomplish his sworn *duty*. However, he should carefully examine those times when his *job* demands such sacrifice, and do so with caution.

Many fighter pilots misprioritize their job, placing it above themselves and their families. Even Christians sometimes put their job above God; to many non-Christians, being a fighter pilot *is* their god. Being a fighter pilot must have its proper place—an important aspect of a complete life, but ultimately just a job to accomplish. As noted earlier, there are times that even this priority may need to be adjusted. A pilot who is attending a rigorous training course may need to commit more time to work in order to excel—it is possible that a Christian may best glorify God by his success in the course. That decision must be well thought out, but it is not unreasonable. The change in priority in order to give the course the attention it requires should be temporary, and, while other priorities may see sacrifices, they should not be abandoned.

By placing the job so low on the priorities I don't intend to imply that a Christian's job should be considered a nuisance or something to be avoided. A Christian cannot become a slave to his squadron, but he also cannot marginalize it. Work is not evil; on the contrary, it is divinely commanded.[5] New Testament verses repeatedly state that those who do not work should

---

[5] Chapter 10 of *Biblical Ethics* by James P. Eckman (Crossway Books, 2004) has an excellent discussion of the Christian perspective on work.

not eat (2 Thessalonians 3:10). Even Paul, whose ministry spread the gospel throughout the world, continued to work as a tentmaker well into his missionary journeys (Acts 18:3, 5; 2 Thessalonians 3:8). A Christian should work at his job wholeheartedly, as though working for God and not men (Ephesians 6:7). He should put his best effort into the work he does and demand the highest quality results from himself. This will ensure that he presents a good image of himself and of the God he speaks so often about. A Christian also shouldn't marginalize his job to focus his spiritual efforts somewhere else; the harvest is plentiful in the fighter pilot community. A fighter pilot who neglects his job to serve God elsewhere may devalue God to his coworkers. Ultimately, the importance that a Christian places on his job needs to be in the proper perspective relative to all his priorities.

Somewhere a military science instructor is rolling over in his grave (or, more accurately, falling out of his rolling office chair) because of where I placed the priority of *job*. Yes, it is true: the second Air Force core value is *Service before self*, and many would consider religious and family priorities to be self-oriented. Service before self means an officer puts the interests of the nation above his own; that is, an officer doesn't make decisions that benefit himself but harm the nation or the mission. In the plainest terms, service before self means pilots should not be selfish. When the needs of military service and the country are greater than a Christian's own needs, then, yes, he should place service first; this goes back to the caveat that there are times that sacrifices and temporary adjustments must be made in priorities. However, each person needs to make sure that he is rightly interpreting what the service *needs*. Does the military really need him to spend 80 hours at work a week? Service before self doesn't mean that he continually neglects himself—or his family, or his God—for the service. A fighter pilot can only deny himself so much before service suffers—*service* and *self* are not mutually exclusive. People accomplish the mission, and if the priority of taking care of "self" (e.g., religious or family priorities) is too low, then the fighter pilot won't be in any condition to perform his assigned mission.

Living Christian Priorities

The primary adversary for all of these priorities will be time. Time restrictions in the fighter pilot world are generally self-induced: an upgrading instructor pilot may spend hours working on a perfect brief, a supervisor may go in on the weekend to write a performance report, and every pilot is "highly encouraged" to attend every conceivable social function. If these events are consistently stealing a pilot from other priorities, it is possible that he is managing time poorly. Many officers spend a significant amount of time socializing or otherwise filling their day with distractions or unnecessary tasks, which results in them departing at the end of the duty day without having completed a full day's work—meaning that they'll have to take work home or work on the weekends to fulfill their obligations. It is tempting in the military, particularly as an officer climbs in the ranks, to come into work on the weekends or take work home. In such a situation a Christian needs to strive to adhere to his priorities, have the discipline to work diligently without becoming sidetracked, or perhaps invest in time management instruction, for which there are a plethora of secular and religious self-help resources.

Poor time management isn't the sole reason some officers have so much work to do. Sometimes officers have many irons in the fire for legitimate reasons; each assigned task demands time, attention, and perfection. What can a Christian do? To paraphrase the law of diminishing returns, the longer he works on a project the less improvement he's making in it. At some point the project must be done, even if it's not perfect. Eventually, the value of the extra hour about to be spent on a project is not worth the value it would have if spent on higher priorities. A Christian officer strives for the Air Force core value of *Excellence in all we do*, but it is not "perfection in all we do." That is unachievable as a human; a fighter pilot will only frustrate himself and add stress to his life if no job is ever complete and no amount of effort is ever sufficient. As a fighter pilot matures, he will be able to look back and see those points where his enormous extra effort yielded little additional result; with experience, he will recognize those points sooner and more readily call the project complete and move on.

This readiness to accept completion is important: a fighter pilot can *always* study more tactics, prepare more for the next flight, or memorize more for a checkride. At some point he must be prepared to accept completion, shut the book, and move on. Even General Patton, in a quote that every Air Force Academy graduate knows, acknowledged that "a good plan executed now is better than a perfect plan next week."[6] Ultimately, a constructive attitude like this will enable an officer to eat and sleep better, complete more projects on time, and have more time for important priorities. This, in turn, will actually benefit his work. While fighter pilots may strive for perfection, they also know the impossibility of that goal—the objective is the best effort to produce the best result given all pertinent constraints.

Time management and priorities may require that a Christian learn to say *no*, even to otherwise worthwhile activities. Christians are often pressured to volunteer for a multitude of events, particularly those related to the church. There are many good things to do in this world. One person cannot do them all or all at once, which is why God gave us wisdom and common sense. Whether it is the phrase *spread thin* or *overstretched*, both imply that a person has extended himself beyond his capability to fulfill his commitments. Fighter pilots have immense obligations in all aspects of their lives; the potential for successful time management can be improved by making discerning choices.

---

[6] "Quotations by General George S. Patton." Copyrighted by the estate of George S. Patton, Jr. http://www.generalpatton.com/quotes.html. Viewed 09 March 2007.

The priorities suggested above are intended to remind a Christian about what is truly important in his life. Ultimately, a balance of all priorities—God, family, and job—is required.

Persecution

It is possible that a Christian who adheres to these priorities may be persecuted as a result.[7] What is a Christian to do in the face of persecution?

First, a Christian should not *seek* it. He should not make decisions with the intent of inflicting self-suffering and intentionally drawing persecution, even as a confirmation of his spirituality. The attitudes of "look how much I'm suffering for my faith" and "look how humble I am" may give a degree of self-satisfaction, but they produce little positive results.

Second, if a Christian feels as though he is being persecuted, he should be sure that he is suffering for the sake of righteousness and not because he's offensive, rude, foolish, or obnoxious. A Christian should not be quick to cry "persecution." Conflict will happen; claiming religious discrimination every time it does will cause others to believe a Christian is a self-proclaimed martyr using religion as a crutch. Simply being a Christian and "mistreated" does not equal persecution. Many a street corner Bible thumper has proudly hailed their time in jail as suffering like Paul; they ignore the legal advice to obtain a permit so they can evangelize without punishment. If a Christian breaks the law or even merely violates common sense he will be justifiably rebuked by those around him, regardless of any religious affiliation the situation may have had.

As an example, many Christians are familiar with the encouragement to "pray continuously," and some in the military may feel the need to do just that to make it through the day. A Christian should take that advice to heart, but qualify it in the workplace: if he is constantly ducking out to pray and his supervisor is consistently unable to find him, he'll bear the wrath of a righteously angry boss (just as a smoker would for constantly being on a smoke break).

The same is true if other "higher priorities" interfere with work, like spending time on a government phone with a spouse (supporting the family priority). While some might argue that such activities would be permissible as long as the quality of work didn't suffer, a Christian who spent such time on non-work related tasks could still generate the *perception* of neglecting his job. A supervisor can rightfully expect that his subordinates should work during duty hours—and, perhaps more importantly, a person's peers can rightfully expect that he shoulder his share of the load. There is a time and a place for everything, and sometimes it's the time to work—even if there is a desire to spend time on a "higher priority." For a Christian to be asked to accomplish his duties is not religious persecution.

---

[7] In the modern American military, true personal persecution is relatively rare; I have never experienced it in my career.

Lt Col Terry Stokka, a retired Air Force navigator and Christian officer, recounted a story about a navigator who would read his Bible while his aircraft was passing through thunderstorms out over the ocean, rather than monitoring the storms and assisting in guiding the aircraft around them. When the members of his crew expressed their displeasure with his *priorities* (placing his religion above them), he felt that he was being persecuted for his faith. He didn't understand that he was being "persecuted" for mistreating his crewmates.[8]

In each circumstance that a Christian dishonors his superiors or his peers while using religious rationale he tends to harm Christ's kingdom more than help it. Those that are "persecuting" him view him as foolish not for religious reasons but for secular ones; when he draws up a religious shield in response (i.e., plays the martyr), his peers see his Christianity with the same disdainful view.

Finally, the possibility exists that a Christian may be truly persecuted for his faith. Incidents of "religious friction"—from slight offense to discrimination—do occur in the military, just as any other form of conflict in an organization with hundreds of thousands of members. The majority of occurrences are resolved at low levels and are thus kept out of the public eye. Some instances could be classified as religious discrimination and would be considered illegal within the military justice system. The primary regulation regarding the military and religious accommodation is Department of Defense Directive 1300.17.[9] In the Air Force, Chapter 8 of Air Force Instruction 36-2706, *Military Equal Opportunity Program* addresses religious accommodation.[10] Both are relatively short and worth reading. If a military officer or action contravenes either of these two regulations then a wrong has occurred. While the regulations do contain a few specific examples, there is obviously significant room for interpretation. A blatant example would be a pilot being patently told that he was passed over for a job because of his religion. Other instances of possible persecution might be more subtle or less defined; for example, a Christian refuses to go with the group to a strip club and is verbally derided and harassed about it for the next few weeks.

A Christian's initial response to personal persecution should be to rise above it. First, to yield is to bend to those who would harass him. Like the child or teenager that finally succumbs to peer pressure, one who changes his behavior because of persecution will only admit defeat. Second, if he becomes overly defensive he implies that God is insufficient; otherwise he wouldn't need to worry about the words (or even the sticks and stones) of those who would persecute him. I believe that *nothing* is an appropriate

---

[8] Stokka, Terry. Lt Col, USAF (Retired). "Professional Development and Job Knowledge," published in *Preparing for Active Duty* notebook for the USAFA Class of 1999.

[9] Department of Defense Directive (DoDD) 1300.17, February 3, 1988, updated 13 November 2003. Available from www.dtic.mil. Last accessed 08 March 2007.

[10] Air Force Instruction 36-2706, *Military Equal Opportunity Program*, 29 July 2004. Publicly available on http://www.e-publishing.af.mil. Viewed 08 March 2007.

reaction for personally perceived persecution; however, more action is required if the persecution affects other Christians, if it exceeds the thresholds of what an individual can handle with no response, or if the discrimination is institutionalized.

For persecution that affects other Christians or that can no longer be ignored, a Christian should prayerfully consider beginning at the lowest level and working his way up in an effort to correct the wrong. The person responsible should be confronted—not in an antagonistic way, but in such a way that he knows the offense he has caused. Realistically, few cases progress beyond this point. Generally, a behavior is changed or an apology made long before any other action is required. If the offender refuses to hear the concern or continues in his path, the next step is to seek redress through the chain of command. In cases that cannot be solved with the chain of command (or when the offender is in the chain of command), the offended party can talk to the Military Equal Opportunity (MEO) office, which will begin an investigation to determine if the religious aspects of military regulations were violated. If those agencies do not adequately address the issue, a complaint can be made through the Inspector General's (IG) office, which is essentially responsible for overall investigative oversight within the military.

All of these avenues will take time to run their course, and the agencies involved should be given the opportunity to perform their assigned duties. If the IG is unable to resolve the issue, there is at least one higher level of official complaint. In what is often referred to as a *congressional*, a military member can lodge a complaint directly with his congressman. The congressman's staff then calls on the military commander (often the General or Colonel in charge of the base) to investigate and generate a report. If a Christian feels the need to take this route, he should first ensure he has exhausted all other means. In the past, well-meaning but naïve airmen have immediately called their congressman over inconsequential matters; the bad press that it provides the base, as well as the fact that the chain of command is entirely vaulted over, can cause hard feelings among those involved (even if they sympathize with the one making the complaint). If the complaint is still not resolved, the offense may be systemic and channels outside the military may need to be explored. For responses to these and other institutionalized religious issues, see Chapter 8 on the Christian Response.

Continuing to live a God-honoring life in the face of persecution is difficult—particularly if it is subtle, constant, harassing, and legal. Christians must depend on God's strength and the mutual support of Christian fellowship.

Chapter 7:
Religion and Military Policy

"Remember this: whoever turns a sinner from the error of his way will save him from death..." – James 5:20

AS NOTED IN THE PREVIOUS CHAPTER, the fighter pilot environment forces a Christian to make reactive moral choices; but what about a Christian who wants to *proactively* exercise his faith? Can he actively witness? Can a Christian evangelize his fellow fighter pilots?

Prior to 2004 the Air Force had no official policy on matters regarding religion other than standard prohibitions against discrimination. It was a vague but simple matter, then, for a Christian to live his life with wisdom, tact, and discretion. So long as he didn't beat his fellow pilots about the head and shoulders with the Bible, he would create no grounds for official complaints.

The religious culture in the military has changed, however, as the military continues to address issues of perceived religious intolerance within its ranks. The impetus to the public debate on religion in the military has been the United States Air Force Academy in Colorado Springs, Colorado. In early 2005 the organization "Americans United for the Separation of Church and State" (AU), headed by Barry Lynn, publicized claims of religious malfeasance at the Academy. The AU cited as religious favoritism the case of former Head Coach Fisher DeBerry placing a banner on a wall that included a reference to the athletes being one team in "Jesus Christ." Other allegations claimed that Christians were given preferential treatment, causing non-Christians to feel ostracized or mistreated. In one specific objection, the AU complained that during basic training a Protestant chaplain told cadets that if they were not "born again" that they would "burn in the fires of hell," and then encouraged them to return to their squadrons and witness to their fellow cadets.

The AU was also concerned that the leadership, in the form of military commanders and Academy faculty, had professed beliefs in a particular religion. For example, every Christmas a religious organization had paid for an ad in the Academy paper that explicitly stated the superiority of Jesus. The ad was signed by various members of the Academy leadership—a move that had been approved by the Judge Advocate years earlier when the question of appropriateness was originally raised. The AU used this as an example of an instance where a subordinate would see his leadership advocate a specific belief and then feel that he, too, must advocate that belief to succeed.[1] The AU also cited as "evangelism" the case of an instructor who introduced himself to the class as a born-again Christian.[2] In another case, a senior officer at the Academy emailed a promotion for the National Day of Prayer, and the AU took offense that a person of such rank and authority would advocate a religious event to his subordinates. The Air Force formed a panel to visit the Academy and investigate these claims of religious intolerance, particularly the much publicized allegations that non-Christian cadets had been "harassed by evangelical Christians."[3]

Prior to the completion of the investigation, the Air Force leadership sent out a preliminary message entitled *Respecting the Beliefs of All Airmen*.[4] The text was also published on the Fox News Channel on 26 May 2005. In the message, the Air Force noted that "religious choice is a matter of individual conscience" and emphasized the need for mutual respect. The majority of the message, though, was focused on discouraging the active advancement of personal religious beliefs within the Air Force. The official message codified restrictions on perceived evangelism when it said that

> "supervisors at every level must be particularly sensitive to the fact that subordinates can consider [their] public expressions of belief systems coercive. [Supervisors that use their] place at the podium as a platform for [their] personal beliefs can be perceived as misuse of office (sic). Where, when, and how [supervisors] espouse [their] beliefs is important." The message also said that while disparaging remarks about a person's religion were "obviously" wrong, "more subtle," but also potentially wrong, were "other well-intentioned expressions of personal religious belief.... In no event should one's expres-

---

[1] *The Report of the Headquarters Review Group Concerning the Religious Climate at the U.S. Air Force Academy*, 22 Jun 2005, Headquarters, United States Air Force. Attachment H, p56.

[2] Ibid., pp55-56.

[3] "Air Force Urges Respect for Religious Differences," May 26, 2005, http://www.foxnews.com/story/0,2933,157829,00.html. Viewed 09 March 2007.

[4] Email received 25 May 2005 from the chain of command. Much of the text was also published on FoxNews.com.

sions of personal belief be allowed to appear overbearing."

The *Respecting* message also addressed the use of government email systems, apparently as a result of religious content in email messages cited by the AU. The use of government email has long been restricted to "official use only," but exceptions were included for morale purposes for those who had no choice but to use the government system—Academy cadets and forward deployed airmen were two obvious exceptions. The new message restricted not only cadet morale email but electronic messages Air Force wide: "The indiscriminate use of mass email address lists to send notices that may espouse a particular religious view, or to market a discrete religious event, is inappropriate." "Indiscriminate mass emails" have been routinely used in the Air Force to advertise everything from briefings to barbecues; this new rule banned the use of email for religious items like invitations to a church or Bible study.

After this restriction was published, another minor scandal erupted when the Cadet Wing Commander (the senior ranking Academy cadet) sent a "farewell" email to the cadet wing; the message contained a 22 page attachment with quotes collected from sources as varied as Erma Bombeck and Gandhi.[5] The quotations from Plato and George Patton garnered no attention, however—just the ones from Jesus and the Bible. The mere fact that "Air Force Cadet Sends Religious Email" (which itself was an exaggeration) was deemed newsworthy is an indication of the intense media scrutiny that Christianity in the military was receiving.[6]

The official Air Force report on the religious climate at the Air Force Academy was released in June of 2005. The panel found seven instances of potentially inappropriate religious conduct, which it forwarded to the Inspector General. Otherwise, the panel indicated that though it investigated all claims (including those that had garnered so much media attention) it had been unable to substantiate allegations of overt religious discrimination. Academy cadets themselves contended that many of the perceived religious offenses were overstated in the media. (In fact, the cadets stated that they first heard of the 'shocking environment of religious intolerance' through the media.[7])

Many of the offended cadets said that accommodation, not discrimination, was the problem; i.e., Jewish and Muslim cadets had difficulty celebrating their faiths on Fridays and Saturdays due to classes and mandatory training events, while Christians did not have the same problem on Sundays. The investigative team even asserted the need for young military offi-

---

[5] Zubeck, Pam. "Air Force Cadet E-mail Casts Shadow on Bias Policy." *The Gazette*, June 1, 2005. Viewed online 04 November 2005; no longer available.

[6] "Air Force Cadet Sends Religious Email." Associated Press, 01 June 2005. http://www.foxnews.com/story/0,2933,158256,00.html. Viewed 09 March 2007.

[7] *The Report of the Headquarters Review Group Concerning the Religious Climate at the U.S. Air Force Academy*, 22 Jun 2005, Headquarters, United States Air Force. p31.

cer candidates to be given the opportunity for spiritual development.[8] In response to the AU complaint about the chaplain's 'hell-fire and brimstone' sermon, the report noted that chaplains are, by regulation, expressly allowed to preach their denominational beliefs.[9] The investigators' report also documented that the media frenzy and official inquiries caused by the accusations had created an uncomfortable environment for Christians at the Academy, who now felt that their every movement was being monitored and critiqued. The report stated that because of the public scrutiny, cadets were concerned that many would begin to wholly steer clear of spiritual topics to avoid being accused of religious insensitivity, to the detriment of open dialogue.[10]

As a result of the public attention given to religious tolerance in the Air Force, the Chief of Staff General John Jumper wrote a "Sight Picture," published on 28 June 2005, which reaffirmed that "the expression of personal preferences to subordinates, especially in a professional setting or at mandatory events, is inappropriate." General Jumper repeated earlier statements that the religious tolerance issue was one of mutual respect and justified the regulation of religious expression by noting that "disagreement detracts from teamwork." The Chief closed his letter by saying that "there will be more specific guidance about expressions of personal religious beliefs. This guidance will emphasize mutual respect and the wingman culture fundamental to all Airmen."[11]

The more specific guidance was released in late August of 2005 when the Air Force published an interim version of religious "guidelines" governing acceptable religious conduct in the Air Force. Public prayer was specifically banned, except in "extraordinary" cases and in circumstances of deep military tradition.[12] With respect to the "individual sharing of religious faith," superiors were "cautioned" that their ideas might be perceived as official policy. The guidelines relaxed the restriction on email, stating that the current rules for use of government computers applied equally to all matters, including religious ones. The guidelines also specifically stated that "nothing in this guidance should be understood to limit voluntary, peer to peer discussions."[13]

The guidelines produced in August were advertised as "interim" and open for revision. Immediately following their release the public backlash from religious groups was significant; most claimed that the steps taken to protect those offended came at the cost of the religious free exercise of mili-

---

[8] *The Report of the Headquarters Review Group Concerning the Religious Climate at the U.S. Air Force Academy*, 22 Jun 2005, Headquarters, United States Air Force. pp7-8.

[9] Ibid., p11.

[10] Ibid., p33.

[11] Jumper, John, General. "Chief's Sight Picture: Airmen, Spiritual Strength and Core Values," 28 June 2005.

[12] Air Force Interim Religious Guidelines, p2. The distributed interim guidelines had no title, specified author, or other pertinent data. The publication was very evidently a rough draft.

[13] Ibid.

tary personnel. In February of 2006 the Air Force released revised interim guidelines that addressed that criticism by specifically emphasizing officers' Constitutional rights of free exercise. Public prayer was still not to be a part of "routine business;" in cases where prayer might be "appropriate," it was to be "non-denominational" and "inclusive." The previous email restrictions were removed, with the guidelines noting that the same rules applied to all email content and emphasizing that chaplains' programs would get the same "communications support as would comparable staff activities."[14]

In light of other ongoing debates regarding the role of religion in the military, in October of 2006 Congress rescinded both the Air Force and Navy's recent changes to their religious policies until the issue could be raised for legislative debate in 2007.

The Military and Religion

The iterative Air Force guidelines are only the latest event in a long history of interaction between the military and religion. The military's relationship with religion has always been somewhat unique, given that it is a government organization with a significant number of Constitutionally-sanctioned religious personnel. The military profession often forces men and women to face their own mortality and thus, through religious representatives, provides them the ability to answer life's eternal questions. Historians and social scientists have recorded the fact that, by self-description, members of the US military are more "religious" than their civilian counterparts.[15] This may be because devoted religious persons—and Christians in particular—are often drawn to public service to contribute to a greater good.

Generally speaking, Christians are often good soldiers, sailors, and airmen because they have already given their life for something greater than themselves. Their religion teaches them to have an unselfish spirit and to serve others rather than seek greatness for themselves. They understand commitment and sacrifice because the devotion they have to their faith is often invisible and unrewarding—not unlike the allegiance they pledge to their country. It is true, too, that the military has tended to favor Judeo-Christian religions—primarily because Judeo-Christian values have dominated the American culture. Military chaplains of other religions have entered the military only in recent years.

The recent media frenzy generated at the Academy has placed military Christians in a defensive position, causing them to second-guess actions that were not previously considered inappropriate. An example is the investigation of a chaplain for advocating his doctrinal religious beliefs. As noted by

---

[14] "Revised Interim Guidelines Concerning Free Exercise of Religion in the Air Force," 09 February 2006. No other publication information was included in the document.

[15] Op-Ed, "Religion in the Air Force," *Washington Times.* June 29, 2005 http://washingtontimes.com/op-ed/20050628-090914-8550r.htm. Viewed 09 March 2007.

the Air Force panel, it is the chaplain's *job* to advocate his religion. That is no more intolerant than the Muslim chaplain proclaiming the superiority of Muhammad or the Jewish chaplain saying that Jesus was not the Messiah. It is not offensive, it is the reasonably expected outcome—but it still resulted in a nationally televised news headline.

Another example of conduct not previously thought improper is an officer expressing his personal religious beliefs. Such actions are not without precedent, and examples of military professionals expressing their beliefs extend from the Continental Army to the present day. In one famous example of religious expression in the military, General George Patton ordered his chaplain to write a prayer and then used vital wartime resources to deliver it to 250,000 soldiers—with "the approval, the encouragement, and the enthusiastic support of the Third United States Army Commander."[16] Patton was not charged with religious discrimination. (It is also noteworthy that Patton believed the prayer worked, as he got exactly what he asked for—clear weather.)

One particularly famous superior officer has recently boldly expressed his personal beliefs: President George W. Bush. In fact, *every* modern President (Democrat and Republican) has used his position of authority and place behind the podium to express religious beliefs. Some spoke not only *of* but also *to* God in front of their countrymen and servicemen. None were reprimanded for being religiously intolerant toward the hundreds of thousands of military subordinates of whom they were Commander-in-Chief.

The relationship between the military and religion is changing, however. Truthfully, the environment *within* the military hasn't changed as much as the world *outside* of it. The American culture is gradually shifting toward one that is strictly secular. Religious absolutes are increasingly considered an affront, and prayer is often considered more offensive than profanity. In particular, public criticism of Christianity has recently increased; this may be in part a backlash to the overt religious expression that freely occurred in the emotional aftermath of the terrorist attacks in 2001. In some respects the American culture is even becoming *anti*-Christian, with people desiring freedom *from* religion rather than freedom *of* religion.

Though the investigation of the Air Force Academy resulted in little substantiation of claims of religious intolerance, the Air Force initially took a decidedly defensive posture and reacted primarily to the critics, rather than asserting the virtues of the Academy's spiritual environment. The glut of negative news coverage and the Air Force's initial reactions—which took issues at the Academy and applied a response to the entire Air Force—effectively initiated the regulation of religious expression. In particular, the vague *Respecting* statement that "well-intentioned expressions" of religious

---

[16] O'Neill, Msgr. James H. "The True Story of the Patton Prayer." From the Review of the News, 6 October 1971. Obtained from The George Patton Jr. Historical Society. http://www.pattonhq.com/prayer.html. Viewed 09 March 2007.

preference are as wrong as epithets could be interpreted as a restriction on *any* religious expression.

Several voices, in addition to those of the "oppressed cadets," have been raised cautioning against swinging the pendulum to the other extreme and restricting legitimate religious expression.[17],[18] Unfortunately, the possibility that the pendulum *will* swing even further is likely given that some in authority do not comprehend the full impact of their words and actions. In the US House of Representatives, a Republican from Texas, Mike Conaway, noted that he was a Christian and that in his faith he was "instructed to go and tell." He said that if he did that at the Academy, then he "could be accused of abusive and coercive proselytizing and be charged."[19] Representative David Obey, a Democrat from Wisconsin, disagreed: "No one is objecting to anyone trying to talk about religion. What they are objecting to is the malicious and mean-spirited attacking of other people for the religious views that they do or do not hold."[20] Unfortunately, it is increasingly likely that Rep. Conaway will be proven correct. Congress may not object to merely talking about religion, but the initial official reaction was to do that very thing.

The military's primary spoken reason for creating rules governing religious expression has been "supporting unity." This was echoed in Congress by Democratic Representative Steve Israel of New York who called it an issue of "military readiness" because religion was "dividing people who need to be united."[21] While the military does have a reputation of breaking individuals down to form a cohesive unit, the goal has never been a homogenous force in the vein of *Star Wars'* clone army. (The Army's recently replaced recruiting slogan was even *An Army of One*.) A Marine from the back woods of Louisiana may have personal differences with one from New York; a soldier from a houseful of siblings may not get along well with one who grew up as an only child; a Republican sailor may have ideological disagreements with one who is a Democrat. In each case the military allows the members to have their differences; it merely requires that they work together as professionals regardless.

The Air Force, too, has long been composed of airmen from a variety of religions, backgrounds, countries, and cultures. The Air Force has thrived not only on the unity of its forces but also on its diversity. To say religious differences "detract from teamwork" unjustly vilifies the role of faith in the

---

[17] Op-Ed, "Religion in the Air Force," *Washington Times*. June 29, 2005
http://washingtontimes.com/op-ed/20050628-090914-8550r.htm. Viewed 09 March 2007.

[18] Wilson, Bill. "Air Force Academy Religious Practices Defended." Focus on the Family, June 29, 2005. Viewed online 04 November 2005; no longer available.

[19] "United States House Congressional Record Department of Defense Appropriations Act, 2006." June 20, 2005, page H4766. Located online at the Congressional Record, http://www.gpoaccess.gov/crecord/. Viewed 09 March 2007.

[20] Besser, James D. "Air Force Debate Turns White Hot." *The Jewish Week*. 24 June 2005.

[21] Brown, Elizabeth Cady. "Prayer Force? Military Must Answer To Higher Power: Congress." *Long Island Press*, 30 June 2005.

military. True, two religious military members may have a disagreement, but there are any number of other things over which to disagree, including money, politics, philosophy, and ideology—and yet differing opinions in those areas are not restricted from expression. The military has never been overly concerned that everyone "get along" for the mission to be accomplished, only that they accomplish the mission despite their differences.

One religious action group quipped that the perception of pervasive Christianity at the Air Force Academy would detract from readiness; they claimed that non-Christian but otherwise qualified individuals would be discouraged from joining, which would deny the Air Force a valuable resource.[22] Given that greater than 85% of the Air Force Academy classifies itself as Christian (as well as 80% of the Air Force as a whole), to enact regulations that may be perceived as hostile to Christianity would seem to have the potential for a far greater impact on military readiness.[23] Additionally, such policies fail to acknowledge the good that religion, and in particular evangelical Christianity, has done for the military. Christianity breeds moral people of selfless character, honor, commitment, and perseverance. To restrict the people who contribute so positively to the military can only be a detriment.

In attempting to justify the new policies, another pilot gave me this example: Imagine how you, as a devout Christian, would feel if your commander introduced himself as a Jew and that the majority of pilots in your unit were also Jewish. I admitted that it could potentially be an awkward situation.

My question to him, though, was equally rational and attempted to follow the path of the policy to its logical conclusion: how protected did I need to be? If I saw my Jewish commander walk out of a Sabbath service, I could be just as uncomfortable as if he'd announced it from his position of authority. Does that mean my commander should not be allowed to attend religious services to protect me from potential discomfort? Even if he *was* prevented from attending religious services, I could still find out that he had a religious belief by a variety of other means. To foster a religiously tolerant atmosphere, should my commander be required to have *no* religious beliefs? If so, wouldn't military policy then favor those with no religion over those without? Regulation of religious expression in the military is a slippery slope.

---

[22] Brown, Elizabeth Cady. "Prayer Force? Military Must Answer To Higher Power: Congress." *Long Island Press*, 30 June 2005.
[23] *The Report of the Headquarters Review Group Concerning the Religious Climate at the U.S. Air Force Academy*, 22 Jun 2005, Headquarters, United States Air Force. p5.

Chapter 8

The Christian Response

I N THE FACE OF PUBLIC SCRUTINY of religion in its ranks, it appears the military is slowly becoming officially secular. The initial Air Force religious guidelines told officers they could not use public expressions of faith, advocate a particular belief system, use "well-intentioned" expressions of belief, or have religious content in their emails. While the guidelines were modified and eventually rescinded by Congress, the potential that the military could one day become anti-Christian now seems possible. In addition to changing regulations, Christian officers must also assess the response their actions may receive in the court of public opinion. Otherwise permissible conduct could still conceivably result in a detrimental news headline, official complaint, or congressional investigation; even if a Christian was acquitted after a complaint, would the cost—to his professional career or personal witness—be worth it? If even chaplains are investigated for religious offense, what is a Christian to do if he desires to have an active witness for Christ?

Rights and Regulations

Given the current direction of faith and the military, the possibility exists that the military may one day regulate or restrict religious activities. Opinions vary widely on how or whether a Christian should react to official restrictions on his religious expression. For many years a majority of American Christians watched their nation become increasingly secularized and did little to oppose it, either because they were opposed to Christian political action or felt that God would intervene if He really wanted to. Even in modern times some have argued that Christians shouldn't rock the boat because they believe that the perceived cost is greater than the benefit. They believe that Christianity may lose face or that non-Christians will actually be driven away as a result of assertive Christian actions. Others believe that by doing nothing Christians are, in effect, acquiescing to the will of the secular opposition.

Beginning in the late 1980s and culminating in the 1990s, Christianity came out of the political closet, giving birth to whole organizations and even inadvertently coining the phrase "the religious right." In 1993 the belief that Christians were yielding to secularization was the impetus for the creation of the Alliance Defense Fund (ADF). The ADF is a faith-based legal entity founded by an array of Christian leaders in response to the ACLU, AU, and like-minded organizations that had for years used lawsuits as a weapon against Christianity. The founders of the ADF decided that *nothing* was no longer a valid reaction to hostile acts toward Christianity.

Given the potential costs of both action and inaction, what should a Christian do? To quote the famous fighter pilot answer for every question, "It depends." Each situation will vary with respect to its facts, intent, severity, and unique details. Firing off half-cocked (without knowing all the details) is the quickest way to making an embarrassing apology; a passionate response to an innocent misunderstanding is the second. A Christian should also calmly assess the degree of the restrictions and the repercussions; in short, is it worth it? Battles need to be chosen carefully. If a Christian is fully aware of the facts, is sure of the intent, and considers the severity significant, he should prayerfully consider taking action to react.

The Christian Reaction

One course of action is disobedience. A Christian can view military regulations as an affront and choose to express his faith even in the face of policies that prohibit or restrict it. The advantage of such action is that those around him will see him boldly living for his faith—there will be no doubt where his loyalties lie. Some may even respect the strength of his convictions and be drawn to God as a result. By boldly proclaiming his Christianity in the face of laws that say he cannot, he will also prevent himself from feeling that he is ashamed of or denying Christ. It is also possible that the military would change its policies as a result.

The disadvantage of such a choice is that the disobedience of regulations might result in punishment and ultimately, if he persists, discharge from the military. A Christian would have his spirituality intact but he would be separated from the military. If he chooses to give up his commission to say "I love Jesus" in protest, he may not be able to reach or influence the military—a unique and hard-to-reach community. If every Christian makes a vociferous stand and is discharged, the removal of God from the military will be aided, not hindered. Also, those same peers may view a Christian who disobeys regulations as hypocritical or as flaunting his religion in the face of authority—thus denigrating Christ to the very lost he hopes to reach. A Christian should carefully consider if violating the rules and getting punished is consistent with the values he wants to uphold.

An example of such Christian disobedience occurred in Alabama in 2004 when Judge Roy Moore defied an order to remove a Ten Command-ments monument from his courthouse. Many felt that Christians needed to take a stand against the erosion of their faith in the public arena. Even now, Christians are divided in their reactions to the outcome of that event, in which Judge Moore was removed from the bench for his rebellion. Some are embarrassed by the actions of Christians who defied the law and "made fools of themselves" in a fruitless cause against the government; some are upset at the loss of a valuable Christian in the judicial system; others are proud that Christians made their voices heard and stood up for their beliefs. All sides can legitimately and morally defend their case.

The opposing course of action is for a Christian to obey, even in the face of rules that restrict his religious expression. Christianity has been slowly removed from American culture over the decades, and there are many other professions where speaking boldly for Christ is already forbid-den; faculty and administration members in public education are one well-known example.[1] To accomplish its mission, the military can legally and legitimately enforce regulations that govern the conduct of its troops. Given the course of the military and public opinion, it is possible that Christianity will eventually be restricted in the military. If a Christian chooses to obey the regulations placed over him—even though they restrict his religious expression—he will be in position to reach and minister to a unique group of people. A Christian fighter pilot, then, truly would be a missionary to a "remote" world. If a Christian feels that God wants him to minister to the fighter pilot community, then obedience may be the only option.

While the first course of action has many gratifying aspects—an almost aggressive defense of Christian freedoms in the military—its shortcomings are significant. There are too many Biblical examples of God's people liv-ing in ungodly conditions—without either rebelling or surrendering—to advocate disobeying those in authority. An American Christian fighter pilot is neither Peter nor John, and the military is not the Sanhedrin ordering him not to speak the name of Christ—yet (Acts 4). A Christian must live within the rules of those in authority so long as they are not contrary to God's Word (Hebrews 13:17, Acts 4). Ultimately, though, only God can say that one course of action is more just than the other.

The Christian Influence on Authority

It is important to note that submission does not imply inaction—I advocate obedience, not acquiescence. Complying with authority does not mean that a Christian shouldn't work to prevent or change restrictions on his faith. After all, Christians participate in the political process, because if they do not then they can't complain about the outcome. If military Christians re-

---

[1] I do not intend to imply that I agree with this policy in public education or elsewhere; I merely state it as fact.

main silent and let organizations like the AU speak for them, can they then complain when their religious expression is restricted? Christians can have a voice, and, yes, even a dissenting one. Until they speak up, those in authority will continue to believe that secularists hold the majority opinion.

How should a Christian respond to military restrictions on his faith? In no case should he compromise his morals. If the law of man violates the law of God, a Christian *must* follow the law of God. Assuming the restrictions limit a Christian but are not contrary to God's Word, he still has recourse while being obedient to restrictive regulations.

Just as in cases of personal persecution (Chapter 6), when faced with potentially discriminatory policies a Christian's first course of action should always be to work within the system at the lowest level to correct the perceived wrong; this is counter to the current trend of running to the news media to publicize (rather than solve) a problem. In the Air Force, these systems include the chain of command, the Military Equal Opportunity system, the Inspector General, and the external congressional complaint process.

When those systems fail, the question becomes whether a Christian should take further action outside the system, whether through legal, political, or public information actions. Some have chosen to do so with varying degrees of success, whether by contacting their political representatives, seeking their own public office, or suing the military to change controversial policies. The legal and political systems can be legitimate and useful means to resolve the conflict between certain aspects of the military and religion; sometimes well-intentioned officials write poor regulations or misinterpret and misapply them. It may take a court of law or congressional action to rectify the error. In any case, it should be done carefully.

One successful example occurred in 1996 when an Air Force chaplain urged his congregation to participate in the "Project Life Postcard Campaign," an attempt by the Catholic Church to persuade Congress to overturn President Clinton's veto of the partial-birth abortion ban. Military leadership believed that such actions constituted political lobbying, which is impermissible in uniform, so chaplains were prohibited from encouraging their congregations to participate. Because the perceived discrimination against religious freedom was institutional, the chaplain stepped out of internal systems and, with the assistance of the Becket Fund, sued and won.[2]

Another positive example occurred in 1999 when an Air Force missileer asked that he not be placed on an alert crew with an officer of the opposite gender. (This would require him to be in the cramped quarters of a missile control center for days at a time with only the company of the other officer.) Because he felt that the potential for temptation would affect his commitment to his wife, he sought relief under Department of Defense regulations requiring religious accommodation. For some time several

---

[2] *Rigdon v. Perry*, as cited on The Becket Fund website at:
http://www.becketfund.org/index.php/case/38.html. Viewed 09 March 2007.

commanders accommodated him; eventually, one revoked the accommodation and gave him an unprofessional rating on his Officer Performance Report (OPR). Fearing the OPR would unjustly hinder his career, the lieutenant appealed to a records correction board to have the OPR amended; they partially edited the "unsubstantiated" statements on the OPR but did not fully meet the request. After several years of working internal grievance processes, the lieutenant sued the Air Force with the assistance of the Becket Fund. The Air Force settled and removed the OPR and all references to it from his records.[3]

Both the chaplain and the lieutenant missileer acted appropriately. The chaplain perceived an inappropriate religious restriction and took legitimate actions to ensure continued religious freedom for chapel congregations. The lieutenant missileer spent *years* exhausting the military complaint systems and moved outside of them when they failed. His actions were metered, thoughtful, and respectful. While he was undoubtedly frustrated, there is no record of him spitefully maligning the Air Force on the national news to achieve his goal. The same cannot be said in the case of a hunger-striking Navy chaplain.

In late 2005 Navy Lieutenant (Chaplain) Gordon James Klingenschmitt, a 1991 Air Force Academy graduate, went on a hunger strike near the White House to protest an effort to have him removed from the military for insisting on praying "in Jesus' Name." He said he would maintain his hunger strike until the President signed an executive order codifying the chaplain's right to pray in accordance with his beliefs. After 18 days, the chaplain ended his strike when his commander wrote a letter stating he was permitted to pray in Jesus' Name while in uniform.[4] He not only failed to work within the military system, he actually worked against it in an adversarial relationship with Navy representatives. His public statements and personal website mocked, criticized, and vilified the Navy and his superiors. His actions did nothing to support either his cause or Christianity. Due to his methods he lost support from even those who may have been sympathetic to his plight. Chaplain Klingenschmitt was ultimately court-martialed and discharged for violating regulations regarding uniform wear at political events. As of 2007, his case is still in litigation.

Finally, the *Weinstein v United States Air Force* lawsuit was unique because military Christians participated in legal action when no personal wrong was committed. In 2005 two Air Force officers—a chaplain and an F-16 fighter pilot—joined the Air Force defense in a lawsuit brought by Mr. Michael Weinstein, a 1977 Air Force Academy graduate who claimed that his Jewish son experienced evangelical proselytizing by Christian cadets and officers at the Academy. According to the Alliance Defense Fund, the

---

[3] *Ryan Berry v. US Air Force*, as cited on The Becket Fund website at: http://www.becketfund.org/index.php/case/2.html. Viewed 09 March 2007.

[4] Chaplain Klingenschmitt's personal website, which contains much of the information regarding his controversy, is located at http://persuade.tv. Viewed 09 March 2007.

two joined the Air Force defense because if Weinstein prevailed, "their ability to share their faith and to candidly discuss religion...would be in jeopardy." The fighter pilot stated that he felt he had the "right to discuss my faith without censorship or fear of retribution."[5] The officers were attempting to influence the outcome of military policy even before it was created, just as politically active Christians have done in government. Such action is not only admirable but is also desirable if Christians want to avoid reactively defending themselves against policies that are hostile toward religion.[6]

Beyond joining in on a lawsuit, however, there is currently no effective system in place through which officers can provide inputs or feedback to military leadership on such topics. Christians can still use the chain of command, though experientially it does little to benefit a line airman attempting to influence Department of Defense policy. (Even the Air Force understands this, which is why when it wants average Air Force opinions it distributes surveys for feedback rather than telling airmen to tell their chain of command what they think.) Also, any officer still has a legitimate right to communicate with his congressmen (to encourage legislative action) to influence both the American political scene and US military leadership.

If internal remedies fail, or if the restrictions are systemic or institutionalized, then legal, political, and public affairs actions may be an effective way to reverse the restriction. The potential costs of action are high, but so are the costs of inaction. Christian officers should work to influence leadership decisions regarding the religious environment in the military, but they must use caution, respect, wisdom, prayer, and the counsel of others to guide them.

There will continue to be challenges to the relationship between the military and Christianity—challenges which Christian fighter pilots and other military Christians may face best from *within* the military. Even now, there is a renewed call to end the US Naval Academy noon meal prayer, just as such prayer is now restricted in the Air Force.[7] Within the limitations of acceptable military conduct, Christians can and should work to influence the military leadership's decisions that restrict religious expression.

Evangelism

The primary question remains: can a Christian fighter pilot evangelize? While proactive Christianity is essential, a Christian must approach active *evangelism* in a professional setting with caution. The Air Force empha-

---

[5] "Members of U.S. Air Force seek to intervene in lawsuit to stand up for free speech," Alliance Defense Fund, 08 November 2005. www.alliancedefensefund.org. Viewed 09 March 07.

[6] In late 2006, the lawsuit was dismissed.

[7] The US Naval Academy noon meal prayer is actually in compliance with new Air Force guidance, but this has not silenced calls for ending it, nor has the Air Force Academy opted to institute a similar event during their noon meal.

sized in its initial religious guidelines that nothing was intended to limit "peer-to-peer" discussions. Any Christian's primary evangelistic audience should be his peer group. So long as he acts with wisdom and discretion in his relationships, there is no official restriction on him evangelizing his peers; that is, those officers in a similar rank to his own. In short, the answer is *Yes*, a Christian fighter pilot can evangelize *his peers*.

If a Christian desired to do so, he would also be free to evangelize his superiors, since he could not exert undue influence on them. (The potential still exists, however, that he might receive unintended repercussions *from* his superiors.) Due to the intricacies of professional relationships and the fact that a superior is generally older and more established, a Christian may have difficulty proactively witnessing to a superior officer, though the desire may be great. It is a veritable military tradition that senior officers "thank God" for their successes in change of command and promotion ceremonies. In their farewell speeches I have heard many officers thank God for their successes, even if they hadn't mentioned God up to that point in their tour. At one event I saw a commander and operations officer both claim God as their "number one priority"—though neither had demonstrated that in any aspect of their lives. In fact, their lives showed that they believed the opposite. Outside of a unique personal relationship with such a superior, there are few opportunities where I feel it is appropriate to confront such a person over the discrepancies in his life.

A unique circumstance that I encountered was working for a superior who attended the same church that I did. Regrettably, his language and life at work during the week did not reflect a Christ-centered relationship. Had he been an equal-ranked peer, I would have had little problem speaking with him about the inconsistencies in his life; however, because of his rank and his position of authority over me (and his apparent comfort with his inconsistent lifestyle), I could find no appropriate situation to have such a conversation. While some may believe it was a missed opportunity, even now I do not know if there was a proper way for me to have such a discussion with my superior.

Most recent guidance on religious expression has focused on an officer's potential influence on his subordinates. The authority of an officer provides immense power over subordinates; the potential for improper influence is the reason that the military restricts superiors from certain actions. Just as a Christian would understandably be bothered by a commander that lauded the benefits of the Wiccan cult from the stage at an official event, those with other beliefs would justifiably be offended at a Christian commander delivering a sermon in the same scenario.

A Christian must understand that in today's military, the idea of an officer—in a position of responsibility, authority, and control—*evangelizing* a subordinate is unpalatable. If someone hears that a superior professionally counseled an overtly religious belief, then they could potentially lodge a *legitimate* complaint. Regardless of the outcome of such a complaint, by exposing himself to an indefensible accusation a Christian endangers his career and professional character. While that may be a price well paid for saving a soul, there will be an entire unit of other souls watching as he is chastised or removed from his position. If it is a step a Christian chooses to take, he must realize that there are legitimate military repercussions for his actions.

Given the number of other unofficial means through which the same information can be communicated, I believe the potential cost outweighs the gain. Referring the subordinate to a chaplain is always an option, and it is also possible to associate with the subordinate at the chapel, church, or a Bible study; by his presence in those places the subordinate voluntarily exposes himself to naturally expected religious topics. Even in such a neutral setting, given the politically sensitive atmosphere surrounding religion in the military, when a Christian has the opportunity to actively witness to a direct subordinate he should walk carefully and seek the counsel of the military chaplain or fellow military Christians. If a Christian wants to *actively evangelize* within his professional setting, he should work closely with the chaplains who should be intimately familiar with the rules, restrictions, and requirements.

There are two distinct, important points here: evangelism from positions of authority, and the potential for legitimate religious complaints. I stressed the first because while evangelism from positions of authority is justifiably inappropriate, this does not mean that a superior cannot evangelize—he can, but he must do so in a manner *separate* from his authority. That is, leading a Bible study may be appropriate; sermonizing at a mandatory official function would not. Even while in his position of authority, I *personally* do not believe it is inappropriate for a superior to mention his religious beliefs. I believe he can thank God, describe himself as a "father, husband, and *Christian*," and say "God bless you" without undue influence on his subordinates.

My second point of emphasis was that a Christian should be wary of taking actions that would open him up to *legitimate* complaints. Any person can lodge a frivolous complaint about any action; if a Christian lives his life trying to avoid all complaints he will avoid all risk and therefore miss all opportunities. If actions are prohibited by regulations, then he should be averse to breaking those rules; on the other hand, he should wisely and boldly take actions that are not prohibited by regulation. Some people may still complain, but if the conduct is in accordance with regulations then there will be no grounds for sanction.

There is little explicit guidance for a Christian living his faith proactively in the military. Ultimately, he must use discernment and wisdom in his words and actions. As was famously said, "The Gospel is offensive enough on its own; a Christian doesn't need to be offensive, too." Still, he must be confident in his faith and ready to give an answer for the hope within him—the same pilots who were hostile toward him one day may be the first to seek him out on another (1 Peter 3:15). It's possible that on his first day as a fighter pilot another pilot will walk up, ask him the reason for his faith, and accept Christ as a result. It's also possible that he may never vocalize Christ to other fighter pilots; he may only be planting the seeds that will open them up to the next Christian they encounter (1 Corinthians 3:6-8, 10).

Every non-Christian peer will react differently to a fighter pilot's life example and Christianity; a Christian must profess Christ to each of them as they will receive it. Each personality will be drawn to—and respond to—the Gospel in a different way. There are those who will be won over by a silent witness and those that will respond only when they're physically shaken. Though they have a reputation for being thick-skinned, fighter pilots, as a generalization, have a personality that will instantly become defensive if their perfection is questioned. It's not that they're sensitive; they're just right. Telling a fighter pilot he needs spiritual help is like telling Donald Trump that he needs financial advice; it's incongruous to them. Ultimately, the mere example of a fighter pilot living a Godly, moral, and successful life will have a significant impact on the men and women around him.

A Christian's Most Powerful Evangelism Tool

A Christian must know military regulations and use wisdom in dealing with his peers, but neither the recent media attention nor changes in regulations should cause him to question his boldness in *living* for Christ. Regardless of rules, government, or social culture, his strongest tool remains his personal witness and God-honoring life. Christianity is not outlawed. Speaking about personal beliefs in the military is not completely forbidden; it merely requires discretion and knowledge of regulations. Bible studies have not been banned; they may just require more effort to form and advertise. Religiously-oriented email might raise eyebrows, but there are other creative and approved ways to achieve the same objective.

There are times when a Christian must vocally proclaim his faith, and there are times when his words will only point out his own hypocrisy or alienate him as a "Jesus freak" from those to whom he wants to witness. A Christian must seek God's guidance and pray for discernment to know when those times are. Ultimately, it is by example—a successful, joyful Christian who has his life in order—that non-Christians will open up to the possibility that there really is more to this life.

While the challenges and risks of being an active Christian in the military may seem daunting, the potential price for not effectively living for Christ may be insurmountable. In the book *Stories from a Soldier's Heart*, author Chuck Holton recounts a vivid example of the importance of living a proactive Christian life. He relates the story of Staff Sergeant (SSG) Jeff Strueker, a US Army Ranger who saw action in Somalia. SSG Strueker was a Christian living an active witness, and "it was no secret among his fellow soldiers that he was a follower of Christ."[8] The positive impact of his ministry of presence soon became evident as the events that would make Mogadishu famous unfolded. As firefights and casualties mounted, the reality of combat set in and

> men in [SSG Strueker's] unit who had wanted nothing to do with God before were coming to him for answers…They wanted to know what happened to their friends who died and what would happen to them if tomorrow it was their turn. Strueker and a Christian buddy spent the better part of the next forty-eight hours sitting on their bunks in the hangar while men lined up to talk to them about God.[9]

SSG Strueker's experience demonstrates the powerful impact of a Christian who is actively living his witness. His ministry of presence opened the door to witness to many as they struggled with faith, uncertainty, and death. A Christian must be willing and ready to speak up when God creates the opportunity; he may not know when that door will be opened, or when it will be locked forever.

There is another significant detail to SSG Strueker's story, however. Just prior to the amazing search for faith he saw in his unit, he was faced with the death of Dominick Pilla, a fellow Ranger with whom he had trained for months. Strueker was known in his unit as a Christian, "but as he stood looking at Pilla's lifeless body, he realized that *simply practicing his faith had not been enough*" (emphasis added).[10] While SSG Strueker had been living his witness, he wondered if by being more assertive—more proactive—he could have had a definitive impact on the soul of that lost soldier. His own perceived failure to reach Ranger Pilla so impacted him that he eventually became a US Army chaplain.

A Christian fighter pilot is *in* the fighter pilot world. The fighter pilot world has rules and laws that—so long as they do not conflict with those of God—he must follow. If he decides that "it can't be done," then he has abandoned either his Christian mission or the fighter pilot world. If he believes that God has sent him into the fighter pilot world, then desertion is not an option. Christians must work diligently every day to find how God would have them achieve His purpose in the world in which He has placed them.

---

[8] Gray, Alice and Chuck Holton. *Stories from a Soldiers Heart.* Multnomah Publishers, Sisters, Oregon, 2003. p75.

[9] Ibid., p77.

[10] Ibid., p75.

Chapter 9:
The Christian Reputation

IN ORDER TO HAVE A CREDIBLE WITNESS, a Christian must have a reputation that is above reproach. A fighter pilot's reputation precedes him everywhere he goes in the military. The Air Force fighter world is not large, and within each particular airframe the population is even smaller. In the F-16 world, which is the largest of the fighter pilot communities, there are five operational bases to which a pilot could be assigned as of 2007 (base closures are reducing that number). Due to the constant turnover of pilots, by the time he is at his second operational assignment he will have met nearly half of the F-16 world. By the end of his first operational year he will have a reputation built not only on his actions and attitude but also on the perceptions of others. As people move out ahead of him, they will leave with their perception of him and will disperse to all the bases to which he could possibly be assigned.

When it comes time for a Christian to change assignments, squadron commanders, flight commanders, and others from his first base will contact their friends and counterparts at his future base and will tell them what to expect. When the pilot arrives at his new duty station, it is likely that the majority of the squadron will already have a good idea of his reputation. Even when I was in pilot training, I remember hearing my instructor pilots mention pilots who were inbound to join them as UPT instructors. If one of them knew the inbound pilot, he'd tell the rest that he was a "good guy," or "dirt bag," or "a good stick." Sometimes a more colorful well-known detail from his flying history might also be told.

Having a reputation isn't inherently a bad thing, and having a name and character known beyond immediate surroundings isn't unusual in the world or in history. The Old Testament frequently recounts the reputations of the individual tribes of Israel, whether for their combat skills, their spiritual qualities, or even their physical characteristics. (Apparently a large percentage of the tribe of Benjamin was left-handed (Judges 3:15, 20:16).) The reputation of David's "Mighty Men" is seconded only by that of David himself (2 Samuel 23:8). A Christian's reputation is unique because it reflects on God, similar to the way that the reputation of the nation of Israel was often linked to the reputation of God Himself (for example, Isaiah 48:9-11, Ezekiel 20:9, 36:20-23, 32, 36)). Given that gravity, for what should a Christian fighter pilot want to be known? A Christian can't control every perception that others decide to think about him, but he can control his actions and attitudes that will shape their perceptions. The character he displays in his fighter pilot life—including integrity, work ethic, devotion to the supremacy of God, and attitude—will form the basis of the reputation that will precede him throughout his career.

Reputations are fragile and transient things. Those of many men and women are made and broken over the choice of a particular word, a seemingly insignificant decision, or even complete misunderstandings. In some cases a single mistake may damage a reputation to the point that the error overwhelms any good that has been accomplished. This is particularly evident in government, when a quick verbal faux pas can instantly end what may have been a promising political career. Even the Air Force has occasionally been accused of being a "one mistake" service when it has discharged those that committed one grievous error without giving them a second chance.

Likewise, a Christian's spiritual "career" can potentially be torpedoed by a minor flaw. In recent history this has been personified by the TV evangelist; some have built virtual kingdoms on their multimedia ministry only to watch it collapse as they are found to have had affairs, visited prostitutes, or misused the money for which they so eloquently asked. In some cases their actions weren't even illegal, but because they were supposed moral icons, their flaws made them spiritual laughingstocks to the rest of the world. While Christians are often understanding of the sins in each other—acknowledging that they are "not perfect, just forgiven"—non-Christians see the incongruity of the actions and speech and label it hypocrisy. After such a fall, a Christian has little credibility with his non-Christian audience. A Christian reputation can be irreparably damaged by a single lapse in judgment or moral failure—or even the mere perception thereof.

For that reason a reputation bears a unique importance for a Christian. His reputation can impact the cause of Christ, just as a famous singer or popular televangelist can hurt or help their faith by their actions. For better or worse, a Christian may come to represent his faith to the pilots around him. While a mistake by another may be laughed at and then forgotten, any errors on his part will draw a unique criticism: "That's what he gets for being different from us."

To the worldly fighter pilot, a pilot who separates himself from certain aspects of the group and fails does so *because* of his distance from the group. Since they blame his failure on his separation from the group, and this separation is based on his faith, a Christian who fails may have his shortcomings attributed not just to himself but also to his faith. The dejection that any pilot would feel in the face of failure is felt many times over as he realizes that the cause of Christ has suffered in his fellow pilots' eyes. By the same token, a Christian who impresses his evaluators on checkrides, advances skillfully through upgrades, has well thought out tactical knowledge, and has excellent flying skills will astound his non-Christian compatriots. They will not understand how a pilot can possess those skills without being party to their secular trysts. It is here that the window is opened and a Christian pilot can say that it is "not by my strength…"

Fighter pilot reputations are often based primarily on individual perceptions. To help young wingmen avoid *mis*perceptions on the way to their first assignment, they are often taught about the basic expectations of a young pilot, knowledge that is sometimes called *Wingman 101*. The primary expectation for young pilots is that they be good wingmen. Wingmen should be anxious to learn and always strive to do the best that they can. The *perception* of a wingman giving his full effort to everything he does and striving to be his best will put him foremost in the minds of the flight leads, IPs, and leadership in his squadron. When the time comes to select those next to be upgraded, such a wingman is more likely to be chosen than his peers.

The number one trait that other pilots look for in a young wingman (and even in other pilots) is a *willingness to learn*. A willingness to learn can be seen by acknowledging, receiving, and using an instructor's critiques. A student pilot who demonstrates that he is attempting to apply the critiques of an instructor will be given credit even if he is only marginally successful. On the other hand, the student pilot who appears to be ignoring the inputs of his instructors demonstrates stubbornness and a resistance to teaching. The *perception* often outweighs reality. The very characteristics that make a person a successful fighter pilot—the Type A personality, confident demeanor, and assertive nature—can actually work against an upgrading student. If a student pilot is unwilling to admit his mistakes, *appears* overly confident for his degree of knowledge and skill, or merely gives the *impression* that he isn't open to the corrections of his instructors, he will be perceived as being unwilling to learn. Once in that position, he marks himself as a "problem" pilot, and he opens himself to the attacks of those who want to knock the chip off his shoulder. This is true for every course of training for a pilot, from basic pilot training to upgrading as an instructor pilot. It is important, therefore, for a pilot to work to prevent the perception that he is unwilling to learn.

Another source of a fighter pilot's reputation is his performance on checkrides and in upgrade programs. Extensive preparation leads to success in checkrides and upgrades. There are substantial regulations for basic flying that must be studied in depth and readied for immediate recall, such as when an evaluator asks questions during a checkride. There are many more manuals on tactics, formations, and techniques that must be studied to prepare well for upgrades. Critically analyzing every sortie and interrogating the experienced pilots as to the reason for their actions will yield a wealth of knowledge that a young pilot will be able to apply to future sorties. Importantly, a pilot's preparation, knowledge, and abilities directly reflect his efforts. A pilot who eagerly asks questions will be *perceived* differently from one who is stoically silent. In the end, a perceived willingness to learn and success in checkrides and upgrades will give a pilot a good reputation as an aviator and will favorably dispose other pilots toward him.

Another misperception a Christian must combat may arise because of his priorities (Chapter 6). Because he may have priorities outside of work—his family and church, for example—his occasional absence may make it seem as though he is not contributing to the squadron as much as others are. In some Air Force units, mission planning for sorties on Sundays is normal; staying at the squadron long after the work has finished is routine. A Christian who goes to church on Sunday, or who wants to leave work to attend a Wednesday Bible study, or who places time with his wife above "goofing off" with the other pilots may generate a negative perception about himself. For a pilot, being a "valuable member of a fighter squadron" sometimes has less to do with flying prowess and more to do with what others see him doing. Regardless of the reality, it is often the *perception* of effort that generates an attitude about a pilot.

While some priorities may be outside of the squadron, a Christian must preclude the perception that his extracurricular activities are impinging on his work. His best means of fighting this perception is to demonstrate a typical Christian trait: an intense work ethic. He must never slack off, whether by showing up late, leaving early, or taking a 2-hour lunch. His work—both flying related and not—must be proactive and impeccable. He should review his products so he submits only a pristine result. He must provide information before it is requested and never miss a deadline.

If he truly finds himself with spare time, rather than diving out of the squadron at the first opportunity, he should ask "What more can I do?" He should improve the processes that he oversees. If he doesn't have enough to do, he should ask for more responsibility. His constant hard work (and initiative to ask for more) and quality products will show the commander and the squadron that he's not only contributing greatly to the squadron, but that he's doing a good job of it. The ultimate goal is to give those who would criticize no means to do so (Titus 2:7-8). With such a display of effort, other pilots will be astonished to see that his work is unimpeachable and he still has the ability to dedicate time to family and God. If they can find fault in a Christian's work, they can connect his professional shortcomings to his faith—an obvious detriment to his witness. A Christian should leave no doubt as to the strength of his work ethic.

Christian Conduct

Beyond just the perceptions of others, a Christian must conduct himself in accordance with the highest standards so that there is not even a hint of wrongdoing. Peter encouraged his readers to "live such good lives among the pagans that, though they accuse you of doing wrong, they may see your good deeds and glorify God" (1 Peter 2:12). Modern times require a great degree of personal accountability in a world that is largely governed by situation ethics. While those around him may bend their moral relativism to fit their personal circumstances, a Christian must live to the standard of moral courage that Christ intended. There is right, and there is wrong—no Christian should dispute that.

Like every other human being, though, Christians face temptations. A modern example is the widespread popularity of digital media, particularly music and movies. The temptation to copy or download "free" music is one that even Christians face. While I was deployed to the Middle East, the local military computer network had a morale section that contained a large quantity of mp3 music files as well as digital copies of movies. Some were obviously pirated—a couple of movies appeared on the military intranet before they were released outside theatres. Even if some of the data was stored with permission, there was an obvious temptation to download and save files for future personal use.

I witnessed another dramatic example during my tour in Korea; I saw illegal copies of everything from name brand purses to Rolex watches. The movie *Star Wars III* was available on DVD on the street outside Osan Air Base less than 24 hours after it hit theaters in the states. Many military members—including some Christians—seemed to have no problem purchasing a $5 DVD even though it was obviously pirated; many rationalized it by citing the sacrifice they were making by being in Korea and noting they wouldn't be able to see the movie legally for months. Whether it is music, software, or videos, honoring a creator's copyright is a clear-cut legal and moral decision. If there is a thought that it might be a gray area, all it takes is one non-Christian asking "if you're so religious, why do you do this?" to pull a Christian back into the proper black and white scale.

The 2007 cheating scandal at the Air Force Academy highlighted, once again, that the temptation to compromise one's integrity is a continuing threat. Nearly three dozen cadets were accused of cheating by sharing answers on an 'inconsequential' military knowledge test. Other cases have revealed that the same temptation occurs on active duty. In 2005 a dozen officers were kicked out of pilot training for obtaining the answers to an Emergency Procedures Quiz (EPQ) prior to the test; an instructor pilot facing court martial for providing those answers subsequently resigned under less than honorable conditions.[1] Again, the EPQ was an 'inconsequential' quiz.

Why would cadets or officers risk their careers over such insignificant tests? Two reasons come to mind. First, at the time, no test seems unimportant. Even though failing the test might have only minor consequences, the

---

[1] "Charges preferred in Columbus AFB cheating investigation," Air Force Link, http://www.af.mil/news/story.asp?storyID=123011058, 15 July 2005. Also, "Air Force News: Pilot resigns after cheating scandal," http://airforceots.com/portal/modules.php?name= News&file=article&sid=114.

fear of failure causes the desire to guarantee success—by cheating, if necessary. Second, the desire for perfection, whether driven by internal or external pressures, makes people seek a 'sure thing.' Someone who might otherwise have gotten a 94 on a test might be tempted to cheat to guarantee a 100. Neither situation is unrealistic. Officers in training and cadets in college often feel that their careers *do* ride on the outcome of that test, inconsequential though it may be. In classes composed of 'exemplary' cadets and officers, where average test scores are already typically high, there can be added pressure not to make a single error, as if one's career rides on a singled missed question. The Air Force values its top-ranked graduates, and few points may separate the members of a class. While the temptation is not unrealistic, giving in is inexcusable. Cheating, in any form, is an unquestionable violation of moral integrity.

The Air Force sometimes uses the phrase "cooperate and graduate" to encourage the members of a class to work together toward graduation, but the intent is not to cheat. The class *should* work together when the rules allow; when individual work is required (on a test, for example), only individual work should be done. In cases where there is doubt whether individual or group effort is allowed, the question *must* be asked. Though to the casual observer it may seem unnecessary to include an encouragement not to cheat, it is likely that a person may one day face an ethical question of academic integrity, whether as a cadet or officer. A prior decision not to violate that integrity will shore his moral foundation.

Another ethical temptation that a Christian will face involves gouge. The term *gouge* apparently has its roots in Navy history; in short, gouge is the 'need to know' or 'quick and dirty' of a situation. Academically, gouge is essentially a previous student's old work. Imagine starting a college math class and having a former student hand you his notes, quizzes, homework, and exams. That information would be *gouge* on the class. Possessing it might or might not be considered cheating, depending on the policies of the school and instructor. At the Air Force Academy, for example, some instructors encouraged cadets to keep their old tests and give them to future students of the course. Those instructors fully planned to write new tests later and presumably thought that the old tests would help the new students learn the material. Conversely, some instructors collected the tests after they were administered and said the specific content of the exam continued to be confidential, meaning that if a cadet even wrote down what he could remember and provided it to a future student it would still be considered cheating. Gouge has a variety of degrees in meaning. In some cases, *gouge* is simply a 'code word' for an answer sheet to or a copy of an upcoming test.

Unofficial Air Force gouge is commonly associated with most official training courses and is often handed down from one class to the next. (In the age of the internet, gouge on virtually any formal training course can also be found on a variety of websites, some less reputable than others.) Some courses clearly state that no material from previous classes may be used, or that you may only use material you personally produce. In those cases, use of gouge would obviously be cheating. Other training courses may not have such restrictions or may even encourage the use of gouge. Ethical dilemmas can develop when officers are in courses with no specific gouge guidance.

For example, an officer may receive material from a friend who just finished a course and find a copy of a test included. The officer must then figure out if he can or should keep or use that particular gouge. I have participated in courses where gouge was encouraged and tests were included in the gouge. My class was forced to make a concerted effort to make sure our instructors knew we had copies of old tests. This enabled them to tell us not to use it or allowed them to write a new test if they desired. If we had not spoken with the instructor and the test they gave us was similar to our gouge, we could easily have been accused of cheating. (Notably, every instructor had no problem with our possession of old tests. Since the course encouraged gouge, the academic policy was subsequently rewritten to take the burden of asking the question off of students.)

Gouge (in either authorized or unauthorized forms) is not restricted to officers or cadets in a student status. Air Force pilots routinely take tests and face the same pressures, particularly if they feel their flying careers ride on the test or if they feel that missing one question may cause them to be ranked lower than a fellow pilot. A unique aspect of Air Force pilot tests is that they generally come from a Master Question File (MQF). The MQF is an open source bank of all questions that might be asked. Studying the MQF (which is often several hundred questions long) is expected and becomes habitual in preparation for testing. There are times, however, when pilots will take non-MQF tests. Because a pilot's habit is to at least have some form of question bank prior to a test, it is tempting to try to "obtain an MQF" for those tests; since such an MQF doesn't generally exist, *MQF* may become a code word for a copy of the test.

If a Christian has ethical doubts about gouge, he should ask an authority figure as to its legality or simply not use it. He must resist the temptation to access bad gouge or use gouge when it is not permitted. The temptation may be strong; again, being a top-ranked graduate carries significant weight in the Air Force. In addition, fellow officers may be using gouge. Both points are irrelevant. Success without moral integrity is no success at all.

Air Force gouge is a veritable ethical minefield; a Christian must step carefully to live his life above reproach. He must follow the rules and obey the regulations to the letter; he must not even permit the perception that he is stretching the spirit of the law (Ephesians 5:3). His credible witness could be destroyed by even the mere perception of malfeasance or vice without there actually being any fault in him.

Good Deals

In the Air Force, obeying the letter of the law is often the easy part; it's during the "good deals" that it's tempting to stretch the spirit of it. There is nothing wrong with claiming good deals that have been legitimately earned—the potential wrong comes in milking them beyond their intent. As an example, when military members are deployed to a combat zone their pay for that calendar month is tax-free (to a limit). There is nothing wrong with taking advantage of that rule and not paying taxes, but I personally believe that the ethical limits are stretched (or exceeded) by those who go out of their way to obtain that benefit.

Most fighter units and many heavy units are deployed into combat areas and are thus entitled to that allowance. Some transport units, though, make runs from outside the combat area to deliver men and equipment rather than actually being deployed into the area. Some stories have been told of such units intentionally scheduling sorties so that they arrive in a combat area on the last day of the month and depart on the first, thus securing two tax-free months for themselves for the price of a single, overnight out-and-back sortie. If such a sortie was truly necessary then there can be no dispute; but if the motivation behind the sortie was simply to garner tax-free money, then I believe it is ethically questionable. The same is true when units load their aircraft with unnecessary crew members to give them access to the good deal.

I have also heard of commanders looking out for their enlisted troops by allowing them to re-enlist while in a combat area—meaning their re-enlistment bonus would be tax-free. That's often a substantial sum for personnel who generally have small paychecks. Again, if the enlisted person is there to do a deployed job, then there can be no argument. But if the enlisted member spends only a few hours in the combat area—just long enough to get sworn in on the tarmac, accept the bonus, and get back on the plane—then I believe the ethical boundaries are stretched. Unfortunately, officers who would never think of committing an illegal act may think nothing about stretching ethical boundaries, whether it's staying in an expensive hotel (reimbursed by the military) when a cheaper one is available, requesting reimbursement for taxis that took them to unofficial locations, or collecting free airline ticket vouchers by giving up their seat while they're on official travel. The conduct of officers in these situations may not necessarily violate any regulations, but they verge on the unethical.

I know two Christian fighter pilots who struggled with this ethical line; one had his reputation impaired by the perception of misdeeds, and the other was strangled by the commission of them. The first occurred when I and another Christian pilot went on an official trip together. As we traveled the Air Force paid for our lodging, and the directive was that we lodge at military facilities. If there were no rooms available, we would be billeted off-base at a local hotel, many of which were in the luxury category and were completely paid for by the military. This made off-base stays very desirable. When the other pilot and I arrived at our first location, he tried every verbal tactic he could think of to convince the airman at lodging that there must be *some* reason we needed to stay off-base, even though there were rooms available in lodging. I was able to rein him in, and we ended up staying in military lodging—in the distinguished visitors' quarters that easily outclassed most off-base hotels.

At our next location there really were no rooms available on base, but this time the pilot's efforts were focused on getting us a "better" (more expensive) hotel than the one that was picked for us. Again, he was unsuccessful, and the perception that he left me with as a fellow Christian was a poor one. His actions were not illegal; they did, however, border on the unethical, as he tried to milk the good deal out of the Air Force. As a Christian, I lost respect for a brother in Christ who was pushing the limits of acceptable behavior to better his good deal. Any other pilot standing in my shoes probably would have been supporting him in his efforts, but I wonder if they would question why this otherwise morally conscientious person was willing to bend so far under these circumstances. I believe his reputation and witness as an upstanding and principled Christian would have been damaged.

In the second case, a different pilot on another deployment borrowed the car of a friend who lived at our deployed location. As a friendly gesture he filled the gas tank before returning the car. Unfortunately, he chose to do so at the government pumps; the military fuel pumps were for official vehicles only, and required only a key to turn them on to get free gas. The pilot used a key that was assigned with one of our official vehicles. In his own mind, he was justified in using the government gas to reimburse his friend, since he was on an official trip and was using his friend's private gas. In this case a Christian attempted to milk a good deal—free gas—out of the Air Force and went beyond the unethical to the illegal. He was caught on camera and charged with theft of government property.

Assuming he really was so naïve as to think he was entitled to use the gas, his ignorance demonstrates a lack of knowledge that a Christian cannot allow himself. The more plausible truth is that he probably suspected that he wasn't allowed to use the military pumps, but rather than ask the question, he chose to see if he could get away with it. The "better to ask forgiveness than permission" attitude is dangerous enough to an average military officer; it is poison to a Christian one. Innocent or not, for the equivalent of a $20 tank of gas his Christian reputation was marred and his credibility was destroyed—not to mention the subsequent legal repercussions.

The Culture of Situation Ethics

Though a Christian will strive to live his life above reproach, his compatriots may live by a completely different standard. A Christian who has not succumbed to modernism still believes in moral absolutes, while his peers often live in the new age of situation ethics. Situation ethics are prevalent in modern society and thus in the military as well; an example is its use in the popular practice of *pencil whipping*. Pencil whipping describes the common practice of accomplishing paperwork for the sole purpose of filling in the blanks; the entries may not accurately reflect reality, often because the paper itself may not even be read. One example might be completing a check-list for a vehicle inspection; a person with situation ethics may decide that it's not that important for them to actually get out and inspect the vehicle. They may place a check-mark in all the boxes without actually performing any of the required inspections. Pencil whipping also occurs when pilots sign off forms indicating they have completed required training events—even when they did not actually do so.

Another common example of the application of relativistic ethics is known as *back-dating*. This occurs when a regulatory deadline passes unno-ticed, and the paperwork is changed retroactively to make it appear as though the deadline wasn't missed. Due to the constant changeover of mili-tary members in every job, it is possible that deadlines required by regula-tion may honestly be missed until an astute troop arrives and points out the error to everyone else. Sometimes, however, rather than having the omis-sion publicized and corrected, forms may magically appear with the "cor-rect" dates on them, even if those dates are in the past.

Regarding the situation ethics of others, the question for the Christian is how strictly he should hold his peers to his personal moral standard. At the Air Force Academy, the question was 'removed' with its honor code. Be-sides swearing to "neither lie, cheat, nor steal," the code requires that cadets not "tolerate among [them] anyone who does." Cadets have been punished for tolerating breaches of integrity when they failed to report a known viola-tion. While the active duty Air Force maintains *Integrity first* as its first core value, it has no such toleration clause. Though in certain circumstances knowledge of illicit events could imply complicity, in general the choice of what to do when a person observes a possible violation of integrity is left to the individual.

Some would argue that the credibility of the Air Force depends on the unquestionable ethics of its officers. Others would say that pressing the lim-its in gray areas may ultimately better support the mission. While I tend to agree with the former, a Christian cannot become the moral monitor of his peers. He can express displeasure with someone if they pencil whip, back-date, use bad gouge or otherwise act with questionable ethics, but if he falls on his sword for every occasion, he'll quickly wear himself out with all the falling down and getting up. If people with situation ethics see their actions as inconsequential, a Christian will be hard-pressed to convince them to act a more difficult way just because *he* thinks it's more ethical. In short, he should choose his battles. Also, when he does choose to press an issue, it's generally more beneficial to frame it in terms of safety and legality, to which even an unchurched person can relate.[2] Ultimately, a Christian should strive to ensure that his reputation is of one who doesn't need to compro-mise his ethics to accomplish his job well. With that reputation his mere presence may strengthen the ethics of those with whom he works.

---

[2] Stokka, Terry. Lt Col, USAF (Retired). "Honor and Integrity on Active Duty," published in *Preparing for Active Duty* notebook for the USAFA Class of 1999.

Regardless of intent and effort, people are imperfect and will make mistakes. When a Christian does stumble, the best he can do is accept responsibility. The only thing worse than violating an ethical or legal standard is to then rationalize it, cover it up, pass the blame, or claim some level of ignorance. A multitude of famous personalities from Hollywood to Washington have proven that errors are forgiven (and forgotten) far more quickly than the failure to take responsibility. Fighter pilots by nature don't like to be wrong, and their first response is generally to become defensive and deny an offense was committed. A Christian must be willing to admit his mistakes and accept the penalty to reclaim his witness. By forthrightly accepting responsibility he actually strengthens his credibility even in the face of a misstep.

Spiritual Reputation

Besides living to ethical and legal standards, a Christian must also live his life *spiritually* above reproach. He must avoid what is perhaps the most damaging perception of a Christian: the belief that he is a hypocrite. A Christian creates this perception when his words are inconsistent with his actions. Claiming to know God but living in a godless fashion is not a new concept. Jeremiah listed it as one of the traits of the wicked in Israel when he told God that "You are always on their lips but far from their hearts" (Jeremiah 12:2). In modern times, the hypocrisy of the church is often cited as the reason non-Christians will not accept Christ. If a Christian fulfills the hypocritical stereotype, any glory he may think he brings to God is more than offset by the damage he inflicts. To avoid the perception of hypocrisy, a Christian must live what he preaches in every detail, spiritually above reproach. While they may not know the intimate details of his religious life, those around him must never have reason to question the integrity of his spiritual life.

With so much riding on his reputation, a Christian may feel that he *needs* to excel above his peers for the sake of Christ; that doesn't mean it will be easy for him to do so. While God will certainly be his help in difficult times, simply being a Christian doesn't mean God will smooth every bump in the road or guarantee success, even if (from our point of view) it would be good for Him to do so.

The most obvious example of this truth was the nation of Israel as it departed Egypt and headed for the Promised Land. More than anyone in history, the nation of Israel *needed* to excel to prove to the world that God was indeed sovereign. As the people sinned and rebelled, God repeatedly told Moses to stand out of the way while He wiped them out—even though they were His chosen people, they were failing in their struggles. Moses argued that if God destroyed His own people He would compromise His Name with the heathen nations who had watched their victorious departure from Egypt (Exodus 32:11-12). David would later use much the same argument when he prayed for success for the sake of God's Name (2 Samuel

97

7:25, 26). These men—Moses and David—are perhaps God's most success-ful warriors and leaders; if anyone in history needed to excel so that God would be glorified it was certainly them—yet they, too, struggled. If their success had come too easily then it would have been tempting for them to take credit for their own achievements, just as it would be for a Christian today.

The story of Hezekiah, recorded in 2 Kings 18-20 and 2 Chronicles 29-32, is another example of a Godly man who still experienced hardship. He was one of the few kings listed as "good" in Judah's history, though he was surrounded by evil. Even though Hezekiah had so faithfully followed God's commands throughout his reign, God still allowed a pagan nation to attack him (2 Chronicles 32:1). Rather than wallowing in self-pity, though, he took confidence in God, and eventually God's own army would fight the battle for the Israelites (32:7-8, 21). In verse 23, the Bible says that as a result of Israel's victory in battle, *"from then on"* Hezekiah was highly regarded by all the nations; God had used the struggle for His own purposes. Christian fighter pilots desperately want—*need*—to excel and succeed so that they can glorify God with their victory. Still, they find themselves struggling as Moses, David, and Hezekiah did. Christians should not lose heart, though, because just as with those men, God uses their weakness to make His strength most apparent.

Chapter 10:
Spiritual Fatigue

A CHRISTIAN IS TO BE A SOLDIER "marching as to war," not searching for a safe harbor in which to drop anchor and rest. He is to be *in* the world, doing the work God would have him do. That work—and the constant spiritual struggle it presents—can be very fatiguing. The daily struggle to live a Christian life in the potently non-Christian fighter pilot world can wear on a person's spiritual, emotional, and even physical being. If after fighting not to be overcome a Christian spends his remaining energy recuperating from spiritual fatigue, he has little energy left for personal growth and nothing left for assertively professing his faith. He may be *in* the world, but if his efforts are focused on not getting drowned by it, he's not doing much in the way of saving those around him.

There were times that I felt as though I had accomplished little more than keeping my head above water. Eventually I earned the respect of my peers as a fighter pilot, but the negative spiritual environment to which I was constantly exposed was spiritually fatiguing. It was a daily struggle not only to keep my life righteous but also to try to influence others; it was discouraging to me that I had made difficult decisions and seen little positive results. I even considered declining another F-16 tour and leaving the fighter community. Ironically, I found strength only when I continued to make the hard and tiring decisions.

Shortly after arriving at Osan I made the tortured decision to skip the Friday night "Show" put on by the squadron, based on the morally questionable events that I thought would take place. Instead, I chose to attend the Hospitality House, an off-base ministry operated by Cadence International.[1] Another F-16 pilot from my squadron was there, and I had barely

---

[1] Cadence International is an organization whose ministry is specifically to the military. See www.cadence.org.

walked through the door when I heard him mention my presence as an answer to his prayers. The young Christian pilot was in his first assignment in the F-16 and had been struggling with being the lone pilot not attending the fighter pilot events. He said he had been seeking brotherly Christian support in the fighter pilot community, and he had obviously grappled with how much he should immerse himself in the activities of the fighter pilot culture. My having skipped the show seemed to reassure him that he was not alone, and that the tough choices he had made were not unfounded. I had demonstrated both ability and desire to not be a part of "the evil." I had been able to lend support in what is probably the hardest place for a young, single, Christian guy to be.

Importantly, though, he was not the only one who benefited from that situation. Unbeknownst to me, my decision to skip the show had lent spiritual support to a lieutenant who needed to know that there were other pilots who had similar beliefs as himself. Unbeknownst to him, the obvious lift my presence gave him in turn gave me strength: finally, I was seeing something good come out of what seemed like an eternity of unpopular faith-based decisions. In what had seemed to be a world of failures, God provided a simple success to reassure me that I was trudging down the right path. The "hardship" remote assignment had the ironic result of giving me the greatest spiritual encouragement I'd seen. Importantly, if either one of us had given in and gone to the show that night, the spiritual bounty would have been lost. Making hard but prayerful choices, and considering their impact on others, had actually allowed *both* of us to experience mutual support.

Fighting Spiritual Fatigue: Understanding a Christian's Purpose

One of the primary ways a Christian can combat spiritual fatigue is to understand his purpose. Imagine that a commander grabs his stopwatch, takes his troops to a track, and tells them to start running. Their ability to perform to their best capabilities will be inhibited because they don't know why they're there: they don't know whether he wants them to sprint one lap or pace hundreds. If he tells them that they're taking an annual fitness test, then they know their purpose and they're able to view the exercise with the proper perspective. Their level of effort may be higher than if it was just a fun run. If he tells them that the test requires them to complete 1.5 miles in 12 minutes, then they know their ultimate objective. If they didn't know the finish line and were struggling at the 1.4 mile point they might be inclined to give up, not knowing how close they were to the end. By understanding their purpose and objective they're able to gain their best performance, even under the hardest of circumstances.

The same is true for the Christian life. A Christian needs to understand his purpose and clearly define his objectives. Knowing his purpose will help him stay focused on the reasons for his labor. When he feels he's suffering without cause he may falter and complain; when he knows that he suffers for a reason, he finds the strength to persevere. A Christian must understand his purpose, define his objectives, and direct his efforts toward his goals.

A Christian's purpose and objectives should be defined by God's plan for him. God has him where he is for a reason, though he may never see glowing lights or hear angelic trumpets as someone explains the divine purpose for his life. Even if a Christian earnestly looks for God's purpose, he still may not be able to discern the specifics of what God wants for him— not everyone has the luxury of knowing the future. In some military training camps there are marches in which those participating don't know the final objective—the commanders have simply said, "March until I say stop." While hardly ideal for personal motivation, it trains the soldiers to follow the order—*start marching*—without delaying to ask questions.

The leadership has the big picture; they can't always take the time to explain the intimate details to every soldier. Instead, they demand immediate obedience and command unwavering trust. Thousands of soldiers will roll up their sleeping bags and move out without knowing their destination or objective—just on the word of a General. Likewise, God has the big picture; sometimes He clues the Christian in, sometimes God tries but the Christian just doesn't get it, and sometimes He tells him just to trust Him. While a Christian would like to have his heavenly Commander tell him the reason he's here and tell him how far he has to go, sometimes that's the only discernible order he gets from God: move out.

Another key to defining a Christian's purpose is found in the answer to a simple question: what does he want to be remembered for? This is a simple filter to differentiate the important from the trivial. In his fighter pilot career and throughout his life a Christian will be faced with choices that will send him along separate courses. Would he rather be remembered as the World's Best Fighter Pilot or the World's Best Father? I use that example not to imply exclusivity, but instead to make the point that every choice he makes will nudge his life down a unique and specific course. He cannot be all things to all people all the time. He needs to define what is important and *that* must be what guides the decisions he makes in his life.

It's also important to remember that most things in this life will be forgotten. An oft quoted means of determining the gravity of a situation is the "Five Year Rule." I've also heard it expressed as the "100 Year," "10 Year," or "Eternity Rule." The premise is the same: in 5 years (or 10, or in eternity), will anyone remember or care what's happening right now? Will you? If, 10 years from now, a Christian will look back and think nothing of what he's going through now, then it can't be that important. On the other hand, if he thinks that in 10 years he may still regret or second-guess the decisions he's making now, then it may be time to alter his course.

God with Us

Spiritual fatigue may also occur when a Christian feels alone in the world. There may be times when a Christian can't find fellowship or support. He may go places or be in situations where he is the *only* Christian, and he has no external spiritual resources on which to call. Whether locked down at an Air Force base in Iraq, on Army patrol in the mountains of Afghanistan, or on a Navy vessel on the ocean, he may be separated from Christian friends and support. In those situations a Christian in the military may feel spiritually separated from the ungodly men and women around him, and he is often physically separated from his spiritual family. Every day he faces pressure to conform to the world, and when he resists he may experience ridicule and rejection. The men and women who are around him are the only friends he could possibly have, and they are the same with whom he may face mortal combat. But because of his Christianity, he risks separation from them and being perceived as an outsider. In such an environment there is a strong temptation to simply—albeit temporarily—become like everyone else. Even in the face of such pressure, a Christian must depend on God's strength to help him persevere in living a life honoring to God. As John said in the frequently quoted verse, "...the One who is in you is greater than the one who is in the world" (1 John 4:4).

The temptation to "bend to blend" is not new—Moses experienced a similar enticement. After being raised as a child of Pharaoh's daughter, he could have chosen to mingle with the Egyptians to avoid the hardship of the Jewish nation. In Hebrews, though, it says that Moses chose to be *mistreated* with the Israelites "rather than enjoy the pleasures of sin for a short time" in Pharaoh's court (11:25). Moses regarded "disgrace for the sake of Christ" as greater than the "treasures of Egypt, because he was looking ahead to his reward" (v26). A Christian who feels as though he is alone in Pharaoh's court can take strength from Moses' model, as well as the examples of other Godly characters that prevailed even when surrounded by godlessness: Joseph, Daniel, and Elijah are just a few.

A Christian living a challenging life in the non-Christian fighter pilot world may begin to question whether he should continue to be a fighter pilot—or if he should even remain in the military. At various points in my short pilot profession I have questioned my career path. While I would not change my original decision to become a fighter pilot, I often wonder if I can (or if I should) successfully navigate the fighter pilot career to its highest rungs. I still sometimes wonder why God has me where I am.

At those times I have found it is encouraging to remember the plight of a unique Old Testament woman. Her people were conquered and exiled, and she had been commanded to join the harem of their pagan captor. Still, because God was with her, she gained favor with all she met and eventually became the queen. As queen she was able to save her people from the attempts of an evil government official to annihilate them. She could never have known that God intended her for that purpose, and she, too, struggled with how she should act in her position as a Godly woman in an ungodly court. The difficulties of a Christian fighter pilot pale in comparison to the struggles of a God-fearing woman forced to marry a godless king who ruled over her vanquished people. When the young Queen Esther hesitated and wavered, her Uncle Mordecai asked her, "Who knows but that you have come to royal position for such a time as this?" (Esther 4:14). God may very well have a Christian fighter pilot exactly where He wants him, for a plan that only He knows.

Joshua, too, undoubtedly experienced spiritual fatigue of his own as he watched the nation of Israel constantly wander from the very God that had delivered them. I've wondered if the man who was Moses' right hand for decades ever considered resigning after all the failures he saw in the Israelite nation. It surely seemed as though there was little good coming of all the work he did. Still, Joshua was chosen to replace Moses as the leader of the Jewish people. With the nation's track record Joshua certainly had reservations about what the uncertain future held. As he prepared to lead the Israelite nation over the Jordan River and into the Promised Land, God repeated a simple, reassuring command: "Be strong and courageous. Do not be terrified; do not be discouraged, for the Lord your God will be with you wherever you go" (Joshua 1:9).

Why Should Christians Bother with the Fighter Pilot World?

Daily spiritual struggles, constant challenges to a Christian's faith, the potential for persecution: with so many negatives, why would any Christian even want to *be* a fighter pilot?

Much has been said about the pessimistic aspects of trying to be an authentic Christian in a sometimes immoral fighter pilot world. This is primarily an attempt to set straight any "starry-eyed" would-be fighter pilots, though it may inadvertently discourage those who honestly know very little (good or bad) about the fighter pilot culture. A dearth of positive topics may lead some to believe that there isn't any good in being a fighter pilot or any respectable reason for a Christian to be one. That couldn't be further from the truth. There are awesome and positive things about being a fighter pilot, and the fighter pilot world even has aspects that make it *desirable* as a Christian career. Though there are negatives, fighter pilots are respected, have access to a unique audience, serve, and have a great deal of fun in their career.

While they may not know the details of a fighter pilot's duties, many people understand that there is a grueling selection process and arduous training that fighter pilots endure; they know that only the best become fighter pilots, and many wish they could be one. With the sole (and arguable) exception of astronauts, more people want to be fighter pilots than any other part of aviation. Many wish they could, but few actually can—it is an elite and select career field. Because of its exclusivity and universal attraction, a Christian that becomes a fighter pilot garners immediate respect and credibility for his professional abilities. That respect and credibility can be an enormous enabler outside the fighter pilot world and can create unique opportunities to work for God. In addition to immediate respect, the fighter pilot profession also creates an instant conversational topic with absolutely any person in the world. The crowd that routinely surrounds fighter pilots at events like airshows is made up of everyone from toddlers to veterans of every armed conflict since World War I. At those times it seems as though every human being either was a fighter pilot, wants to be a fighter pilot, wants to talk to a fighter pilot, or has a piece of their mind they'd like to give a fighter pilot. Combined with the credibility of his profession, his universal conversational topic gives a Christian fighter pilot a distinct and far-reaching witness opportunity. Thus, by choosing to become a fighter pilot a Christian can gain respect, credibility, and a platform from which to accomplish the work God would have him do.

Though the popularity of being a fighter pilot may give a Christian unique opportunities with the public, there are some distinctly personal reasons that some may choose the profession. Fighter pilots have the noble purpose of serving the greater good, and they have the unique ability to individually make an enormous impact on the outcome of a conflict. While many people are involved in the intelligence and support of a successful operation, it was a single fighter pilot that skillfully employed his laser guided bomb and killed the leader of al Qaeda in Iraq in June 2006. Few people outside of the fighter pilot community get the opportunity to individually have such a significant impact (or to have their personal accomplishments displayed so prominently on the international news). People want to be fighter pilots to make a significant, lasting, and valuable contribution to the defense of democracy. They are willing to risk their lives (and take lives, if necessary) to preserve the freedoms of others.

Though less noble, it is important to remember that being a fighter pilot is also just plain fun. Fighter pilots fly multi-million dollar aircraft that have guns, missiles, bombs, can pull 9 Gs and go Mach 2; they can fly upside down, hold formation within inches of other aircraft, fly so high they can see the curvature of the earth or so low they can count the spots on the cows. Being a fighter pilot is a continuous, changing tactical challenge. No mission is ever the same. Fighters are often considered the "race cars" of military aviation. Flying a fighter is unquestionably exciting and gratifying.

While those aspects of *flying* fighters are enviable, if the *life* of a fighter pilot is so tough, why become one? Though spiritual fatigue is a genuine threat, the potential opportunities for a Christian are colossal: being part of the salvation of a dead-to-God fighter pilot, making an eternal impact on enlisted troops with a Christian leadership example, providing spiritual support for a struggling younger Christian fighter pilot, being a Godly example during combat operations, influencing the direction of an entire fighter squadron with moral and ethical leadership....the possibilities are endless.

Still, they are just possibilities; a Christian may go for a long time before seeing *any* impact of his witness. Paul said in Galatians that a Christian should "not become weary in doing good, for at the proper time we will reap a harvest if we do not give up" (6:9-10). The author of Hebrews encouraged him to "persevere, so that when you have done the will of God, you will receive what He has promised" (10:36). While there is promise of reward, neither encouragement said when that "proper time" would be. If a Christian couldn't see the positives and still struggled under spiritual pressures, why would he be willing to go through that difficulty? Why does a football player subject himself to punishing physical exertion everyday for a dozen games a year? Why does a marathon runner punish his body every day for weeks on end for an individual race? In today's age of publicity and muckraking, why would any humble man of integrity aspire to be a politician?

The answer to those questions is easier than it seems. Why would anyone seek any profession that is difficult? The reason people participate in challenging careers is because they enjoy what they do, as odd as that may seem to an outsider. A football player treasures the glory of the game and the feeling of victory. A marathon runner relishes the rhythmic pounding of his feet on the pavement and the knowledge that he's pushing his physical limits. People join government because they value the political process and the feeling that they are helping their constituents. People become fighter pilots because they enjoy the freedom of flying a fighter and the knowledge that they are serving their fellow man. *People choose difficult professions because they enjoy them.*

Believe it or not, the answer is the same for a Christian. If a Christian enjoys the thought of flying a fighter and serving his fellow man in armed conflict, then a fighter pilot career may fit him well. If he *doesn't* enjoy the basis of his potential profession—flying a fighter—then he may want to consider another career. What about spiritual issues? They are nearly irrelevant. Yes, a Christian should always try to understand as much as possible about the spiritual environment he's going to encounter (as this book tries to do for the fighter pilot). If a Christian honestly believes that there is no way he could live that life without being miserable or giving in to the pressures of the world, then perhaps he should consider another profession. If he thinks he can positively impact that spiritual environment, then that may be *one* factor in his career choice.

Otherwise, outside of direct divine guidance, I believe a Christian should pursue a career he thinks he will enjoy. One who chooses a career that he does not enjoy may end up being unhappy in it; spiritual struggles in that career field will only make him more miserable. Again, the statement is similar for every career: *Christians become fighter pilots because they <u>enjoy</u> the freedom of flying a fighter and the knowledge that they are serving their fellow man.* Religious and secular stresses take place in every profession. A Christian in a career he enjoys is best equipped to persevere; the question, then, is not what *should* a Christian do, but what does he *want* to do?

I question those who would abandon their talents, expertise, and job satisfaction, even if they do so for the mission field. It's one thing for someone to move their qualifications to missions, like a military pilot who chooses to enter the field of mission aviation. It's quite another for someone to abandon them, like an avid computer scientist who moves into a field without running water or electricity. Is that where God wants him? Possibly, but God also gave him a passion and unique set of skills.

I don't believe that people with drive, desire, and talent should necessarily give up what they love because of the potential for spiritual hardship or the thought they can do better for God somewhere else. Someone with a Masters in Physics who has never touched a hammer will probably be miserable if he tries to become a carpenter simply because of the lost souls in carpentry or the spiritual struggles in the Physics community. I believe someone who loves computer science should be the best Christian computer scientist he can be; one who enjoys Physics should be the best Christian physicist he can be; one who enjoys flying should be the best Christian pilot he can be. I believe God gave us passion and skills so that we could *use* *them* to His glory.

A Christian should choose the life he thinks he'll enjoy, and *then work for God* in it. The reason that there are Christian politicians, rock stars, motorcycle gang members, and fighter pilots is Christians who were drawn to those lifestyles entered those worlds and worked for God. Besides, Christians were commanded to *go into* the world. If Christians avoid careers that aren't friendly toward spiritual values, large portions of the world will be abandoned, and humanity will be no better off for our place in it.

As previously mentioned, one of the greatest impacts a Christian can have in his profession is the positive influence of his morality and ethics. Though the American military has a fairly positive reputation in the world and is held in high regard by the American public, it has committed vile acts and atrocities in the past (My Lai and Abu Ghraib, to name two famous examples). This has caused some to wonder: Where are the ethics? Where are the morals? *Where are the Christians?* If Christians avoid spiritually challenging parts of the military world then they can only lament the state of American military ethics from afar. If they want to positively impact their world—the fighter pilot world—Christians have to be in amongst them.

Should a Christian be a heavy or fighter pilot? Should he even be in the military? Ultimately, any Christian should seek God's will in his career choices. Once assured that his options are within God's desires for his life, I believe a Christian should do whatever he wants to—he should pick the career path that he will enjoy living. There are potential spiritual negatives to any career, and, yes, the ones for the fighter pilot are particularly acute—but that doesn't mean it shouldn't be done. A Christian working his hardest at what he loves will make the greatest impact for God in this world.

Chapter 11:
The Fighter Pilot and God's Will

IN MY LAST YEAR at the Air Force Academy I developed the same question that I'm sure every Christian in their last year of college does: what is God's will for my life? While all cadets would be commissioned in the military, the variety of options available meant a plethora of possible career—and thus life—opportunities. Lt Col Stokka, the Officers' Christian Fellowship staff member at the Academy, taught a lesson to the first class cadets (seniors) that I'm sure he did every year. In it he basically taught that we shouldn't only seek God's will when we have a significant decision to make. Rather, we should strive to live as God would have us live everyday. This is rooted in Romans 12:2, "Do not conform any longer to the pattern of this world, but be transformed by the renewing of your mind. *Then* you will be able to test and approve what God's will is—His good, pleasing, and perfect will." If a Christian reads the Bible, prays, and seeks God's will everyday, then the decisions that he makes should be consistent with the will of God. Rather than depending on emotions and feelings—what he *feels* God's will is—he should make his decisions based on the Word of God.

Lt Col Stokka assuaged some of our fears about our future assignments by relating some of his personal history. As an Air Force officer he faced reassignment every 2 to 4 years. The Air Force assignment system allows the military officer to create a list of ranked choices for upcoming assignments. Once that list is submitted, the assignment is at the Air Force's whim. Ideally, they will be able to give the officer one of his choices, but there is always the caveat that "the needs of the Air Force" are paramount. If the Air Force needs a pilot somewhere he doesn't want to be, he'll still be assigned there. Lt Col Stokka related that as he approached these assignment opportunities, he prayed about where God wanted him to go. Short of the voice of God telling him what to submit, he listed his choices based on thoughtful discussion with his wife and their life goals. Lt Col Stokka noted that he never felt that God was directing him to take or ask for a certain assignment; *but*, looking back, he could see how God had guided his assignments to bring him to the place where he was.

Such decision points will occur regularly for the fighter pilot. As early as pilot training he will need to choose between a fighter and non-fighter training track. The second phase of pilot training is designed to direct student pilots into the type of flying for which they have showed the greatest aptitude. Based on class rank, student preference, and instructor pilot input, student pilots could go on to fly helicopters, the T-44/C-12, T-1, or T-38. The helicopter training was with the Army and was obviously for those who would go on to fly helos. The T-44/C-12 was a precursor for those who would fly the C-130; the T-1, for heavy airframes like tankers and cargo aircraft; and the T-38 was for those who would fly fighters and bombers.

While for many the choice was obvious, I thought a long time about what I really wanted to fly. I didn't particularly want to fly helicopters, but the thought of leading a crew into combat did make the C-130 track appealing to me. Each track also had its own distinct lifestyle, with pros and cons for personal, family, and professional life. Additionally, some student pilots considered their "follow-on" careers; they wanted to fly the military equivalent of a civilian airliner so that they could obtain the experience they needed to eventually land a comfortable airline job after leaving the military. Ultimately, I decided that flying a small, powerful airframe and delivering weapons on the enemy was what I wanted to do, and I put the T-38 track at the top of my list.

As we completed pilot training, we were ranked within our track, and we submitted our choices for what airframe we wanted to fly in the operational Air Force. A "drop" came from headquarters listing the aircraft our class was allotted. The leadership then took our preferences, class rank, their own opinion, and airframe availability and assigned everyone an aircraft. As I considered the aircraft I could potentially fly, I decided I wanted to help the soldier on the ground, so my desire was to fly a bomb-dropping airframe. While the totally air-to-air F-15C held the potential for achieving aerial glory, as it would likely be the first to shoot down enemy fighters, it had no air-to-ground role and one more significant shortcoming: most conflicts in recent history had met little air resistance, so the pilots of the F-15Cs had been utterly bored. Ultimately, my choices going into the drop were F-15E, A-10, F-16, and F-15C. There were no F-15Es in our drop and only one A-10. On our assignment night we were notified of our new jet, and mine was an F-16. In less than two years I experienced several significant decision points that would set the direction for the rest of my career. Each time I prayed that my choice was within God's will.

Searching for God's will is one of the great conversational topics within Christianity. If anyone ever publishes a book titled *How to Know Exactly What God's Will is for Your Life*, it will be a bestseller if it contains even a modicum of truth (and perhaps even if it doesn't).[1] In trying to explain God's will, one of many analogies I have heard describes it as a field or park. The park is fenced and a Christian is free to roam within it; it has a variety of potential paths that he can take, and many activities to accomplish—all equal before God. A Christian is free to make whatever choice he desires within the park, so long as he stays within it. As applied to life, this might mean that there isn't one particular assignment that God wants him to have, or even perhaps one particular mate that he should marry. Within the will of God, there may be several acceptable choices for either. A military Christian struggling to figure out which assignment God would have him take might be surprised to learn that God might not care. Assuming both choices are "within His will," He may have a plan to bless and advance the pilot regardless of which choice he makes. Taking a path that is outside of God's will, though, is like climbing over the park's fence. Unfortunately, that fence is rarely as obvious as a Christian might sometimes wish.

God is in Control

A Christian who lives in God's will must take confidence in God's control of his life, which is difficult for anyone to do. Giving up control—"letting go and letting God," as some have said—is one of the more difficult things for a Type A fighter pilot to do. Fighter pilots (even Christian ones) tend to view the world logically and mathematically. They hope that their hard work, effort, and diligence will be recognized and will be rewarded with increased rank and responsibility. They measure their accomplishments and anticipate a given sum: "I've done A, therefore I deserve B." When life disappoints and the sacrifices do not bring the expected rewards, a Christian pilot risks developing a bitter attitude: "I'm making all these sacrifices and getting nothing in return;" "the people around me—who are doing less and living easier, more carnal lives—are getting by as well as, or even *better* than, I am."

A Christian's bitterness can easily become resentment because he feels slighted. He can start to view his life, his peers, and even his Christianity with scorn because he feels that he is suffering injustice. When he begins to feel justified in his contempt for the people and environment around him the potency of his Christianity evaporates. A bitter Christian is no more an asset to God's kingdom than an atheist or a Buddhist. A bitter Christian has forgotten the sovereignty of God; his religion is based on a deity that isn't all powerful, all knowing, and *just*. By accepting a negative attitude—which is easy to do in the military—a Christian can start down the slippery slope that leads to a bitter and ineffective life.

There were times in my career when I felt in my logical and mathematical opinion that I was being passed over for jobs I was due. I had hoped

---

[1] Since this book was begun, other books have come out trying to address that very topic—and have had immense success.

to be the Christian that God was obviously blessing, evidenced by the great professional success I was having, but instead someone else got the accolades. While men hope that God will reward them with success, they may work with all their heart only to see others advanced ahead of them. I must accept that I may not be recognized in this life. At times like that a Christian must not become discouraged but must remember that regardless of what happens—someone is promoted over him, his hard work goes unnoticed, he is criticized despite his best efforts, whatever "injustice" he may suffer— God has a plan for his life, and God is in charge. As the ultimate Creator of his life, God has plans for him that only He can know. Because a Christian is a part of His plan, God won't leave him flapping in the wind. For a Christian, there is an immense amount of encouragement in remembering that everything happens for a reason—God's.

Flying and Living by the "Seat of the Pants"

Though they may experience happiness, grief, frustration, or joy, Christians must trust God over those emotions. While stereotypically fighter pilots fly by "the seat of their pants," they are actually trained to trust their stoic, mechanical instruments over their feelings, because all five senses can fool a pilot's brain. At night or in the weather, a pilot's eyes, ears, and the seat of his pants can convince him that he is flying straight and level even if he's in a turn, roll, or dive. It is a tragic fact that many pilots have died because their senses convinced them that they were flying safely when in fact they were hurtling toward the ground.

Several years ago I was flying on the wing of a tanker after refueling. The tanker began a turn into me, and I became convinced that the tanker was turning steeper and steeper, making it impossible for me to stay with him. An instructor pilot on my wing keyed his radio and asked "2, everything all right?" As soon as he did, I checked my instruments and realized that the tanker was in fact in straight, level flight. Checking my instruments "caged" my brain, and I regained my awareness. What had happened was that the tanker had actually rolled out, but I had kept my aircraft in the same relative position to him—I almost ended up directly above the tanker, convinced that he was rolling into me. A short radio call from my instructor and a quick check of my instruments enabled me to regain my composure and potentially saved my life.

The loss of such awareness is called "spatial disorientation." Because the sensory inputs are so strong, to combat the sometimes fatal effects of "spatial d" pilots are taught to depend on their instruments, which are calibrated, redundant, and provide a trustworthy frame of reference. Many pilots—just as I did—have "felt" like they were flying one way and have been saved when they saw that their instruments told a different story. Just as a pilot must depend on his instruments, a Christian must rely on his solid frame of reference. His senses, feelings, and emotions are not always trustworthy, which is why he must depend on what he knows is faithful: the constancy of God. While his mood may change for any number of reasons, God's Word never changes, and he can take confidence in that.

Still, it is tempting for a fighter pilot to try to take control of his career. To do so many officers spend immense effort maximizing "visibility" or "face time" with the commander or other senior officers. Much as in the business world, it used to be said that to get ahead pilots had to know how to play golf—because all the Colonels and Generals did. While golf doesn't hold the prestige that it once did, getting face time with senior officers is still a priority for many. Some feel that face time with the leadership will give them name recognition, so that they'll be favorable in the leadership's mind when they have an opportunity to hand out a good deal. I have known pilots who spent more time trying to get visibility with senior leadership than concentrating on doing a good job. Such politicking is generally easy to spot, but it is still frequent and often at least partially successful.

A Christian must remember that he should not resort to politicking or other career management tactics to further his position in life. Politicking implies that he is making choices and taking actions that are more for show than for the effective completion of his job; it also implies that he's working to look good—while he's being watched. Such a motivation is contrary to the commands in Ephesians 6: first, to work wholeheartedly as if for God (and not to please men), and second, to work with sincerity and respect not only when being watched (v6, 7). If God is truly in charge, then a Christian doesn't need to seek face time with senior officers or promote himself. To do so would imply that God was insufficient and that he needed to take matters into his own hands. Instead, he needs to grow and prosper where he is planted, and let God handle the rest.

Even though a Christian knows not to politic to advance himself, he is still faced with career pressures to succeed. A fighter pilot must accomplish military education, aircraft training, upgrades, and a variety of other military functions to advance professionally. Unfortunately, many opportunities for advancement as a fighter pilot require a significant amount of self-assertion; in the simplest terms, sometimes an officer needs to toot his own horn. Even before being commissioned I was warned by officers to make sure that I looked out for "number one" because nobody else would—they'd be too busy looking out for themselves. Much to my dismay, I've sometimes found that statement to be true. If officers hear of an award for which they feel they might qualify, it is often contingent upon them to research the award, write their own package, and submit their name. Superior officer recommendations are often written by the subordinate for the leadership's signature. The necessity of self-promotion conflicts with a Christian's inherent need to be humble and receptive, rather than assertive and diffusive.

Christian Ambition

One of the greatest challenges to a Christian letting God control his life is personal ambition. In the military, there is a fine line between ambition and initiative that only the individual Christian can discern. Many fighter pilots have grown up dreaming of being nothing less than a combat ace, squadron commander, or general. A person who sets his sights firmly on a prize can benefit from the strong motivation and drive to succeed. Unfortunately, such focus may bring danger with it. A Christian risks planning God out of his life and not even seeking His will or guidance. He may become so fixated that being a fighter pilot consumes his life and is his idol. Worse, when his goal is achieved and he becomes what it is he desired, he will be tempted to think that he has "made" himself.

Excessive ambition may drive a Christian's life away from God, but a lack of sufficient ambition may cause his career to stagnate. Career advancement is necessary for both professional and spiritual reasons. Obviously, if an officer fails to progress professionally, the military will fire him. More subtly, a Christian's degree of professional advancement has a direct impact on his witness. If an outspoken Christian is successful in his career as an officer and a fighter pilot, his witness gains immediate credibility— particularly if he gives the credit for his success to God. If he is slow or fails to advance, regardless of the reason, his mediocre performance in a world of successful stand-outs could be a detriment to his spiritual witness.

A Christian does not need a complete lack of ambition, but he must prevent ambition from consuming him. There is disagreement even in the Christian community about the appropriate level of ambition.[2] Paul notes in Galatians that "selfish ambition" is "obviously" an "act of the sinful nature" (5:19-21); on the other hand, a healthy degree of ambition can provide a drive to succeed and achieve goals. I believe a Christian can express interests in jobs and advancement opportunities, and he can work everyday to do his best and show his ability to handle more rank and responsibility. He can and should search out and apply for positions or schools in which he is interested; goals are admirable. However, when he tries to manipulate the system and slides into the single-seat cockpit of his career, he pushes God out of it. Instead, he should express his career and job desires clearly to his superiors and then concentrate his efforts on doing his job well, allowing God to control promotion, advancement, and recognition.

Certainly there is nothing wrong with taking actions and making prayerful choices that are consistent with personal desires—assuming that a Christian believes those desires to be within God's will for him. In fact, when it comes to the direction his life will take, it is unlikely that God will divinely commandeer the military assignment system, so at some point a Christian will have to make a wise and informed decision. God has given

---

[2] An interesting book on Christian ambition is Hugh Hewitt's *In, But Not Of* (Thomas Nelson, Nashville, 2003). Regrettably, most of the chapters are simply about securing success; a few have a caveat about how a Christian shouldn't have pride. Mr. Hewitt says to succeed you need to endear yourself to the appropriate people: "People rise in the world because they attract the attention and approval of powerful people" (p50). On the topic of being a successful Christian, Mr. Hewitt asserts that one cannot be both a pastor and influential in the world because "a preacher has next to zero credibility on any issue of politics or public policy…" (p62).

man a heart and a brain for a reason; he is to wholly depend on God, but he is also to make wise choices. Though this sounds like he is to be an independent creature totally dependent on God, there really isn't a contradiction. For example, I believe that God protects me, but I still look both ways before I cross the street—I trust God, *and* I attempt to make wise choices. God has given men the ability to make choices and subsequently reap the consequences of those choices.

To live out his life a Christian must make decisions; he can't merely sit on the couch and demand that God *make* His will happen. Some use to say that "God helps those who help themselves." Whether that adage is true or not, there is some basis for human initiative within God's will. There is a popular uncredited joke, told in many variations, about waiting for God's action in life:

> A man lived in a house that was threatened by a flood. As the waters began to rise, neighbors drove by and offered the man a ride out. "No thanks," he said, "God will save me." The water rose to his doorstep, and a Good Samaritan in a boat came by to carry him to safety; still he refused. The water continued to rise and the man was soon forced onto his roof. A helicopter crew saw his plight and lowered a rope to rescue him. The man sat on the roof, arms crossed, knowing that God would save him. The water eventually covered the house, and the man drowned. When he arrived in heaven, he asked God, "Why didn't You rescue me?" God said, "What are you talking about? I sent a car, a boat, and a helicopter!"

"Waiting for God" does not imply inaction on a Christian's part; often, he must prayerfully step out in faith first, and only later will he see how God was working in his life. He can't pray "God, I really want to cross the street," and then do nothing until God sends angels down to carry him across. After all, God parted the Red Sea, but the Israelites still had to walk across. In the same way, a Christian can't pray, "God, I want to be the world's best fighter pilot" or "a four-star general" and then take no initiative to that end. He should not take *control* of his life toward that goal, but that doesn't mean he shouldn't *work* toward it, *if* he prayerfully believes that it is within God's will for his life.

At one point I considered taking control of my career and had the error of my ways pointed out to me. My wife and I were expecting a child and I thought about actively avoiding assignments that might place me back in combat. After mentioning my feelings to Lt Col Stokka, he gave me a pretty succinct reminder of God's sovereignty. He told me that if God wants a person to die, then he will—whether that person is in combat or sitting behind a desk. If He wants him to live, then he will—whether it's surviving through a AAA and missile barrage or a morning of briefings.

King Ahab of Israel is the perfect Biblical example. God told Ahab that he would die for disobeying His command (1 Kings 20:42). The prophet Micaiah would eventually tell Ahab that he would die in battle against the Arameans (1 Kings 22:20, 28); in response, Ahab entered battle in disguise as an ordinary soldier so that he could not be singled out. For all his efforts, Ahab was still struck by an arrow "drawn at random" by an unknown soldier; the arrow sailed through the air to strike Ahab in the only place he could be hurt—the joint between the sections of his armor. He bled to death that day, struck by an ancient golden BB. God had declared he would die, and despite Ahab's best efforts, the Word of God was fulfilled. God's will is supreme, and a Christian must understand that God has a plan. A Christian must make wise and prayerful choices and then take comfort knowing that God is in control.

Chapter 12:
Spiritual Requisites for a Christian Fighter Pilot

A CHRISTIAN FIGHTER PILOT engages in spiritual combat on a daily basis. His foundation is threatened, his faith is tested, and his righteous life is challenged. To survive, he requires a firm spiritual foundation and Christian mutual support.

A Christian needs a firm foundation to be an effective witness to the world. His foundation is based on the strength of his faith and beliefs; he must know what he believes, why he believes it, and he must have *confidence* in it. If a Christian believes without question that God parted the Red Sea for the nation of Israel, allowing them to cross on dry ground and drowning the Egyptians after them, then to him it is as certain as fact. Conversely, if he *thinks* that God parted the sea, but isn't sure if it was just a marsh, or maybe the Egyptians just got caught in the mud, then his faith is based on indefinites and his beliefs are indefensible. When challenged, the Christian with firm beliefs will not waver and will rely on the underpinnings of his faith; the Christian whose faith is based on possibilities will have no fortress to fall back to when his faith is challenged, and he may retreat to a secular position or simply surrender all together. To stand firm, a Christian must know where he stands; the cliché says that if you don't stand for something then you'll fall for anything. Isaiah said that if you don't stand firm in your faith, you won't stand at all (7:9).

Tactical Expertise

A Christian can strengthen his foundation by increasing his knowledge. The fighter pilot equivalent is tactical expertise. Pilots must know their aircraft and all its systems, the weapons it can carry, the support provided by their

115

allies and sister services, their enemy, and their enemy's defenses. Volumes of data cover the classified and unclassified features of every aspect of a fighter pilot's tactical world, and they are constantly revised and updated. The only way to maintain currency on the plethora of material is constant study. Proficiency also requires more than just memorization; the best understanding comes with analysis, scrutiny, and the desire to understand the foundational concepts. To fail to keep up with the most current data or to forget critical pieces of information is to invite disaster on a mission. No combat pilot would dream of entering a hostile area without ensuring that he had the training and knowledge needed to emerge victorious.

In the same way, a Christian must know himself, his God, his support, and his enemy. The manual that he can reference is the Bible. First, *reading* what he claims to believe is essential to *knowing* what he believes. I once heard a preacher say that he knew many who claimed to *believe* the Bible "cover to cover" but had never *read* it from "cover to cover." While the task may seem daunting for even the most avid Christian reader, there are many suggested blueprints available to accomplish the feat; now, many Bibles even include one in the "extra" pages. A Christian *must* know his Bible. In 2 Timothy 3:16, Paul says that "all Scripture is God-breathed and is useful for teaching, rebuking, correcting and training in righteousness." Importantly, in verse 17 Paul continues, "so that the man of God may be thoroughly equipped for every good work." The Bible is God's tactics manual, and it is the source of knowledge for every aspect of a Christian's spiritual life, guiding him in how he should live for God. The Bible is *the* means by which the man of God is equipped for *every* good work in his personal, professional, and spiritual life. Only through constant study and perpetual saturation in it can he hope to stay current in his spiritual walk with God.

Additionally, like tactical proficiency, more than simply knowing or memorization is required. A Christian must strive to analyze, discover, and comprehend the intricacies of his beliefs and the qualities of the character of God. Resources that can help him understand what he believes include Josh McDowell's *New Evidence That Demands a Verdict* and Paul Little's *Know What You Believe*.[1,2] I recommend that a Christian use resources such as these to strengthen his understanding of the *basics*. Just as a fighter pilot must learn how to take off and land before he learns how to dogfight, a Christian benefits most from having a firm grasp of the fundamentals. Once he is proficient in the basics, *then* effort can be expended on the advanced:

---

[1] McDowell, Josh. *The New Evidence that Demands a Verdict*. Thomas Nelson Publishers, Nashville, 1999. Josh McDowell is famously introduced as the man who sought to prove Christianity a farce and became a Christian in the process. His book is written on an intellectual level and contains not only the basics, but also advanced theology and apologetics. This book is highly recommended for those who want to know more about the intricacies of their faith.

[2] Little, Paul E. *Know What You Believe*. Cook Communications, CO, 1999. This is an excellent resource for understanding the basics of the Christian faith.

in the case of the fighter pilot, advanced tactics; in the case of the Christian, apologetics.

A Christian can also strengthen his foundation by remembering what he believes. The easiest way for him to do this is to write down his testimony; that is, the way in which he came to know Christ. Every person who claims Christianity has a testimony; Christ is not inherited or just "happened upon" one day. Becoming a follower of Christ is a choice—an act of will. Writing down his testimony will force a Christian to remember that act of will, articulate the choice he made, and list the reasons he made that choice. It will give him the starting point from which to support his decisions. A choice that cannot be expressed cannot be defended. It is helpful if he writes down the condition of his life before and after his conversion. If he was saved at a relatively young age, then it is likely that there isn't too much to the "before" picture; in any case, he should be able to enumerate his Christian choices as he's grown and be able to explain and justify them. This will help him answer the question of why he lives the way he does, beyond the fact that "he's a Christian." His ability to know, understand, and defend the reason for his faith will give him a firm foundation on which to stand when the world challenges him.

Ebenezers: Reminders of the Journey

When I began to fly combat sorties in OIF, I was quickly educated on the popularity of creating combat souvenirs. Whether it's a trinket carried into space on a shuttle mission or a memento carried around the globe on an aircraft carrier, people like the idea of having a souvenir with a unique story. For those who worked near combat aircraft, the souvenir of choice was a US flag. Photos of airborne aircraft flying combat missions—many are taken while the aircraft is on the boom of a tanker—often show a flag up against the fighter's cockpit glass. As many pilots did, I carried American flags with me when I flew. It seemed that every crew chief, intelligence officer, and random airman wanted to own a flag that had been flown in a fighter aircraft in the hostile skies of a foreign country. We actually had a large box of "waiting to be flown" flags by our operations desk, and pilots were encouraged to take a few to fly on every sortie. After the sortie, the data from the sortie would be written down and the flag owner would get a nice certificate to accompany his combat-experienced flag. Fighter pilots, too, like having mementos to remind them of their combat experience. I flew flags for my friends and family.

A Christian's testimony reminds him of his spiritual origin; to remind him of the journey he should collect 'spiritual souvenirs;' some have called such spiritual markers *Ebenezers*. Popular Christian self-help books have made *Ebenezer* almost standard Christian-speak; it was originally in the old hymn "Come, Thou Fount of Every Blessing" ("Here I raise mine Ebenezer; hither by thy help I'm come...").[3] The source is 1 Samuel 7:12: under the guidance of Samuel, the Philistines had finally been defeated, but not by Israel. God had caused the Philistines to be thrown into such a panic that they were routed before the Israelites. In recognition of God's protection, Samuel set up a memorial stone and called it *Ebenezer*, which means "stone of help." This was not the first time the Israelites had created such monuments. In Exodus 16:32 Moses commanded the Israelites to save a jar of manna to show future generations the provision God had made for the people. When Joshua led the nation across the Jordan, he commanded them to collect 12 stones from the dry riverbed and erect them as a memorial.

In modern times, with the popularity of catch phrases and pithy mnemonics, Christians have taken to referring to any "life turning point" or "memorial stone" as an Ebenezer—a standing stone that marks a location of God's help. As Christians mature in Christ, they will face many struggles, and only by the grace of God will they continue to walk in His ways. They will also have moments of joy and success that only God could provide. As they come through such struggles and joy, Christians need to scribe those moments in their memory, or perhaps even create a physical reminder of them; write them on the inside cover of a favorite Bible, keep them in a journal, or put them on index cards and post them on the wall.

The objective is to remember these spiritual highs and lows for two reasons. First, they remind a Christian of God's provision during the good times and in times of struggle. Ebenezers will mark his spiritual growth and provide a reminder of the constancy and dependability of God. In my own life, my failure to raise an Ebenezer caused me to forget that God had provided me encouragement. Near the end of one of my assignments— throughout which I had struggled under the weight of my unpopular Christian decisions—one of my fellow pilots experienced significant personal problems that eventually led him to God. Because of my actions in the squadron over the previous years he knew that he could talk to me about his spiritual life. We had many good conversations, and I can only hope that I was able to provide him some strong spiritual support. I left that assignment not much later, though, and failed to even realize that God was showing me that my "sacrifices" in living a Godly life were not fruitless—someone had positively responded to my Christian character. Only when the story was recounted to me later did I realize my need to remember that God had shown me my choices would ultimately have good results.

The second reason for Ebenezers is that other people might see concrete examples of God's provision in a Christian's life. A Christian will be able to articulate to other people the times in his life that God sustained him. This will show them the reason that he continues in his faith; it will also enable him to provide comfort and reassurance to those who go through similar circumstances.

---

[3] Robinson, Robert. "Come Thou Fount of Every Blessing." Public Domain. Published in *A Collection of Hymns Used by the Church of Christ in Angel Alley*, Bishopgate, 1759.

Finally, there is another use of Ebenezers that is somewhat different but almost more important. As demonstrated by Joshua after crossing the Jordan, when the Israelites erected an Ebenezer it was intended as more than a memorial; it was also to inspire conversation. The reason for the stones by the Jordan was to cause future Israelites to ask "Why are these here?" and enable the elders to speak of God's provision for their people (Joshua 4:20-22). Similarly, at various times in history God directed His prophets to have "conversation pieces" to draw the attention of the Israelites and convey His messages. (As an example, the Judah/Ephraim stick of Ezekiel in 37:15-18.) As a member of the military, fighter pilots may have difficulty finding ways to physically create this kind of Ebenezer, but these Christian conversation pieces can be extraordinarily effective ministry tools. Each situation will have unique circumstances, but whether it's a cross around a neck, a bumper sticker, a fish emblem on a car, a T-shirt with a Christ-centered slogan, or Christian music blaring on a stereo, these Ebenezers can be ways to inspire others to say "What's the reason for this?" and open the door to say "my hope is in Christ."

I have only recently been able to raise my favorite Ebenezer. Air Force flight suits are littered with unit and name patches that are attached by Velcro. Most fighter pilots remove a flap of Nomex that covers the pen and pencil holder on the upper left arm. (This semi-official uniform alteration is sometimes a distinguishing mark between fighter and non-fighter pilots.) When they remove this flap, it leaves a small portion of exposed and unused Velcro. Depending on the rules and regulations of the command, many pilots have small patches made (generally ½" by 1") that fit neatly on the exposed Velcro. Most are off the wall emblems like a "fun meter," an acronym, or other graphic.

At one base a group of pilots had made a squadron-colored patch that had a blatant profanity on it. While it shocked me, it appeared that the leadership was doing nothing to stop them from wearing it. Since there were no clear rules at this base on the legality of these small patches and the offensive one was allowed, I had my own made. It was bordered in black and had an olive drab background, subdued much as our combat name tags were. The content of the patch itself was simple: the outline of the Christian fish. I was, almost literally, wearing Christ on my sleeve. In some respects it was merely a parry to the vulgarity of the other patch; ultimately, though, I hoped it would be an Ebenezer to the pilots around me, and that someday someone might ask "What does that mean?"

Mutual Support

Even once confident in his foundation, though, a Christian requires the reassurance of mutual support. Mutual support is not only crucial to mission success, it is also essential to coming home alive. The key to mutual support is a wingman. Fighter pilots almost always enter combat in formations of multiple aircraft. A flight of aircraft is composed of a flight lead and a wingman, referred to as #1 and #2. In a four-ship, #3 is another qualified flight lead, though he is subordinate to #1. #4 is another wingman. According to the mantra once taught in pilot training, the wingman was only allowed to say three things: "2," which was an acknowledgement of a directive from #1, "bingo," which meant that he'd reached the fuel state at which he had to go home, and "Lead, you're on fire," indicating that he saw a problem with #1's jet. Some joked that the wingman could only say "Lead, you're trailing smoke," because being "on fire" was a judgment call. (An oft-quoted corollary to #2's permitted calls was "I'll take the fat one," a description of a wingman accepting the less desirable young lady to support his flight lead in a social situation.) The subservience of #2 to his flight lead was heavily emphasized and was based on both the wingman's lesser experience and the need for a firm leadership structure in the flight.

Over the past few years, however, the supremacy of #1 in the eyes of the Air Force has slowly faded. By the time I had left pilot training and moved on to operational aircraft, the concept of "Crew/Fighter Resource Management" (C/FRM) was more common. The Air Force knew that many flight leads had broken things and gotten people killed while their wingmen had the situational awareness to prevent the mishap. Decades of telling #2 to be quiet had taken their toll, though, and most would only speak up in rare circumstances. C/FRM, as taught and emphasized by the Air Force, placed a priority on communication and sharing information. #2 was still supposed to be subservient to #1, but if #2 saw things were going south in a hurry, he was encouraged to speak up and ask the question rather than watch silently as #1 fouled it away. The wingman was encouraged to provide proactive mutual support.

In a rudimentary sense, each aircraft in a formation provides mutual support by checking the other's "six." Using a clock as a reference, the area directly in front of the aircraft is 12 o'clock, the left and right are 9 and 3 o'clock, and the 6 o'clock position is directly behind the jet. Six o'clock is the least visible area for a pilot. Each aircraft flies in a tactical formation that allows the other to "check six" for his wingman—a pilot depends on his wingman to defend his most vulnerable area. With increased technology and more advanced weapons systems like the F-22, visual formations are less important and pilots may not even be able to see each other. Still, the presence of other friendly aircraft in close proximity provides mutual support; regardless of what happens to either aircraft, a squadron mate is close by to lend a hand if required.

A Christian needs mutual support in his spiritual life just as a fighter pilot requires mutual support in combat. The support, accountability, and encouragement provided by a friend in Christ can determine the success or failure of his mission in life. The support of a fellowship of believers has an unquantifiable impact on the life of a Christian. While it is true that God is the source of a Christian's strength, there are few Biblical examples of those who God intended to be alone in this world (though there are a few).

In Ecclesiastes, God said, "Two are better than one, because they have a good return for their work: if one falls down his friend can help him up. But pity the man who falls and has no one to help him up." And further, "Though one may be overpowered, two can defend themselves. A cord of three strands is not quickly broken" (4:12). Many people quickly assume that the "cords" apply to those who are married, representing the husband, wife, and God. While it does have a unique application to a marriage relationship, there is no evidence the author intended it to be restricted to that use, and the phrase is just as pertinent to those who are single. The first two cords are the Christian and God, the third cord is his wingman; depending on the point of view, the wingman could be fulfilled by church fellowship, a Bible study group, or a faithful Christian friend—importantly, a friend of the same gender—to whom he can confide and maintain a relationship of accountability. The mutual support of a Christian wingman is an important asset in all facets of a fighter pilot's life. Twice in my short career another Christian and I have uplifted each other's spirits by supporting each other in a common struggle. A Christian fighter pilot needs a spiritual "wingman" on this earth just as much as a tactical wingman in combat.

A Christian requires many of the same things in the spiritual world as he does the tactical one. The typical fighter pilot exudes confidence in his abilities and expertise in knowledge; a Christian needs a similar confidence and wisdom in his spiritual foundation. In combat he needs a wingman to back him up; spiritually, a Christian brother does the same. Strength in these qualities assures mission success in the fighter pilot's tactical and spiritual worlds.

PART 3:
PRACTICAL CHRISTIAN OFFICERSHIP

Chapter 13:
Establishing a Spiritual Lifestyle

THE TRANSITION FROM CADET LIFE to the active duty military is a significant one, particularly for cadets from the military academies. While cadets from civilian colleges have lived "real" lives for the past few years, most Academy cadets are straight out of high school. The only life they have known has been the enforced structure of a military school, dorms and meals provided. Since my graduation the Academy has changed significantly, in part due to progress, in part due to scandal. Still, the fishbowl life of the Academy remains unique in its structure and rigidity. The first time that most cadets experience "freedom" is immediately after graduation when they are given 60 days of leave before reporting to their first assignments. Some take the opportunity to travel, others get married, some spend time with their families, and some do nothing at all. Unbeknownst to them, that leave is a quiet transition between the "too much homework" of the Academy and the "too many things to do" of the "real" Air Force.[1]

Many Christian Academy cadets graduate with high aspirations of the things they'll do when they're finally free and clear, whether it's going to church regularly, finding a Bible study, starting a personal daily Bible study, or beginning to tithe. Some cadets, for a variety of reasons, find they can't do those things while at the Academy. With the academic, military, and physical demands of the Academy, cadets can be so busy that it may be difficult to even establish a daily Bible reading routine, much less conduct a Bible study or focus on spiritual growth. Financial giving may also be diffi-

---

[1] Buxton, Cleo and Louisa. *Into the Real World – Young Officers Comment on Their First Duty Assignments.* Command Magazine Bicentennial Issue, 1976. Reprinted in the USAFA Firstie Notebook, *Preparing for Active Duty*, June 1999. This quote is from Rob Alexander, USMA '74.

cult. When I first entered the Academy I earned $60 a month; while we didn't have many expenses, that $60 was quickly erased by phone cards, snack foods, and credit card bills generated by purchasing Christmas airline tickets. Because I felt financially strapped, I felt unable to give God back even a mere $6 of my small paycheck. Like many cadets, I often reassured myself that I would correct those oversights when I finally graduated. Unfortunately, the sudden and complete freedom of 60 days of leave often convinces new officers to delay their resolutions until after their leave is over. Once they report to their first assignment, they find themselves so involved with their first job that their previous resolutions—Bible reading, tithing, church attendance—fall by the wayside.

For that reason, new officers—particularly Academy graduates— should use the freedom of their post-commissioning leave as a time to set the foundations for their active duty life. The cliché that it is best to "start now, because it will never get any easier" has been used to describe things as varied as investment schemes to daily Bible reading, and it's true. Those who are too busy or too tired will never find the day when they are not. It is important to create a routine even when it is difficult; eventually, the forced repetition will become habit and the habit will become a lifestyle. What habits does a Christian need? Establish a daily time with God. Set up a daily Bible reading time (or quiet time, whatever it's called), and make it part of a routine even while on leave and there really is no routine. Establish financial stewardship. Contribute a portion of those first significant Lieutenant paychecks back to God's work. Whether or not a Christian believes in an exact tithe, 10% is a nice round number for which to aim. Throughout a pilot's career he'll find that he's frequently moving and doesn't have a steady church to financially support; at those times I recommend contributing to a national Christian organization like Officers' Christian Fellowship (OCF), Focus on the Family, or national Christian radio.[2]

A Christian's objective is to start his active duty life with strong spiritual habits in place. Those habits will help him with two aspects of his new active duty life. First, because he's left college or the rigid structure of the Academy, he'll have significantly more freedom with his time. If he hasn't already decided what to do with some of that time, it becomes easy to fill it with other activities. By having a planned Bible reading time in his daily life, for example, he'll prioritize it in the free time of his routine. Second, after his leave ends and his life gets busy again with work, he will be able to carry on with his established spiritual habits. Just as college life was busy with homework, classes, and the demands of the cadet military life, a pilot's active duty life will soon seem overwhelmingly occupied with the demands of academics, training, work, and the extracurricular activities of professional development. On those days when a hectic schedule pushes the Bible to the side, the *lifestyle* of Bible reading will be missed. Without that estab-

---

[2] Sister stations K-Love (www.klove.com) and Air-1 (www.air1.com) are two examples of national Christian radio stations.

lished lifestyle, when the days get busier (as they certainly will), the Bible will get pushed to the side and won't even be noticed. By establishing spiritual habits early, a pilot will set a precedent in his active duty life that will support him through varied and challenging times.

Unfortunately, it's easy to say things like "set aside a daily Bible reading time" and much harder for a fighter pilot to actually do it. A pilot's life revolves around the flying schedule—he may come in before sunrise one week and land after sunset the next. There is little "routine;" a fighter pilot does not live a predictable "9 to 5" job. Unfortunately, that has always been true for Christian pilots. In the 1970s, Officers' Christian Fellowship conducted a survey of recent graduates, asking them for what they were best and least prepared, and asking what information they could provide for upcoming graduates. A 1971 Air Force Academy graduate, describing the hectic demands of a pilot's schedule, said, "Flying at different times, TDYs, and alert all tend to make it hard to set aside a regular time each day for prayer, and make planning ahead for meetings difficult. Regular weekly attendance is impossible."[3] The challenges he described in the early 1970s are *exactly* the same as those I have faced, and they are challenges that Christian fighter pilots *will* experience in 2007 and beyond. A Christian faces a continual struggle to establish and maintain those stakes in the ground of daily Bible reading, prayer, study attendance, fellowship, and the other basic Christian needs.

---

[3] Buxton, Cleo and Louisa. *Into the Real World – Young Officers Comment on Their First Duty Assignments.* Command Magazine Bicentennial Issue, 1976. Reprinted in the USAFA Firstie Notebook, *Preparing for Active Duty,* June 1999. This quote is from Tim Duff, USAFA '71.

Chapter 14:
Finding a Church

ARRIVING AT A NEW BASE often makes a military Christian feel as though he's been thrown into the water by himself—the only options are to sink or swim. The single most important thing he can do is establish his spiritual support. Finding a church and Bible study are important to prevent him from feeling that he is standing alone.

When I arrived at my pilot training bases, I first attended the chapel, primarily because it was convenient; the teaching was sound, but rarely deep or challenging. At Laughlin and later at Luke I did eventually find an off-base church after I met someone who was familiar with the local area; in neither case, though, was it a proactive search on my part. I simply ran into someone who attended an off-base church and casually found out about it. From my time as a young cadet to my arrival at F-16 training I believe my Christian life was hindered by my inability to find a strong church.

I was sluggish to find a church for a variety of reasons. Like many fighter pilots I find comfort in routine and have a small comfort zone; it took effort on my part to stroll confidently into a new church on Sunday morning, particularly if it was small enough that everybody made a big deal about the visitor. By being slow to try new churches I didn't risk my comfort zone often. I was also busy with flight training, and it was easy to forget about church until Sunday morning, at which point it was easier to go back to the convenient chapel rather than scout a new church. Also, much of my early flight training (UPT, IFF, B-course) took place in different locations for only a few months each. Because I was in one place for a short time it was easy to convince myself to put off finding a church until I got to my first *real* assignment.

The primary reason I was so lackadaisical in church-hunting was a simple lack of motivation. So long as I had *a* church to attend, my stagnant spirit was placated. It was easy to tell myself that so long as the church had sound doctrine it was good enough until I could get to my next assignment, which is where I'd finally find a good church. I would tell myself that I'd find a real church home tomorrow, or next Sunday, or at my next assignment—always later. Settling for spiritual mediocrity allowed me to funnel my desires for spiritual growth, maturity, and strength into flying.

It wasn't until my first operational assignment—after two years on active duty—that I made an early, proactive, and concerted effort to canvas local churches and decide which would be my church home. It was not as if I suddenly received a divine dose of spiritual stimulus to find a church. Instead, my motivation was based on the upcoming arrival of my new wife. Only after I had attended the local churches and sought a home for my new family did I realize I should have been doing that all along. Attending a church for a sound spiritual reason (rather than convenient geography) enabled my wife and me to take root in it, benefit from its teaching, and contribute to its fellowship. By finally having a church home I was able to revive my stagnant spirit and once again experience spiritual growth.

My experiences have taught me that when a Christian moves to a new location (whether a new assignment or temporary duty), his number one priority (short of eating) should be finding a church to attend. (At some churches, his meal may be taken care of as well.) It is a fundamental step in establishing a spiritual foundation at a new base. As I found out, if a pilot doesn't establish the base of his spiritual support early, then he has no foundation on which to build. Without establishing an anchor when he first arrives, he risks floundering until he moves on no better spiritually than when he arrived.

The Military Chapel

My recommendation is that the *first* Sunday a pilot is at a new location, even if he arrived only the night before, he should attend the base chapel service. If nothing else, this will keep him in the habit of going to church; if he rolls over and goes back to sleep because he hasn't decided where to go, it becomes progressively easier each consecutive week to come up with a reason not to find a church. Besides helping to keep a routine, attending the chapel allows the opportunity to meet the base chaplains, with whom a Christian is certain to have some interaction over the length of his tour. Most chapels today have Catholic as well as traditional, contemporary, and gospel forms of Protestant services. Traditional tends to be more liturgical, with a scripted service and probably an integrated communion. Contemporary tends to have the modern style of music and a somewhat more casual atmosphere. Gospel services are, of course, oriented in the style of southern gospel.

Base chapels are a convenient starting point with familiar surroundings, though the quality of a base chapel is entirely dependent on the chaplains and the support of the congregation. I have been to bases where the service is nothing more than "Christian light," a watered down religiosity that is sure to offend no one. I have also been to chapels where the preaching, teaching, and fellowship would rival even the best established, well-funded, and largest churches in the United States.

Attending the base chapel does have its advantages. The chaplain is intimately familiar with the military lifestyle and will likely apply his teachings in an environment that a pilot will understand. Also, when stresses like checkrides, inspections, and exercises are restricting a pilot's schedule, the location and military integration of the chapel will help both his continued attendance and pertinent spiritual application. In addition, by attending the chapel that first day a pilot may get all the information he could desire on local fellowship opportunities, as many Bible studies and para-church groups use the chapel as a meeting point for new arrivals. Finally, the chapel is normally the first stop for those in the military who have felt, but may not understand, a hunger for God; by attending the chapel, a Christian pilot may expose himself to other members of his squadron who may be attending as they seek life's answers.

The military setting of the chapel program also has its disadvantages. Because the chaplains are responsible for the spiritual well-being of all military members, it is possible that they may neutralize their message to avoid offense. On the other hand, regardless of a Christian's church past, it is likely that the chapel will expose him to things to which he's not accustomed. Counter to some denominational beliefs, there are female chaplains. It is also likely that a Christian will meet the local Muslim chaplain; in July of 2004 the Navy commissioned the first US military Buddhist chaplain.[1] I was stationed at a base where information on a Wiccan meeting—conducted under the auspices of the base chapel program—was listed directly below the schedule of church services. It is an imperfect system in an imperfect environment.

A Christian should seek God's guidance in prayer as to where God would have him. Whether he chooses to attend the chapel or not is his personal preference; it has much to do with his spiritual maturity, needs, and desires. As a generalization, I would say that *on average*, most chapels lack in-depth teaching and strong spiritual fellowship. For most newly commissioned officers (particularly those who are young in their Christian walks), I personally think that active duty life will provide enough of a challenge that they'll need to attend a church with strong teaching and fellowship. If that is not the chapel, then so be it. Conversely, if they are spiritually strong and mature Christians, then the base chapel may actually be the best place for them so they can have the greatest impact on the military community. Prayerfully, it depends.

A young Christian may need to find a church with strong teaching so that he can grow; a mature Christian may attend a church with weaker

---

[1] Kerns, Rob. Journalist 1st Class. "First Armed Forces Buddhist Chaplain Commissioned," http://www.news.navy.mil/search/display.asp?story_id=14387, 22 July 2004. Viewed 09 March 2007.

teaching to further some other goal. While some base chapels may lack depth in teaching, they are still the focal point of ministry to the military. A Christian might do well to attend the chapel solely as a means of outreach, even if it doesn't afford depth of teaching or is weaker in other areas. Officers' Christian Fellowship (OCF) emphasizes support of the chapel program for this reason; as OCF considers itself a ministry to the military, the chapel provides a crucial means to that end.[2]

I wholeheartedly agree with the OCF principle of attending the chapel as means of outreach to the military community. I personally believe, though, that the decision to make potential spiritual sacrifices should only be done with understanding of the ramifications of that choice. There *may* be weaker instruction or a loss of other niceties of a civilian church, like strong children's teaching. When a Christian is sufficiently mature in his walk to knowledgeably make such choices—a point which will vary for every individual—I believe that he not only can, but should. A Christian's greatest potential ministry is to the military members that surround him, and the chapel is a critical channel to that goal.

Community Churches

Should a Christian decide not to attend the base chapel, many locations have the opportunity for a variety of off-base services. A pilot will likely be able to find a church of his particular denomination. If he prefers non-denominational services or cannot find a familiar service to attend, he may be forced to attend a church sight unseen. Ideally, the way to find out about off-base churches is through contacts who have attended there. A new arrival's first choice should be to ask members of a Bible study or equivalent fellowship, if he's found one. Second, most chaplains will have information on local churches' styles and formats of worship that could help him make an informed decision.

The last option, which could potentially be the only one available, is to crack open the base paper, local newspaper, or phone book and find a church. Christians may be able to get information on the church by calling them and asking them about their doctrine and style of worship. In my case, when I couldn't get recommendations I went to churches that I drove by or found in the paper. I recommend caution when finding a church with that method; the risk is not in finding a church with completely bizarre beliefs, but in finding a seemingly reasonable church with subtle but important doctrinal discrepancies. While every person's spiritual development is at a different place, it is helpful in those cases for a Christian to have a firm grasp on what he believes, and to listen with some skepticism at first. Once he determines that the doctrine of the church is in line with Biblical teaching, whether by attendance or by direct questioning of the pastor or other mem-

---

[2] Roush, Paul. Col, USMC (Retired). *Supporting Your Chaplain.* OCF of the USA, 1987.

bers of the congregation, he can then open himself up to the teaching of the church.

For people who grew up in one church or a particular denomination their entire life, the first experience of finding a new church in a new place can be rather daunting. The churches that a Christian will survey as he searches for a new church home have a significant challenge to overcome: to make him comfortable and willing to worship there, they need to be much like the church he's used to. As he attends new churches, the very characteristics that have made him a fighter pilot may begin to surface: he'll find himself critically analyzing the sermon, the building, and the budget; being judgmental of the doctrine, worship style, and structure; and wondering if he'll ever find the "perfect" church. It's important to remember that unless a Christian happens upon the First Church of [Your Name Here], no church a person ever attends will be perfect in his own eyes. (Someone once said that if you do find a perfect church, don't join it—you'll ruin it.) There will always be something one can find "wrong" with a church.

A Christian must know what is important; he must understand that which cannot be compromised and that which really doesn't matter. If it is a doctrinal discrepancy or other fundamental belief that cannot be reconciled with the Bible, then that church should not be considered. If the beef is stylistic, geographic, demographic, or some other minor issue, a skeptical pilot should approach it with an open mind and heart. A church with sound teaching should not be abandoned simply because they pass the plate at the end of the service instead of the middle. If the difficulties a new arrival has with the church are distracting him from his ability to learn, worship, and fellowship, then he must decide if he can plant himself there. If he cannot get himself beyond those distractions, then perhaps that particular church is not for him; I urge caution, however, because if the difficulty is truly a minor one and he cannot let it go, then he seriously inhibits his ability to find *any* church where he will ever be comfortable. Such a Christian runs the risk of church-hopping through all the local churches and never having a steady place that he might call his church home.

Some Christians may be comfortable in any church setting. For them and for relatively new Christians I recommend caution that they don't allow themselves to be *too* accepting of a church. Ideally, a Christian should have some spiritual foundation and a familiarity with the Bible so that he can test what the preacher says; in the least, he should have a trusted friend to talk to if he hears an unusual teaching. This caution is neither closed-minded nor unfounded; it's actually a Biblically demonstrated practice. In Acts 17:11, Paul commended the Bereans for checking the Scriptures to see if Paul's preaching was true, rather than simply believing everything they heard.

I put myself in a situation like this when I attended IFF in 2000. I was there for only a few weeks, and I decided to try a generically named church that I had passed on my way to the base. The first Sunday I attended I was quite impressed. The style was a bit conservative but was similar to what I had known growing up, and the teaching had depth and knowledge. I gladly attended again the second week; the next week, however, the sermon seemed to be teaching a concept with which I was vaguely familiar. When I approached the pastor of the church after the service, he confirmed that what he had preached could be described as a sermon on the fifth tenet of Calvinism. Had I not had some knowledge of Calvinism prior to that sermon, I may not have recognized it. My point is not to comment on the Calvinist doctrine but to emphasize that when "experimenting" with churches, Christian pilots potentially expose themselves to the gamut of doctrinal leanings. If what a pilot hears just doesn't sound right, he should look it up and see what the Bible says about it. If a church insists on teaching that which is contrary to the Bible, then he should look for another church. There is no need to run at the first sight of a challenging teaching, but a Christian shouldn't accept a difficult concept without careful study, either.

Changing Churches

My final thought on finding a church is the ever-controversial topic of "leaving" a church. There used to be an old Academy gripe that cadets were judged unfairly: if a civilian changed colleges, it was called *transferring*. If a cadet left the Academy for a civilian college, it was called *quitting*. Similarly, it seems the modern Christian culture cannot abide those who depart one church to attend another. Rarely is there a quiet church move; there is generally a doctrinal tussle, a social falling out, and the lingering effects of gossip between those that remain and those that have left. As a military member a Christian will obviously have many opportunities to enter and leave church congregations as he moves between various locations. There may be times, though, when he feels the need to change churches for other reasons. For example, advocating a non-Biblical doctrine is obviously grounds for leaving that church.

Departing a church body doesn't need to be hostile, though; it might be quite possible that an individual simply feels that his spiritual needs may be better served somewhere else, or that his spiritual gifts may be better utilized at another church. While all churches generally make up the body of Christ, each tends to have its own personality and specialization. Some churches are mission-oriented and focus the majority of their resources on outreach; others are gospel-oriented and focus their efforts on evangelism. Some focus on families, military members, discipleship, or fellowship. Humans have personalities and churches do as well. Occasionally those personalities may not mesh well regardless of a common faith. A church may have a focus that is slightly different than a Christian's, and he may feel that another church would be more appropriate for him. Also, as he grows, he may find that the church that was once his near-perfect home is now not quite suited to his spiritual gifts or needs.

My wife and I experienced this at one assignment where we attended a fellowship-oriented church. The friends we made there were invaluable, and it was a great positive influence on our young marriage. Close to the end of our tour, though, we saw that as we had developed spiritual maturity the church had not, so its teachings were no longer helping us grow. By changing to another church we were able to encourage our overall spiritual development, both individually and as a couple.

When we moved churches we didn't make a scene of it, but simply and quietly moved from one to the other. When we met some of our friends who asked us why, we explained, without demeaning our previous church, that it had become time for something different in our spiritual lives. As a Christian is stationed at various locations he'll be forced to "plant" and "uproot" in many places, and many factors in his personal life, spiritual state, and other areas will influence his decision in what he calls his new church home. Regardless of why he leaves a church, whether for military or spiritual reasons, it does not need to be a drama.

A Christian must make an active effort to find a church he can call home. The base chapel and community churches have their advantages and disadvantages. Whatever his choice, a Christian should recognize his critical nature and prayerfully consider his spiritual gifts and needs and the teaching of the church. A Christian in the military will move and travel often in his career, and finding a church is a critical first step in continuing his spiritual walk.

Chapter 15:
Finding Fellowship

ATTENDING A FELLOWSHIP or Bible study is a close second in importance to finding a church. Occasionally, a Christian will find both a compelling church and a strong Bible study, but more often one will be weaker and it will be the combination of the two that will provide him sufficient teaching and growth. I experienced something similar as a cadet. Though I had difficulty finding a strong church, I was able to find an excellent Bible study fellowship.

At the Academy, Officers' Christian Fellowship (OCF) conducted a Bible study on Monday nights as part of the chapel-sanctioned Special Programs in Religious Education (SPIRE) system. The staff of OCF also hosted a Saturday night Bible study at their home just outside the Academy gate. The sponsors were Lt Col Terry Stokka and his wife, Artha. Lt Col Stokka had been a navigator on an AC-119 gunship in Vietnam. As a retired Air Force aviator he garnered immediate respect from cadets. When I attended the first OCF gathering, I was impressed with the Bible study; it involved Lt Col Stokka and some cadets playing guitar and singing praise and worship songs, and then the group divided for in-depth Bible studies. The organization and structure of the gathering impressed me, and Lt Col Stokka's leadership style and obvious spiritual maturity reassured me that I could be comfortable and learn in the environment of OCF.

Once I began attending OCF, my spiritual foundation became significantly stronger. I found in that fellowship what I had lacked in the local churches I had attended. My spiritual growth was exponential in my last year and a half as a cadet not because of church attendance but because of the teaching and mentorship of OCF. In some cases it came about simply by being around and observing other Christians. It was at OCF that I made the rather surprising discovery that it is possible for two dedicated Christians to utterly dislike each other. I met another cadet whose aggressive and outgoing attitude grated against my more withdrawn personality; I knew from his actions that he had a genuine faith, but his personality was not one I enjoyed being around.

It was also at OCF that I saw a mature and effective Christian leader who had served in the same Air Force in which I was about to be commissioned. Lt Col Stokka's experience as a Christian both in combat and in the Air Force prepared him well to answer the questions of the soon-to-be officers. More than that, though, I saw how a humble and unimposing man led a large group of raucous cadets. He was almost always soft-spoken and jovial, yet he still managed to command the attention, obedience, and respect of the cadets around him. The means with which he did that—humbly, gently, but firmly when required—amazed me and gave me a model to emulate. Even in my short time in the Air Force I had seen leadership, but here was a man who was a Christian *and* a leader, with detriment to neither. My positive experiences with OCF as a cadet prepared me well for active duty.

There are many national military fellowships and most have contacts at nearly every military location. (OCF even provides the ability to search contact names by location on their internet site.[1]) These people have volunteered to be a point of contact for new arrivals and can provide information on the local Bible study and often off-base churches.

Integration in a Bible study outside of a Sunday morning service is important; while virtually any Bible study will do, I would encourage attempting to find one with other service members. A Bible study with other fighter pilots is even better. One reason for participating in a Bible study is personal spiritual growth, but another is interaction with others. Interacting on a spiritual level with other military officers can provide invaluable opportunities for learning, accountability, and growth. In those situations a Christian fighter pilot has the greatest opportunity to be mentored by, or be a mentor to, other members of the military. It can also give him a feeling of community—he is not alone in his Christianity in the military—and, with a group of peers, a place for accountability.

While I'm not necessarily advocating an exclusionary Bible study, one composed of fighter pilots would provide particularly unique and interesting opportunities. On the other hand, that composition is almost impossible to accomplish. With varied flying schedules, additional duties, training upgrades, and deployments, it is nearly impossible to get a group of Christian fighter pilots in the same room at the same time during the week. Weekends provide greater opportunity, but with Sunday generally filled with church activities and Saturday the sole free day for family and recuperation, many pilots will find it difficult to commit to a weekend study. Though difficult, attending a study outside of church should be a goal for the Biblical exposure, growth, and experience it provides.

These studies may take various forms, from small, simple Bible study groups to large gatherings at a dedicated building. Some, like OCF, are con-

[1] Officers' Christian Fellowship has a website with links to various resources as well as a lookup table for points of contact at various locations. See http://ocf.gospelcom.net.

connected to national organizations. When I arrived at Osan I found a local fellowship ministry called the Hospitality House, which was run by an organization called Cadence International. "The House" served a meal on Friday nights, and a meal with a time for singing and a Bible lesson on Saturday night. It was hosted by a couple sponsored by Cadence and had become a refuge for many at Osan seeking both spiritual support and Christian fellowship. I was amazed at the depth and strength of the fellowship.

It's important for a Christian to have an open and positive attitude toward the fellowships he may find at a new location. When departing a base with a large, well-run fellowship and moving to a place that only has a small group, it is tempting to despondently remember how good it "used to be." Even though Academy cadets eagerly await graduation, I have seen some bemoan their departure because they feared their new base wouldn't have a fellowship like the one they were leaving. Even though remote tours contain some of the harshest spiritual, emotional, and physical conditions I have known, I have seen airmen lament their departure from Korea for fear they'd be unable to duplicate the unique and intimate fellowship they'd experienced there. Throughout the rest of the Air Force, this is known as the *Base X* syndrome. When someone arrives at a new base, they tend to compare everything to their last base: "At Luke we did it this way. At Spangdahlem, we did this differently." Eventually, it becomes, "At *Base X*, we did it this way." People who have that attitude develop a reputation for complaining—they are constantly bemoaning the perfect way their old base was and letting others know how their new base doesn't do things so well.

Moving to new places and new situations is the nature of the military, and Bible studies will vary in each new place. For example, the Academy OCF group had as many as 200 cadets involved in the fellowship, with multiple planned studies both on Saturdays and Mondays. OCF provided ample opportunity for Christian music, strong spiritual teaching, and an intimate fellowship. After I departed the Academy and arrived at my pilot training base, I and another student pilot formed the OCF study there. At any one time there may have been 3 or 4 people attending, with meetings sometimes moved or canceled because of schedule conflicts. No two Bible studies, churches, youth groups, or ministries are the same; some may be better than others, but the diversity and change a Christian experiences as the military moves him from one to another contribute to his growth and maturation.

Finding a church and Bible study to attend are important *first* steps a Christian can take when he arrives at a new base. Once he finds a church and study to call home, he needs to do more than merely count time. In the military it's easy to think, "If I can just survive this assignment, at my next base I'll...," "Once I get back from this TDY I'll...," "After this remote I'll...," or, more famously, "When I retire and have a paycheck and free time I'll..." Instead of capitalizing on the opportunities the Christian has *now*, he treads water while waiting for the time he'll *really* be able to do what is important.[2] In short, he's wasting time. He should be utilizing what he has to make the most of the time he is given. Once he has found a church and Bible study, merely attending is one way in which he can count time, content with the status quo. Instead, he should contribute to the body of Christ by participating in the congregation and study.

Participation in the local church's activities builds fellowship and relationships, which gives a Christian a network of friends on whom to depend. Interactive participation in a Bible study—including leading when the opportunity presents itself—builds knowledge, confidence, and abilities; one day when a Christian arrives at a base with no Bible study, those tools will give him the ability to start and lead his own Bible study.

Starting a Bible Study

If a pilot arrives at a location (either a new assignment or temporary duty) and doesn't find an active Bible study, he should consider starting one on his own. Often Christians who see such a need choose to start a fellowship under the auspices of a national organization such as OCF, the Navigators, Cadence, or any of a host of others. An important note for those pilots is that outside religious organizations that operate *on base* must do so "under the umbrella of [the] senior chaplain's program."[3] This is normally not a problem since most organizations that minister to the military encourage an active relationship with the local chaplaincy. Given the current Air Force climate regarding religion in the military, though, it is important for a Christian to make sure that he is in compliance with the appropriate procedures.[4]

There are many resources that can guide a Christian in starting a group Bible study.[5] Many publishers create not only the text of the study, but also teacher's notebooks with schedules and guided discussion questions. The specifics of how to conduct a study can be found in any of those sources; still, there are unique challenges to having a Bible study as a military member and fighter pilot. I learned most of the following concepts from Lt Col Terry Stokka's pamphlet "Preparing and Leading a Bible Study," published in his *Preparing for Active Duty* notebook for the Class of 1999.[6]

If a Christian needs help running a study, the content for a do-it-yourself Bible study can easily be created using preformatted materials. The format can vary widely; popular modern studies often have music, prayer, a

---

[2] Grosse, David, Chaplain. *Now That You're in the Military Service*. Beacon Hill, Kansas City, 1978. p39-40.

[3] *Respecting the Beliefs of All Airmen*. Email received 25 May 2005 from the chain of command. Much of the text was also published on FoxNews.com.

[4] See "Religion and Military Policy" in Chapter 7.

[5] As an example, OCF's *Leading Effective Small Groups* and *A Step by Step Guide to Starting an OCF Local Fellowship* can be found on the OCF website: http://ocf.gospelcom.net

[6] The pamphlet was a locally produced and printed handout for senior OCF cadets. In one section of the handout it is cited as an OCF pamphlet, but no other documentation is noted. The pamphlet does not seem to be available from OCF.

study, and perhaps some snacks or a meal. As already noted in other facets of a fighter pilot's life, coordination for a group Bible study will be difficult. If a pilot does start a study, he should maximize predictability for all who attend so that they can fit their unstable schedules around a stable Bible study. To that end, he should advertise the start and end times and then adhere to them. Once a study is established and a group of people is attending, stability can be ensured by considering continuity. For example, sharing leadership responsibility can prevent the study from relying too much on a single person; such reliance might cause the study to fail when that leader is unavailable, or might cause the study to take on too much of that individual's ideas.

Different personalities make Christians comfortable in different situations, and military Bible studies will draw members from all career fields and across all personalities. In general, to maximize the possibility that all will feel comfortable, including those that might just want to sit and listen, I agree with Lt Col Stokka's opinion that no one should be pressured to read, pray, or share with the group. One method that I saw him use was what the cadets sometimes called *Popcorn Prayer*. Rather than praying around a circle, Lt Col Stokka would start and end the group prayer (or give an open invitation for someone to do so); in between the opening prayer (often jokingly called *dialing*) and the closing prayer (*hanging up*), anyone was allowed to pray as they desired. After a slight awkward silence, the person saying the closing prayer (generally the leader, so he could control when it ended) would finish for the group. This allowed those who wanted to pray the opportunity to do so, and it didn't force those who were uncomfortable with public prayer to be embarrassed by nervously awaiting their turn around the circle. If a Bible study leader calls on people and they have a reserved personality, they may be put off and choose not to return. Lt Col Stokka used to say that he'd rather have someone sitting silently in a Bible study week after week than not being there at all.

Conversely, it's important not to let those who are assertive dominate the study. Type A fighter pilots tend to have strong opinions and have little fear of sharing them. If they dominate the study, they may overpower those who are more withdrawn but have questions to ask or constructive thoughts from which all could benefit. Also, a religious topic that is assertively communicated may be construed as correct simply because of the confidence of the person speaking it, particularly if it isn't contradicted just as assertively. The leader or facilitator needs to seek a balance so that everyone can get the greatest benefit from the study.

Another popular part of modern Christian gatherings is food; integrating food into a Bible study will depend on resources, time, and timing. Whether a full meal or mere snacks, fancy food is not required—or desired. In many religious circles it is easy to get into a culinary competition with each contributor attempting to outdo the other. To prevent a food fight, food should be a side item to the gathering, not the primary focus. In the mixed group that forms the study there may also be families with children, which means figuring out how to integrate them without alienating them (if they are in the minority) or focusing too much on them (if they form the majority). Depending on ages and numbers, children may be able to be integrated into the study; if not, childcare may need to rotate within the group or be arranged outside of the study.

Relationships in a Military Fellowship

Relationships within the group are an important aspect of a military Bible study or fellowship group, as it will likely be composed of varied ranks, government civilians, locals, and even other military services. In general, the Air Force environment is such that personnel in a Bible study or fellowship can probably be on a first name basis, though it is highly situation dependent. Trying to balance military professionalism with personal Christian relationships is an aspect of a military fellowship with which many struggle. Ultimately, it is true that eternity will last long after the military ceases to exist, and there is no rank between Christians in God's kingdom. Still, there needs to be a balance of personal and professional relationships. Though the Air Force rules on fraternization do not specifically mention using first names, it could obviously be an 'indicator' of an unprofessional relationship, which is forbidden.[7] In addition, there are several court martial cases that have involved the use of first names as evidence of fraternization. (Notably, those cases appear to have had other more serious charges, and fraternization was an 'additional' charge.)

Military customs and courtesies dictate that personnel act professionally in official circumstances. Thus, if members of a Christian fellowship choose to use first names, as many do, the separation of personal and professional must be carefully explained and followed. Members of a Bible study should be able to interact on a first name, personal level during a fellowship and work together professionally—with appropriate customs and courtesies—during other times. If there are those that cannot, they may need to have the importance of such a personal/professional balance explained to them. If the members of the group can continue to have professional relationships during other times and do not show favoritism or other indications of an improper relationship, then there should be no grounds for complaints against them. They should still exercise caution and default to military customs and courtesies if questions arise.

The idea of having such a personal/professional balance is just that—an idea. It is by no means an overarching directive or universal truth. It is possible that a Christian may be at a base, location, or environment where a given level of familiarity is either not possible or simply not a good idea.

---

[7] For specific information on permissible relationships, see Air Force Instruction 36-2909, *Professional and Unprofessional Relationships*, 01 May 1999, and "Talking Paper on Professional and Unprofessional Relationships," Col Passey, AFJAG, 21 June 99, available in the www.af.mil library.

Fellowships that serve basic training camps or formal training courses may be better served accepting "sirs" and "ma'ams" rather than attempting to impose a foreign informality. Groups with Army or Marine service members, particularly with mixed ranks from those branches, may see the unique personalities of the different services. If, for example, an Air Force officer works at an Army base and has a study composed primarily of soldiers, it may be better to fit into their environment (of more formal and regimented standards) rather than try to force his relaxed standards upon them. A Christian must prayerfully determine what the appropriate level of familiarity is within each circumstance.

Finally, in any group where there are single, mixed-gender Christians, men and women will tend to pair off and become involved. I have yet to see a singles group, young peoples' Bible study, retreat, or mission trip that hasn't resulted in romantic involvement between at least one pair of Christians. The complications of military-to-military relationships are a topic for another time; instead, it is important to note the possibility that closer-than-friends relationships may develop between officers and enlisted who are in the same military Christian fellowship. Each of the services has its own rules regarding fraternization, though they are similar. Air Force Instruction 36-2909 governs the specifics of relationships in the Air Force.[8] It recites Article 134 of the Uniform Code of Military Justice (UCMJ), which prohibits any non-professional relationship that would be prejudicial to good order and discipline.

It is highly unlikely that an officer and enlisted member could conceivably have a cross-ranks relationship that was legal under military law. Dating (or any "social substitute" used as an equivalent) between enlisted and officers is expressly prohibited. Depending on the situation, the potential for the temptation to begin an unprofessional relationship may dictate the need for segregated fellowships (divided either by gender or rank); in the very least, group leaders and mentors should watch for such interactions and actively talk to people who may appear to be involved in them. Though each instance is situation dependent, the potential for such relationships demands extreme caution. For example, an 'all-ranks' Sunday School class at the base chapel may be appropriate. A half-dozen officers and enlisted going on an overnight retreat may not be. (It is also important to note that officers/enlisted of the same gender can also have 'inappropriate relationships' in which they have a personal friendship. Romance is not required.)

I also believe it is highly unlikely that God would "call" a Christian to do that which is illegal; on the contrary, the New Testament repeatedly states that a Christian should obey and respect the authorities over him. If military regulations or an order from a commander prohibit a relationship, I do not believe it is morally right to ignore such a directive with the belief that God has "ordained" that two people be together. In such a situation, the couple needs to determine if they really are in God's will. It is a distinct

---

[8] Air Force Instruction 36-2909, *Professional and Unprofessional Relationships*, 01 May 1999.

possibility that God would have them be together, but perhaps their *timing* is not His. In short, in a military Bible study the potential exists for relationships to develop between men and women of all ranks. Extreme care should be taken that the reputation or witness of the group is not hindered by the existence or perception of inappropriate relationships.

Sharing the Gospel

Whether a Christian assumes the leadership role of a Bible study or simply gets the opportunity to witness to a non-Christian, it is crucial that he know how to communicate his faith. How does a pilot share the gospel with those around him? There is no simple, distinct answer to that question. There is no formulaic response that will enable a Christian to take a checklist, approach a fellow pilot, and convert them by ticking off the boxes.

There are two canned answers I can provide. First, a Christian must be living his witness. St. Francis once said, "Preach the gospel at all times. If necessary, use words."[9] Joseph Aldrich, President of the Multnomah School of the Bible, said that "evangelism is allowing the non-Christian to turn the pages of the book of your life, read the fine print, and hear the music of the Gospel."[10] A Christian's actions are yelling louder than his words ever will. Still, as noted earlier (see Part 2), this ministry of presence must be augmented with proactive Christianity. The second canned answer is that a Christian must know how to communicate the plan of salvation. If someone questions him, he must have an answer ready (1 Peter 3:15). The conclusion of that oft-quoted verse is also important, though: "But do this with gentleness and respect." Again, there is a plethora of books, pamphlets, and websites on the subject, and Part 2 goes into greater detail on proactive Christianity in the military environment. While there is only one plan of salvation, the way that it needs to be presented will vary for every person. Still, I can recommend the basic framework, which I first heard in a sermon during the F-16 B-course:

1. What: You need to be born again. (John 3:3)
2. Why: Being "born again" means you need to be saved from the consequences of your sins.
   Romans 3:23 - All have sinned.
   Hebrews 9:27- All will be judged.
   Romans 6:23 - Sin results in death, but God's
   gift is eternal life.
3. How: Acts 16:30, 31 - Believe in the Lord Jesus Christ—it's more than "just knowing."

---

[9] Francis of Assisi, http://www.cdu.jesusanswers.com/photo5.html. Viewed 09 March 2007.

[10] Aldrich, Joseph. "Evangelism." President, Multnomah School of the Bible, 1992. Reprinted in *Preparing for Active Duty* notebook for the USAFA Class of 1999.

> Romans 10:13 - Call on the name of the Lord
> and be saved.
> John 3:16 - Believe…

4. Believe (a) Jesus Christ bore your sins, (b) died in your place, (c) was buried and resurrected.
5. Receive forgiveness of your sins, accept God's free gift of eternal life.

Or, as some have described, the "Romans Road:"[11]

1. Romans 3:23 - All have sinned.
2. Romans 6:23 - The wages of sin is death, but the gift of God is eternal life.
3. Romans 5:8 - While we were still sinners, Christ died for us.
4. Romans 10:9-10 - "If you confess with your mouth "Jesus is Lord," and believe in your heart that God raised Him from the dead, you will be saved. For it is with your heart that you believe and are justified, and it is with your mouth that you confess and are saved."
5. Romans 10:13 - "Everyone who calls on the name of the Lord will be saved."

When explaining the reason for others to share the hope within you, there is no single right answer, but there is at least one wrong one: none at all. Christians must have an answer ready.

Attending a fellowship or Bible study in concert with finding a church home will give a Christian a strong start in establishing a spiritual lifestyle in his career. The spiritual support will strengthen his foundation and allow him to grow spiritually and teach and mentor others. Ultimately, the fellowship will give him the spiritual support he needs to live an active Christian life in the military.

---

[11] Stokka, Terry. Lt Col, USAF (Retired). "The Romans Road to Salvation." As printed in *Preparing for Active Duty* notebook for the USAFA Class of 1999.

Chapter 16:
Assignments, TDYs,
and Family Separations

MOST AIR FORCE OFFICERS relive their search for God's will every few years as they work with the Air Force Assignment System. Because of the length and variety of training assignments, fighter pilots may go for 3 to 5 years before they even have to deal with the regular assignment system; prior to that, fighter pilot assignments are either automatic or are the result of class standing at the end of training. Many young fighter pilots will make Captain—a rank most consider mature—and have no clue how to deal with the assignment process. The assignment system can be a challenging process for anyone to understand, though there are generally plenty of older pilots who will gladly offer their mentorship for younger officers considering their future assignments. Unfortunately, few view the military—or even life—the same way a Christian does, so their advice must often be taken with a grain of salt. I was assigned to my first operational base after two years of fighter pilot training at various locations. I wouldn't have interaction with the assignment system until 6 months prior to my departure date in late 2004—nearly 5 years (and a multitude of assignments) after I'd been commissioned.

As of 2006 the Air Force is revising the assignment system for officers, though the general concept appears to have remained the same. A year before I was scheduled to leave my first assignment, I received notification that I was on the "vulnerable movers list" (VML), meaning I was eligible for a new assignment in a window of a few months. Before that window began, I needed to complete a Preference Worksheet (PW), which is now called a Transitional Officer Development Plan (T-ODP). The PW contained a rank-ordered list of the assignments I wanted. There was a segment for my comments, which enabled me to put down reasoning for the assignments I desired as well as communicate my long-term goals. The comments section allowed officers to communicate specific details to his assignment team. For example, I know a pilot who adopted 2 kids and didn't want to go remote due to the "bonding time" he needed with them; the officer included that information in the comments to help the assignment team give him an appropriate assignment.

The last section of the worksheet was a space for my commander's comments. This was an important part; if a commander recommends that the Air Force Personnel Center (AFPC) deny an officer a particular assignment, it is unlikely (though not impossible) that he'll get it. In general, the commander would let his subordinate know ahead of time for what he would or would not recommend him. Also, the personnel center had certain metrics to meet; they strived to give people one of their top three choices.

Some officers try to manipulate the assignment process (or "game the system") to control their careers. For example, while I was filling out my PW the pervading perception was that if a pilot was not a true "worldwide volunteer"—meaning he would accept *any* assignment, including remotes— then he hurt his chances of getting what he wanted. This led many people to say that they would accept a remote even though it wasn't what they really wanted, just so they would look better in the eyes of AFPC. I once heard a story about a pilot who put his real desire as his second choice because he heard no one ever got their first. Imagine his shock when he got his first choice, which he didn't want at all.

Regardless how the system changes over the next few years, the best advice I ever got regarding the Air Force assignment process was from my flight commander at Spangdahlem. His advice was simple—put down what you want. So long as an officer's PW is consistent with his desires, the worst that can happen is that AFPC has to give him something not on his list. If he puts down fake choices in an attempt to game the system, AFPC may very well give him one of them—will he then blame the Air Force for giving him what he asked for? If a pilot says he's a remote volunteer to sweeten the opinion of him, AFPC may give him that very remote. A Christian shouldn't try to manipulate the system. He must acknowledge that he is not in total control of his future; when he attempts take control he is pulling it from the hands of his Creator. A Christian faced with an assignment decision must make prayerful choices and then, as difficult as it may seem at the time, let God handle the details.

There are many potential assignments that an Air Force fighter pilot may receive. There are operational fighter tours, UPT instructor slots, staff jobs, unmanned aerial vehicle (UAV) assignments, Air Liaison Officer (ALO) jobs that attach pilots to the Army, and others. Each has distinct challenges and varied impacts on a pilot's personal and professional life. There are operational tours around the globe, with the expected potential deployments and commitments. In the F-16 world right now, receiving two consecutive operational assignments, or going "ops to ops," is rare. Normally, operational assignments are alternated with other kinds of tours. UPT instructor pilot assignments are relatively stable tours—a pilot is at one base for three years, and official travels are infrequent and short. The stability of the job generally gives a pilot the ability to be with his family regularly. Though stable, the days are long—UPT IPs may fly as many as three times a day multiple days in the week, as well as attend to other duties.

The non-flying staff job gets officers face time with higher ranks and commands, but it also tends to require long hours making paperwork and reports look perfect. While not faced with the demands of an operational fighter squadron, the demands of Generals and Colonels will draw just as much time, if not more. UAV jobs tend to be much like fighter pilot squadrons without the imminent danger of flying. Deployments to dangerous locations still occur, though under somewhat different circumstances. In some cases, a small contingent will deploy with the aircraft while the rest of the squadron flies the aircraft via satellite from home station. ALO jobs are unique in the opportunity to interact with the Army. An Air Force pilot is assigned to an Army unit and does everything with them—including deploy, should that occur. In combat, that pilot's job is to coordinate the air support for the Army. Ultimately, every potential assignment brings its own inherent difficulties and challenges, both to single fighter pilots and those with families.

Deployments

In addition to his demanding daily commitments, a fighter pilot will inevitably be called upon to deploy—meaning he will travel to another destination to accomplish even more responsibilities. These deployments vary in nature and include short-term temporary duties to attend a training class, indefinite commitments to conduct combat operations, and assignment to remote tours that are a year or more long. Each situation presents unique challenges to a fighter pilot's Christian walk, finances, family, and more.

Most Air Force deployments are *temporary duties* (TDYs) that involve an officer departing his home station and going to another location to fulfill a mission or training requirement. It could be as benign as a single officer being sent to another base to receive some form of training, or it could be as complex as an entire base deploying to a front line location to engage in combat. Fighter pilots also occasionally get the opportunity to fly cross-country, meaning they fly to a different location for a weekend or so. Contingency deployments are also frequent, with pilots and jets departing the home station and traveling to any of a variety of worldwide locations. There are few "standard" TDYs.

The most frequent TDY for a fighter pilot is in support of an Air Expeditionary Force (AEF). A few years ago, the Air Force attempted to add predictability to deployments by instituting the expeditionary air force concept, with each unit assigned to an AEF cycle. Each AEF, in which there are multiple units from a variety of bases, is vulnerable to be deployed during a given window of several months. Previously, when an AEF window approached it was obvious that a unit would deploy to either Operation NORTHERN or SOUTHERN WATCH, which started soon after the Gulf War. Those operations ended in 2003 with Operation IRAQI FREEDOM, and subsequent TDYs have been much more varied and less predictable. With the close of those two operations, deployment is not guaranteed but still likely to support operations in Iraq, Afghanistan, or another less famous part of the world. When the AEF rotation is complete, the units enter a re-cuperation phase before beginning the next months of training for their next AEF assignment.

The tenor of the TDY varies widely with the nature of the deployment. When a unit "deploys" to a location in the United States or near a popular city, it is very much a good deal TDY. Las Vegas, Nevada, is the first location that comes to mind because it hosts *Red Flag*, which is a large scale exercise with aircraft from around the world. A pilot might be lodged in base billeting, or he could potentially stay in a luxury hotel in the city— costs paid. There are plenty of amenities, including cable TV, hotel pools, base gyms, and, of course, the local sights and sounds. On the other end of the extreme is a deployment to a near-bare base location. Rather than a posh hotel, pilots may be sleeping on a cot in a tent with 12 or more other guys. If there is access to a TV at all, the programming will be at the whim of the group. Meals are generally provided by a mess tent, and there are no other expenses. Often there are few other activities in which to participate, and the ability to go off-base and see the sights may be limited.

When deploying with a unit, a Christian could face greater pressures than at home station. During 'good deal' TDYs, many fighter pilots will want to go out on the town frequently; this is partially because of the desire to experience the locale and also due to the fact that most billeting rooms or hotels will have few, if any, cooking facilities, which necessitates going out to eat. Going out often may concern someone who doesn't want to spend too much money or has a family back home with whom he is sharing finances.[1]

In the majority of the deployments I have been on, I have found that there can be a balance of social events. It can build comradery—as well as just be fun—to go out to eat with fellow pilots and experience the local cuisine of a unique location. If the other pilots desire to go to other places (in particular, bars or "gentleman's clubs"), a Christian can generally bow out

---

[1] While they can sometimes be stressful and cause family separations, some military members actually look forward to deployments because they can sometimes generate a veritable financial windfall. During a TDY there is often a daily stipend (per diem). Depending on the location, military members of all ranks may also receive hazardous duty pay, hardship duty pay, and a family separation allowance. If the location is classified as a combat zone, then an officer's base pay will be tax exempt, which translates into another healthy increase in take-home pay. It is not unusual to return from a TDY and receive a significant sum of money that more than covers any expenses. Some people enter a TDY as if they already have that money; they will tend to spend money more freely while they are deployed. This is often to their detriment, particularly if they miscalculate what the Air Force is going to pay them at the conclusion of their trip.

and get a ride back to lodging. There may be some pressure to join the group, but firm refusals generally work well, particularly if a Christian has already established his moral reputation. For those who need encouragement after getting ribbed for not going along (or for those who are tempted to join the group), a Christian can find many words of wisdom and encouragement in the Bible.

For example, when faced with ridicule for refusing to patronize bars, strip clubs, and other less than positive places, there's an unlikely source of support in the usually dire book of Ecclesiastes. It says that "it is better to go to a house of mourning than to go to a house of feasting, for death is the destiny of every man; the living should take this to heart" (7:2). Solomon was saying that, as odd as it may seem, it's better to go to a funeral than a festival. At a funeral, death reminds a person that the casket up front will one day be his. The stark reminder forces him to mature and live his life appropriately. If a person spends all his time at bars and parties, he will never be motivated to mature and realize the consequences of this life. He will end up going nowhere, and will be shocked at the end of his life when he realizes he's accomplished nothing.[2] So while some fighter pilots may frequent "houses of feasting," there are benefits to avoiding constant partying.

One of my earliest TDYs was near the end of pilot training. Our final sorties required a cross-country, and it was then that I was introduced to the half-joking "two TACAN rule," which is similar in concept to the "two time zone rule" in business travel. TACANs are navigational transmitters located at military and civilian airfields. When a pilot departs one base he will dial in the TACAN frequency of the next base to fly there. The two TACAN rule simply meant that after dialing in his second TACAN, the pilot was far enough away from his home that he could misbehave and the information wouldn't make it back to his unit or, more often, his wife. Later in my career I learned the phrase "what goes TDY, stays TDY," which essentially implied that the shenanigans that went on while TDY weren't to be spoken of once back home. Obviously, no one was protected while TDY and people would find out—one way or another—what had gone on. From a Christian perspective, God knows everything anyway—"I the Lord search the heart and examine the mind" (Jeremiah 17:10). A Christian lives in the knowledge that God knows everything he does or thinks.

Whether the TDY is as an individual or a group, once the distance to home increases there will be great temptations; for men, the most notable temptation is in the sexual area. For many young fighter pilots, the first time they go TDY will be the first time they realize they can anonymously access adult TV channels, computer pornography, and strip clubs. Most hotels have cable TV with varying levels of pornography that is immediately accessible. Also, fellow fighter pilots—both married and single—may carouse

---

[2] This example is from a Bible study of Ecclesiastes, taught on video by Tommy Nelson, entitled *A Life Well Lived*. The book is published by B&H Publishing Group, September 2005.

with the local women or patronize the local strip clubs. To deal with the television temptation, most hotels have the option to call the front desk and have the adult channels turned off in a room. If that isn't an option, or the TV itself is the temptation, unplugging it, closing the cabinet, or covering it over are good alternatives. To deal with the temptation to go to strip clubs or the like, having a planned activity like a Bible study or a designated time to call family can also provide a good excuse for not joining in when others go.

There are two other valuable techniques that I have heard to help men deal with the sexual temptation of being alone in a far away city. The first is to get accountability from other Christians in the group, which is addressed in the mutual support section of Chapter 12. The other technique is an anecdote I heard related many years ago. A businessman frequently went on official trips and experienced the same sexual temptation that many men do. It came to a head on one trip when he found himself leafing through the escort section of the yellow pages, tempted to call someone to his hotel room. When he realized what he was doing, he felt so guilty that he immediately called his wife. To his amazement, she was not only *not* upset, but she also understood the temptation he was experiencing. They talked about it at length and developed a means to help them deal with temptations together. When he faced those same lures in the future, he was to call her—regardless of what time it was in either of their time zones. They also developed what could be described as a code word or phrase that he could say to tell her that he was tempted, thus not requiring any detailed explanation. His greatest help was in knowing his wife supported him so fully.

Whether an accountable Christian brother or a spouse with whom the situation has been discussed, there is great benefit in having some plan of defense to call upon when the temptation occurs. If a Christian has access to neither—perhaps he has no family to call upon and is the only Christian on the trip—then the most important thing is to depart on the TDY with the knowledge that the sexual temptation will be there and attempt to prepare himself for it. There are many Christian books wholly devoted to dealing with sexual temptation, and I could do little justice to the topic here.[3] A Christian must rely on God, through prayer and Bible study, and know that God provides him a way to stand up under assault (1 Corinthians 10:13).

The unpredictability of a TDY makes it difficult to plan Bible studies, attend chapel services, or even have a personal Bible time. There is rarely a normal schedule or a routine—in general, by the time one is developed, it's time to leave, thus the temporary nature of such a deployment. This is a

---

[3] As an example: Arterburn, Stephen and Fred Stoeker. *Every Man's Battle.* Waterbrook Press, Colorado Springs, 2000. The *Battle* series is immensely popular. While it's not perfect and I don't agree with everything they say, it is a good book with plenty of advice for dealing with sexual temptation. Notably, I was surprised to see them mention the evil of the double entendre, something I had yet to see addressed outside of the pilot community (p13). On a less positive note, the authors set out to "bust the myth" that men can't control themselves, though in at least one instance they qualify masculine traits by saying *How could he help it?* (p184).

perfect example of a time when having established spiritual habits will bear fruit (see Chapter 13). A spiritual lifestyle will make a Christian miss the absence of his Bible study or fellowship and he will then put the extra effort into accomplishing them. While at a TDY location, it is generally easiest for a Christian to attend the base chapel. He's generally there for too short a period to become connected to an off-base church; in forward deployed locations, there won't even be an off-base option. Chapels in forward deployed locations have been some of the best I have attended, even though the chaplains are only temporarily assigned themselves. The chapel is built around the mission of the deployed location, though not always perfectly.

When I was TDY at Incirlik in Turkey, the chapel had dedicated chaplains and even a Christian coffee shop that supplied free food, games, and Christian music. Operation NORTHERN WATCH (ONW), though, which Incirlik supported, had been ongoing for years, so it was a fairly routine deployment; the chapel was able to work around the relatively predictable schedule.

When I deployed in support of OIF, our airbase had a chapel program that I attended. Before hostilities started I was able to attend regularly; however, as the war approached, I was one of the group chosen to fly night sorties. I took off after sunset and landed before dawn on most days. Once I was established on the "night train" it became virtually impossible to attend what was equivalently the midnight chapel time. I came to rely primarily on my own Bible study time. I and several other Christians had a happenstance Bible study group. Since the combat sorties were so long, we often woke up, went straight to work, flew, landed, and went straight to bed. When we had the occasional day off it rarely coincided with the downtime of other Christians, but those of us that were available would do a short Bible study when the time presented itself. The best that a Christian can do during such an unpredictable TDY is have a strong personal study and make the effort to do more as the opportunity arises.

Though it may be unpredictable and rare, at some point during the deployment a fighter pilot will likely have some free time. During some TDYs, free time will be so rare that a Christian may be satisfied with simply doing *nothing* as a change from the constant demands of work. On the opposite extreme, some TDYs are a vacation from the fast-paced life of a home base. Particularly when those types of deployments are anticipated, a Christian should plan things to occupy his time. He could take books to read, an instrument to play, or materials for a class in which he's interested. Obviously, a Bible is a requirement, and he might also consider Bible reference or study materials. Modern electronics have made some travel requirements easier, and an officer might consider taking Christian music on an mp3 player or Bible study tools on a PDA or laptop. A helpful military Christian spiritual tool is a pocket-sized Bible. A fighter pilot can take it with him wherever he goes; I carried one in the pocket of my g-suit on every combat sortie. While it didn't see any use in the cramped cockpit of my night sorties, I carried it in the event I was downed in Iraq.

Most Air Force locations will have some form of library that will have books, magazines, videos, and possibly internet connectivity. I think I can safely say that every military location has some form of gym. Regardless, exercise is a good thing to incorporate into a deployed lifestyle; it burns off excess energy and improves health and morale. Once at a TDY location, a Christian should fill his extra time with these activities, rather than giving in to the temptation to watch hours of television or party constantly. This will give him some mental and physical exercise and prevent cabin fever. The repetitive nature of many TDYs causes some people to relate their lives to *Groundhog Day*, the movie in which Bill Murray relives the same day over and over. The monotonous lifestyle and limited extracurricular activities encourage many to engage in wild (and often unwise) activities to release steam. By having edifying activities in which to participate, a Christian can have something positive to do that will also benefit his overall well-being.

Remote Assignments

Remote tours are, in many respects, similar to TDYs, with the key difference of length. (As of 2007, the maximum TDY length in the Air Force is 179 days. It is worth noting, however, that the Army is serving tours of a year or more in Iraq. A few Air Force members have served that length there as well.) Receiving an Air Force remote assignment means being assigned to a base in a far-off location for a year-long tour, most often separated from family. Pilots in every Air Force fighter aircraft have some form of remote requirement to fill. Virtually every F-16 pilot is supposed to complete a remote tour at some point in their career, though it is not a given. Some may go an entire career and never go remote. Due to the costs associated with remote assignments (many expensively-trained people, including pilots, have separated from the Air Force rather than go remote), the Air Force is in the process of re-evaluating the status of some remote locations. What they ultimately determine (whether some bases close or are turned into normal accompanied assignments) could significantly alter the outlook for fighter pilot remote assignments.

Supposedly, fighter pilots have a requirement for a single remote tour in their career, though many pilots may voluntarily take another. Also, the needs of the Air Force may dictate that some receive a second. Depending on the availability of assignments, accepting a second remote assignment may be the only way some pilots can stay in a flying job and avoid an ALO or UPT tour. Some more senior pilots are offered command of a squadron in a remote location. If they turn it down, they probably won't get another offer of command, and their career progression may grind to a halt. So while the requirement is for one tour, to get what they want (more flight time, a command) some officers may volunteer for another.

Air Force remote tours are actually rather stable and predictable; pilots are generally fixed in one location and rarely go TDY. Air Force members on a remote tour generally live in dormitories, the enlisted may not have a car, and all will have the majority of their personal household goods either with their families or in storage back home. Remotes are often in austere locations or in foreign surroundings, which limit the amount of activities in which to participate off-base. Because there are so few activities outside of work, fighter pilot lives tend to revolve around the squadron—either officially, with pilots working long hours and through weekends, or unofficially, as pilots create a myriad of social functions with which to fill their free time.

Feeling trapped on an island of a base, combined with the fact that remotes are so much shorter than regular duty assignments, causes many to view a remote as an extended TDY rather than a permanent assignment. This may lead to a destructive short-term attitude: people may put off "problems" because they know that if they can delay long enough, their tour will end and it will become someone else's predicament. With few activities and a TDY perspective, little excuse is needed to spend much of the available free time either getting drunk or recovering from a hangover.

There are several remote tours in Greenland, the Middle East, and Asia (mostly non-flying ones), but the more likely place that a fighter pilot will fill his remote tour is Korea. Kunsan Air Base and Osan Air Base host the two US flying units in Korea. There are also several staff and ALO positions throughout the peninsula. If a Christian is unable to bring his family on a remote tour, he's faced with the prospect of being separated from them for the greater part of a year. Depending on the assignment, he will probably get one 30 day leave to go home with them, and he may get one or more opportunities for his family to come and see him for 30 days. This separation can be challenging for young marriages or families with children.

Dealing with Separation

With family, a spouse, or a significant other, the separation of a TDY or remote will be a challenge to the relationship. As noted earlier, the family must remain a high priority for a Christian. While the sexual temptations have already been addressed, communication with family is important for another more subtle reason as well. While pilots are separated from their families they will have reduced interaction with their family and increased contact with the people they see every day. In today's military, virtually every deployment—including combat—is mixed gender within the officer and enlisted ranks.

Besides the sexual implications, it can be tempting to develop an inappropriate emotional relationship with a peer of the opposite gender. If a pilot finds himself befriending someone of the opposite sex and talking to them more than he communicates with his spouse, he is at risk for developing an intimate emotional relationship outside of his marriage. Such an emotional relationship can be just as damaging (and perhaps more so) than an illicit sexual one. The same logic applies to singles that are engaged or simply involved in a serious relationship that they intend to continue. In any case, a Christian who gives the appearance of having a special relationship with a friend of the opposite gender while TDY will endanger his witness based on the smallest hint of impropriety. The mere appearance of an inappropriate relationship can threaten the stability of a Christian's marriage. His family relationship should always take precedence.

Regardless of the reason or the distance of the separation, it is important to have as much communication as possible between those that have gone and those that are left behind. Most Air Force bases have a variety of connection methods even in the harshest environments. During OIF, our mail was dependable, a library with email computers was fairly accessible, and military phones were available for us to make morale calls twice a week for 15 minutes. There was no privacy on the phone, though; not only were there airmen parked on phones on either side, it was distinctly possible that the command post or base operator that had connected the call had decided to have a listen as well. There was also the obvious possibility that the calls were monitored for security reasons. Still, the phone calls were better than email and far superior to nothing at all. Some locations now have high speed internet so that military members deployed to even remote locations can communicate with their families via internet video phone, which has the benefit of both audio and visual interaction.

Maintaining a family is one case where I would elevate the relationship over financial concerns. It's difficult to grow a relationship over distance; just to maintain it requires immense effort and significant communication. Long phone calls are standard—particularly if one party is upset with the other—and pictures, videos, video phone calls, and emails are essential to keeping a visual connection with home. If a Christian keeps his phone calls short to minimize phone bills and doesn't want to pay for high speed internet, then I think he risks endangering his family for the sake of a few dollars. Plane tickets will certainly be expensive if official travel isn't available, but the potential emotional benefit to both the pilot and his family is unquantifiable. It does no good to come back from a deployment well-off financially but having damaged or lost a family. There may be some financial sacrifices to make, and a Christian should budget and search for the best financial deals, but ultimately I believe that maintaining the family relationship is more than worth the cost.

Besides continual communication, commonality helps keep a family connected. One important example would be to have a common Bible study or devotional. This has the advantage of keeping a pilot and his family spiritually oriented *together*. When I initially deployed in support of OIF, I did not know how long I'd be gone. To keep our spiritual lives somewhat linked my wife and I decided to study through a book of the Bible together, reading 10 or so verses every day. I chose Psalms; in retrospect, with its 150 psalms and hundreds of verses, it may not have been the best choice to encourage my wife of my speedy return. Still, by having a connected study, we were able to have our minds on similar Biblical topics. On the occasions we were able to talk or write we were able to communicate our thoughts about the study, knowing that the other had read the same verses recently. If creating such a study isn't possible, Christian bookstores and online resources have a veritable plethora of pre-fabricated studies.[4] It is easy enough to purchase two copies of a Bible study and have both complete the studies throughout the week; the couple can talk about the studies on the weekend or email each other the answers to the study questions.

The quality of the relationship during the separation will be based on the attitudes on both sides. Both the person deployed and the family at home must remain committed to the relationship and willing to put the time and effort into maintaining it. Separations are not easy, but if both sides understand its necessity and temporary nature, it will be more bearable. There are many Christian and secular resources on maintaining relationships over distance that have more ideas and cover the difficulties in greater detail.[5]

TDYs can be one of the more enjoyable aspects of a fighter pilot career, though for a Christian they can also be one of the more challenging. Remote assignments offer opportunities to see unique place, though they too can be spiritually taxing. The separation caused by TDYs and remotes, though temporary in nature, can be hard on families. With knowledge, preparation, and active spiritual effort, a Christian can succeed and thrive even in the face of such challenges.

---

[4] For example: Christian Book Distributors (www.cbd.com), Family Christian Stores (www.familychristian.com), Focus on the Family (www.family.org), Thomas Nelson, Inc. (http://www.thomasnelson.com/consumer/), Ravi Zacharias Ministries (http://www.rzim.org/), Promise Keepers (http://www.promisekeepers.org/), Heritage Builders (www.heritagebuilders.com), Family Life (www.familylife.com), Intervarsity Press (http://www.gospelcom.net/ivpress/) are just a few of the sites I have found for books and pre-fabricated studies. Cadence and OCF also have resource related links.

[5] For example: Kay, Ellie. *Heroes at Home* (Bethany House, 2002) and Fishback, Jim and Bea. *HomeBuilders: Defending the Military Marriage.* Campus Crusade for Christ's *Military Ministries* and OCF's *Wives of Warriors* are also excellent sources of information.

Chapter 17:
Paperwork and Reality

ONE OF THE MORE IMPORTANT (and unfortunate) things that a fighter pilot will discover in his military career is the preeminence of paperwork. One day a pilot may go out and save the world, but unless it's documented on an official military form, it's as though it never happened. Like it or not, an officer's career may live or die based on his performance evaluations, which are called Officer Performance Reports (OPRs) in the Air Force. A pilot's supervisor will be required to complete a report on him regularly; normally, every 12 months, but depending on the circumstances, from every 6 to 18 months. Pilot training and other formal courses create Training Reports instead of OPRs, so a young pilot could be well into his first operational assignment—more than two years after being commissioned—by the time he receives his first OPR.

The first time one is coming due, a predictable thing will happen: his supervisor will ask him what he's been doing for the past 12 months. In a perfect world, the leadership would monitor their subordinates' successes and failures and document them accordingly. Unfortunately, in the real world the leadership will be so busy that unless the subordinates are being derelict they'll likely go unnoticed. For that reason the leadership will ask those below them to provide "bullet statements" of the things that they have accomplished since the last time they received an OPR or training report. They'll use this information to fill in all the "white space" on the report.

Because young fighter pilots generally haven't received an OPR in their first two years, they're often caught off guard by the first request for bullet statements. It is helpful if a pilot makes a habit early on—ideally, as soon as he arrives at his first assignment as an officer—of keeping track of his activities and achievements. There are a variety of ways to do this: a calendar, a record book, or a journal is a good place to record accomplishments. I have found that a convenient way to achieve this in the computer age is to create a document on my computer and save it to an obvious location in plain view. I update the file with bullets as significant events occur. It's not important for it to be fancy, just dated and factual.

A pilot should write down awards he receives, official activities in which he participates, dates he is deployed, and contributions he makes to the unit and the mission—for pilots, this often means sorties in support of exercises or inspections. For that reason I also recommend a logbook to record sortie information—not just flight time, which the military will record as well, but also details like mission type, other pilots in the formation, ordnance, and significant events.

I maintained a flying logbook from my earliest sorties, but I regret not including more details, particularly when it came to my combat sorties. I remember some events that I witnessed but cannot recall the specifics of when they occurred, like the Patriot intercepts or Army surface-to-surface missile launches I observed. A combat logbook or war journal with those kinds of details, as well as newspaper articles, email traffic, and other bits of information and paraphernalia may mean little at the time but will later serve as a reminder of what actually happened. Whether it is an OPR or an award for which someone wants to submit a name, a pilot will definitely be asked for a list of things he's done. Having a ready and up-to-date list of items, even if they're simple and plain, will prevent him from having to recall details months later. In addition, as he progresses in his career he may appreciate having maintained a record of the events of his professional life.

Let's say a new pilot is standing around one day and his commander tells him to figure out a way to get the dumpsters emptied because they're making the squadron parking lot look a mess. The young officer figures out that Civil Engineering (CE) is responsible for that duty on base and calls them; CE gives him the phone number to the contractor and soon the trucks roll out and empty the dumpsters. He might record:

> (Date): commander asked to get dumpsters emptied;
> called CE, emptied 2 hours later.

While that may sound lame, he'll turn that information into his supervisor a year later for his OPR, and the OPR will read:

> Hard charger—hand picked by commander to spearhead
> bioenvironmental cleanup effort; coordinated with multi-
> ple base agencies and ensured continued mission success
> with record-setting response.

While the content of the example bullet is a little unlikely, the change from "fact" to "performance report" is not far from the truth. In many cases it is not unusual for an officer to review his own OPRs (officers generally don't see them until after they're written and signed) and not recognize his own accomplishments. Glorification is, unfortunately, a virtual requirement for success in the military and has been for many years. It used to be said that an OPR needed to make an officer look like he "walked on water." Now, an *average* report makes him look that way—to be above average, he needs to walk on water and freeze it behind him so that others may follow; in some cases, he merely needs to make the water that others will walk on.

Embellished Records

Unfortunately, generating "amazing" reports from "normal" things is a relatively common occurrence in the military. As the initial portion of OIF wound down and the combat sorties for my squadron decreased, the leadership started telling pilots to write down their war stories so they could create awards packages. For us, the hunt for the enemy was coming to an end, and the hunt for medals was on. On the surface, the squadron's leadership appeared to be looking out for their people to reward outstanding conduct. The problem was that every single pilot was put in for an award of one kind or another; there was no distinction of one man excelling above another. Each pilot was already getting an award purely based on the number of sorties he had flown. These "sustained flight medals" were awarded for completing a certain number of combat flights, much as similar awards were given in previous conflicts.

Part of the reason that everyone was submitted for an award was that other squadrons were submitting all of *their* pilots. Some pilots were concerned that if our peers in other units got medals and we did not, we would be at a disadvantage; ten years later at a promotion board to Colonel, the fact that one guy had a medal and another did not might be the distinguishing factor that would get one promoted and the other passed over. Each pilot was put in for multiple medals resulting in hundreds of submissions from dozens of squadrons involved in the conflict. So many packages of questionable content were submitted that the medal review board actually sent a message out telling commanders to forward only those that were actually worthy of recognition; they noted that they had rejected a huge percentage of submissions.[1]

The overall attitude of the medal hunt—that we should scrounge for decorations and embellish our escapades so as to be awarded higher honors—was epitomized by a member of our unit who received the Bronze Star Medal (BSM), one of the highest medals given out in combat. Apparently, it is practically a military tradition that certain members of combat units get a BSM at the close of hostilities. Therefore, in due course our unit submitted a BSM package for specific members of the squadron, and it was subsequently rejected—the requirements of the BSM dictated that it only be given to those involved in "ground operations against the enemy," and regulations specifically directed that it not be awarded for action involving aerial

---

[1] The Air Force Central Command (CENTCOM) review board indicated that they had rejected over 70% of the awards thus far submitted.

flight.[2] We were a flying squadron and hadn't conducted ground combat. Still, upon receiving the rejected awards package the squadron staff did the routine thing and added the phrase "in ground combat against the enemy" to the decoration narrative. They resubmitted it, and it was approved. Left out of the package was the fact that our unit was based on a peninsula in the Persian Gulf that was nearly 400 miles from the nearest hostile force. True, the base had been locked down for fear of terrorist act (much as every base—including those in the United States—had been), but no hostile act ever took place against the base. No member of our flying squadron participated in ground operations against the enemy, and therefore no member of our squadron deserved the Bronze Star Medal. The desire to receive accolades prevailed over the truth of what actually happened.

Inflation and magnification in OPRs and military awards packages are not anything new. Anecdotally, the current attitudes toward combat medals probably started in Korea or Vietnam, where awards and medals were given to compensate men forced to be in an unpopular part of the world in an unpopular war. I have been told that the Distinguished Flying Cross (DFC) was given as a "tour completion" medal in Vietnam, much as Air Medals were given out after OIF.

Given what I know now about the military and medals, it does not surprise me that people might question why an award might describe one person's harrowing and life threatening experience while a fellow soldier, airman, or seamen might recall a much different story of the same event. Members of my squadron received medals whose citations described amazingly dramatic and frightening events, but other pilots who flew that same night (or perhaps even in that same flight) might have considered the sortie routine and dull. Such disagreement in memory was also the case in the political run-up to the 2004 presidential election, when Senator John Kerry's Silver Star was questioned by some who claimed to have been there but didn't see what the medal citation described. One man sees truth, another stretched truth, another exaggeration, and another sees a lie and a fraud. Who is correct? Only the men who were there, and their God, will ever really know.

During my unit's medal hunt, I told my commander that all of my missions had been routine, and that I would not submit a report that described them as otherwise. When my flight lead began to write an awards package for himself, he suggested that he might change some of the details and submit one for me. Because I knew that no worthy awards package would contain a sufficient degree of truth, I told him and my leadership that I would neither sign nor accept any award based on such evidence. The issue was dropped. In making my personal choice I did not imply that every person

---

[2] Air Force Instruction 36-2803, *The Air Force Awards and Decorations Program*, 15 June 2001. Table 2.1 lists the achievements for which each decoration can be awarded. The BSM has this footnote: *Do not award for normal performance of duties.* Paragraph A4.1.2 dictates the opening sentences for the decorations. The choices for the BSM all include *ground combat* or *ground operations* "against the enemy" or "an opposing armed force."

who received an award did so through exaggeration. Undoubtedly, many medals were painfully earned, and many were probably never awarded that should have been. Individually, though, a military Christian will see—and will be a part of—reports, forms, and packages that describe everyday events in spectacular terms. Depending on perception, it is possible that at some point those documents will cross the line from "fantastic" to "fantasy." It is up to the Christian's moral turpitude to determine what he will allow.

From OPRs to awards packages and every other form of paperwork, official documentation reigns supreme in the military. Supervisors want their subordinates to succeed and will try to write an evaluation to guarantee advancement. Commanders want to reward the courage of their troops and will submit their names for medals. For Christian superiors, "doing right by your people" is not wrong, nor is accepting what is deserved and earned. As pilots and officers, Christians must use discretion and wisdom in what amount of praise they are willing to accept. As supervisors, Christians must strive to take care of their subordinates by writing competitive OPRs and medal packages. In no case, though, should they stretch, slant, or sacrifice the truth. Paperwork may be supreme in the military, but One is Supreme over all.

Chapter 18:
Professional Officership

C HRISTIAN FIGHTER PILOTS are military officers, and there are things that pilots will do simply because they are the appropriate thing for their professional position. A pilot's presence may be expected at the annual military ball, the wing Christmas party, or an enlisted promotion ceremony. Each of those events has its own unique structure and traditions. While some less socially-inclined pilots may view such activities as an inconvenience, there are generally no moral arguments for avoiding them. On the contrary, they often give a Christian the opportunity to interact with many officers and enlisted whom he rarely sees. Still, he must decide if the activity is appropriate for his attendance. In my experience, wing and group functions tend to be more formal and controlled, while many squadron parties I have attended have been more raucous.

One frequently mentioned part of officership is the Officers' Club. The O'Club is a tradition that spans decades. It generally provides relatively inexpensive (and sometimes free) food as well as ample opportunity for social gatherings. The dues vary by base, anywhere from $5 to $25 a month, depending on the location. To obtain a club card an officer is currently required to apply for a club-sponsored credit card, as it doubles as the membership card. Over the past few years the popularity of the Air Force Officers' Club has waned, probably because the military culture has changed. One commander attempted to correlate membership at the O'Club with membership at a country club, which only seemed to emphasize the generational gap between his peer group and ours. Being part of a country club was prestigious to him and his colleagues; to the younger group, it was the equivalent of a retirement community.

Also, with military obligations around the globe drawing members' time, fewer are willing to spend time or money at the club. A few years ago, being a member of the club was a virtual requirement; even today, a base's senior leadership will still encourage its new arrivals to join the club, though they no longer maintain lists or harass the non-members to join. In general, they'll make their pitch and drop the issue. Though there is nothing wrong with it, I chose not to become a club member primarily because I didn't expect to patronize the club much; I didn't want to pay dues for something I wasn't using. In the past several years I have had one or two occasions where membership would have benefited me. Otherwise, I have seen no negative impact as a result of not being a club member. For those that are continuously "highly encouraged" to join the O'Club, though, joining may be the less controversial decision, as described in Chapter 5.

Another "officer thing to do" is known as the Company Grade Officers' Council (CGOC). Composed of officers from all specialties from lieutenant to captain, the CGOC gathers for social events, organizes trips, and often participates in volunteer and charitable activities. Unfortunately, the CGOC and the fighter pilot communities tend to have strained relationships with little shared professional respect. Pilots have a flight rating, and are therefore referred to as *rated* officers, while non-pilots are called *non-rated*. At one base, the pilots referred to the non-rated officers as *trees* (a reference to the camouflaged uniforms that they wore), while the non-rated officers called pilots *bags* or *zipper-suited sun gods* (a reference to the flight suit).

Because fighter pilots have fluid and full schedules, they rarely have the availability to attend CGOC meetings, which often means that the attitude and actions of the CGOC do not reflect those of the rated officers. The frequent CGOC gatherings—particularly those during the duty day—give pilots the impression that non-rated officers don't work as hard as they do, which only widens the gap between the two groups. Some people participate in the CGOC only to gain face time with senior commanders, but the CGOC can be a good organization; more importantly, it is composed of a pilot's non-rated peers. Statistically speaking, pilots will probably be in the minority in any group of officers, and this includes gatherings like Bible studies. They should attempt to foster good relationships with non-rated officers, and a good relationship with the CGOC is one means to that end.

A somewhat smaller but no less important group that a Christian will interact with is his superiors. A fighter pilot must respect, obey, and support his superiors. If he's given a directive with which he disagrees, he may voice his reservations in private, but once the superior ends the discussion, he should support it in public. He should never speak poorly of his superiors in front of his subordinates. There may be times when it feels difficult for a Christian to support a non-Christian superior. So long as a superior's actions and orders are legal and ethical, a subordinate is bound to obey and support him. If a superior's directives are in conflict with the commands of God, then they are probably inconsistent with military law, making them illegal. In such cases a subordinate should express disagreement and, if necessary, refuse to comply. Officers are not compelled to obey unlawful orders. Taking a principled stand in the face of a superior officer requires strong personal ethics and moral courage. Knowing *when* to make such a decision requires prayerful discernment. Ultimately, a Christian must remember that God has established authorities, and he is commanded to obey them.

Another military group that Christians can significantly influence is the enlisted corps, primarily the small contingent of life support, intelligence, and aviation management specialists in the squadron. Unfortunately, pilots have little contact with the greatest concentration of airmen and sergeants located in maintenance. (As of 2003, maintenance separated from operations to form their own squadrons.) The relationship between operations and maintenance can be tough. Pilots want to fly the jets and get frustrated when jets are either not available or break and disrupt the mission; maintenance—and crew chiefs in particular—often get frustrated with pilots for breaking their jets.

Crew chiefs, the most visible maintenance troops, are young airmen who often wanted to be pilots. Some still hold aspirations of obtaining a degree and becoming an officer—some for the sole purpose of becoming a pilot. When a pilot reaches a place where he is actually assigned *his* jet (and is so lucky as to get his name on the side of it), he will also have a dedicated crew chief for that plane. That presents him with a unique opportunity to have a distinct professional relationship with that airman or sergeant. Knowing his name and caring about his family and personal aspirations will go a long way to fostering a positive relationship. A little praise goes a long way, and spending a few minutes actually talking to them when a pilot steps to his aircraft will do wonders for their perceptions.

Generally speaking, enlisted troops look up to pilots by virtue of their rank. The example a Christian pilot portrays as a leader has the ability to directly affect the personal conduct and eternal future of many. Unfortunately, some fighter pilots have poor relationships with enlisted troops. They may maintain undue familiarity with enlisted personnel and show them little professional respect. Because fighter pilots maintain familiarity with each other, often calling higher ranking officers by their callsign rather than their rank, they tend to transfer that familiarity to the enlisted troops in their squadron. Strange as it may seem, enlisted troops generally appreciate officers who maintain a professional bearing. More than most pilots, enlisted troops tend to take pride in their bearing, appearance, and overall job professionalism. By maintaining a professional relationship with the troops in the squadron a Christian will almost certainly be different than the majority of others. By being professional with them, he compliments their professional conduct and gains their respect.

A Christian officer should strive to be the best professional military member that he can. A professional fighter pilot and officer sets the example in all aspects of his personal and official life. This means that he follows the rules: he gets his car registered on time, files his voucher before the deadline, and accomplishes the training he's been ordered to—regardless of how asinine he may feel that it is. He should always be on time or early, never late. (An old, cynical Air Force Academy quote used to be, "If you're early, you're on time. If you're on time, you're late.") If that means he has to keep a calendar or appointment book then he should do so—he should never expect someone else to remind him of his duties. While it may seem obvious to say "follow the rules," there are some pilots who choose to ignore such "minor" details. Occasionally, an officer can get away with skipping or ignoring mundane tasks where an enlisted troop could not; this is one of the many unfortunate examples of *RHIP*, or *Rank Has Its Privileges*. A professional military Christian officer should avoid the perception that he avoids certain requirements by virtue of his rank; rather, he should hold himself to the same standards as those around and below him.

An officer's professional military bearing includes wearing a uniform within regulations. Many non-rated personnel who wear Battle Dress Uniforms (BDUs) or blues/Class As that require ironing and maintenance already look down on pilots for having easy-wear flight suits. Also, with a few exceptions, pilots rarely have shiny boots. A pilot with a well-kept uniform and shiny boots will likely be favorably noticed by the enlisted, and may also receive some jibes from fellow pilots. A pilot should at least keep his boots polished enough so that they stay black. By being a professional officer, a Christian will garner the respect not only of those who look up to him, but also of his superiors.

A Christian should always strive to live his life to the highest moral standards. There are some things, though, that are neither moral nor immoral—they are simply the expectations of an officer. Whether it's attending a social event or relating with non-rated officers, superiors, or subordinates, a Christian should be the most professional officer that he can. By holding himself to the highest professional standards a Christian will gain credibility and the respect of all around him.

CONCLUSION:
Working for God in the World

WHILE THE WORLD EXERTS PRESSURES on a Christian no matter where he is, those placed on the fighter pilot are particularly acute, earning the fighter pilot world the well-deserved reputation for rebellion and immorality. The acerbic character of the fighter pilot world is on an unequaled level, and the fighter pilot's invincible nature has buttressed bad habits rather than challenged them. If a Christian chooses to become a fighter pilot, he will be deeply *in* the world. His spiritual foundation will be attacked, his faith tested, and his righteous life challenged on a daily basis. Christian fighter pilots are faced with career pressures, family separations, ethical stresses, and social pressures to participate in traditions that are not God-honoring. The ultimate goal of such pressure is to conform a Christian to a world filled with profanity, sexual innuendo, and immorality.

A Christian who enters that world must not only maintain his own faith but must also bring a ministry of presence and proactive Christianity to his fellow fighter pilots. The life he chooses to live must be based on God, himself, his objective, his witness, and the potential perceptions his choices may bring. He must clearly define his priorities—God, family, and job. Those priorities and his life choices will form the basis for the reputation that precedes him throughout the military. He must develop good habits for his personal and spiritual life. He requires a firm spiritual foundation and Christian mutual support—as well as the spiritual fortitude to stand alone if he must. If persecuted for his Christian life he must not shrink from it but continue to live a God-honoring life. In the face of spiritual fatigue he must not only persevere but also find the strength to show joy. He must find encouragement in knowing that God is in charge, no matter what "injustice" he may experience, and that everything happens for God's reason. The life of a Christian fighter pilot may often be hard, but, like Joshua, he needs to "be strong and courageous...not terrified...not discouraged," for God will be with him wherever he goes.

It is hard to be a Christian in an ungodly world, and it's hard to be a Christian and a fighter pilot. Though there will be difficult times, it's important for Christians to remember not only the soaring and noble aspirations of lofty spiritual goals, but also the down-to-earth reasons for doing the things we do. Fighter pilots have a really cool job. Few other people in the world have the opportunity to fly a fighter jet everyday. On each of my sorties I chide myself if I don't do two things: take a moment to enjoy the awesome view of God's creation (which I must confess is unparalleled from the air), and fly upside down—one of the most fun and simple maneuvers that surprisingly few pilots are allowed to do. It's a job I enjoy, and it's a place that I can make an impact by being a living witness for God. What can compare?

While much of this book appears to state Christian principles matter-of-factly, they are often not so simple to actually live out. I formed many of the *"A Christian fighter pilot should..."* statements *after* I had *not* done what I recommended and had come to realize that the choice I made was in error. Experience has sometimes been a less than pleasant instructional tool, but God has been a patient Teacher. To this point in my career and life I have often erred on the conservative side, which often meant I made the 'more controversial' decision. While I have protected the sanctity of my personal Christianity, there may have been times when I could have yielded a little and improved my relationships with other fighter pilots as a result. I have proven to myself that I can withstand the pressures of the world. As I mature as a Christian and fighter pilot I may need to expand my comfort zone and more frequently consider making decisions that are harder for me but will improve the relationships I have with the non-Christians around me. Living as a Christian for God in this world is a goal but hardly a destination. There is no single, all-encompassing answer that covers every situation, place, and time. Only God has the answer and can provide the true guidance Christians need.

This book is intended to be a source of information and preparation for those that would desire to live a Christian life in the fighter pilot community. It does not replace nor even augment the Bible, which should be the basis for every Christian's life. A God-fearing, Bible-believing Christian can be an extraordinarily effective tool for God in even the deepest parts of the world—perhaps more so *because* they are the deepest parts of the world. The most challenging places for Christians to be are where the harvest is greatest—but the workers are fewest. A Christian can not only survive but can thrive for God as a fighter pilot, proving that *Christian Fighter Pilot* is not an oxymoron.

IS "MILITARY CHRISTIAN" AN OXYMORON?

Praise be to the Lord my Rock, who trains my hands for war, my fingers for battle. – Psalm 144:1

BEFORE EVEN CONSIDERING the phrase *Christian fighter pilot*, many would argue that *Christian* and *military* are mutually exclusive themselves. Particularly for new Christians who have recently been introduced to Christ's teachings, or Christians who grew up in peaceful times and areas, the concepts of a "warring Christian" who is a child of a loving God can seem contradictory. There are many books and pamphlets written on the topic, and most categorize their analysis in two categories. Those that oppose Christian military service focus on the pacifist teachings of Jesus, while those that support it focus on the Just War doctrine. Well-researched books quote Augustine and Thomas Aquinas (generally credited with the formulation and articulation of the Just War theory) and cite lists of well-known theologians who opposed and supported Christian military service. Whole volumes analyze this subject from a much more learned position than I can. The objective of this section is only to briefly address the question, "Is 'Military Christian' an Oxymoron?"

Pacifist Theory

The controversy of Christian military service is not a modern notion. Throughout the ages, church leaders, theologians, and men of faith have dissented over the divine intent of the Christian and his relation to armed conflict. Many early church leaders actually prohibited Christians from participating in military service. There are, in truth, many arguments against Christians being in the armed forces.[1] Since God gives life, all human be-

---

[1] While there are non-combat roles in the military, for the sake of simplicity I will assume that serving in the military requires actively killing another human being.

ings have a sacred right to life, and the pacifist view asserts that killing them denies them that divinely-given right. Due to the warring nature of Israelite history, there are few pacifist phrases in the Old Testament—with two notable exceptions. The first and most obvious is the Sixth Commandment, in the King James: "Thou shalt not kill" (Deuteronomy 5:17). The second was Isaiah's prophecy that the Messiah would be the "Prince of Peace" (9:6). Since the tone of the Old Testament is often brutal, many pacifist teachings focus on the New Testament as the culmination of the process of divine revelation. By arguing progressive revelation, they minimize the Old Testament and assert that a Christian's conclusions about war should be based primarily on New Testament theology. As Jesus is the crux of the New Testament, His teachings are used as the basis for pacifist doctrine.

Pacifist interpretation of the Sermon on the Mount implies that it should be a prescriptive instruction for Christian conduct, not just a descriptive attitude a Christian should have when faced with conflict. As a prescriptive doctrine, "blessed are the peacemakers" is a command for Christians to act in no ways but peaceful ones (Matthew 5:9). "Do not resist an evil person" and "if someone strikes you on the right cheek, turn to him the other also," are active directives that a Christian must not oppose evil or violence, even upon themselves (Matthew 5:39). Christians should not fight but are "to love [their] enemies [and] do good to those who hate [them]" (Luke 6:27). Probably the strongest pacifist Christian doctrine centers on the example of Christ himself. First, in one of the few interactions Jesus had with a weapon, he told Peter to "put [his] sword back in its place...for all who draw the sword will die by the sword" (Matthew 26:52). This directive of peace, even though it was Jesus himself that Peter was defending, is an example of the attitude pacifists believe Christians should have. Finally, pacifists assert that since Jesus died as an innocent victim, Christians, seeking to be like Him, should be willing to suffer and die even in the face of injustice.

Pacifism Answered

History does show that early church fathers prohibited Christians from military service; the social context, though, was that Roman soldiers had to swear allegiance to the emperor as a god.[2] Two things occurred that changed the culture of those times: one, Constantine came to power and ended the persecutions of Christians; two, Christians were derided for enjoying the *benefits* of Roman society without bearing any of the *responsibility* for it.[3] The result was that church leaders began to allow and even encourage Christian military service. Examination of God's Word in its entirety—including the Old Testament—allows great insight into God's

---

[2] Driver, John. *How Christians Made Peace with War*. Herald Press, Scottdale, PA, 1988. p31.

[3] Ibid. p38.

perspective on war. There is no arguing that life is sacred: God created man in His own image (Genesis 1:26-27). However, man is fallen, and war is a direct result of his sinful nature (Psalms 51:5; James 4:1-2). Pacifists have made much of the Sixth Commandment; but those who adamantly proclaim "thou shalt not kill" are unable to reconcile God's own directives in the very next chapter that death be the punishment for criminal offenses. First, the source text for *kill* in the commandment is more accurately translated *murder*, which is how the majority of modern translations scribe the verse.[4] Murder is never permitted in the Bible, while killing is not only occasionally allowed but is also divinely commanded. Second, God's command that death be a judicial punishment indicates that there are just reasons for taking a life; therefore, killing is not inconsistent with the character of God. Finally, while it is true that the Messiah was predicted to be named the Prince of Peace, He was also called a Jealous God, a Judge, and Warrior (Exodus 15:3, 34:14, Genesis 18:25). The God of peace was also the God of war.

Does the Bible require a Christian peacemaker to obtain peace at any cost? Do the commands to not resist evil and to turn the other cheek mean Christians should surrender, even if evil prevails? Are Christians commanded to accept peace, even if it is the peace of a "slave camp or cemetery?"[5] Does "loving our enemies" mean Christians should love the evil they represent? As has been said, peace is not merely the absence of war, but the securing of justice, law, and order. In an active sense, a *peacemaker* does not simply avoid conflict but *restores* and *maintains* the peace.[6] Romans 12:18 says that Christians are to live in peace "if it is possible," indicating that there may be times when it is not feasible to do so. Christians should work for peace, and, by humbly turning the other cheek, should give an offender every opportunity to accept that peace. When the antagonist refuses peace, a Christian is not commanded to surrender. He is to love his enemies, but just as a parent has conflict with a child they love, the love he has for his enemies does not mean he will not fight them. The love a Christian has for his enemies will inevitably conflict with the love he has for those whom his enemies would threaten. A Christian is not commanded to sit idly by and watch as his wife, children, or parents are ravaged in the name of his Christ-like peace—to do so would actually violate a Biblical command to provide for one's family (1 Timothy 5:8). Allowing an act of aggression, rather than defending against it, does not equal peace, love, or righteousness. On the contrary, tolerance toward such conduct often en-

---

[4] Eckman, James P. *Biblical Ethics.* Crossway Books, Wheaton, IL, 2004. From page 61: "The Hebrew term *rasah* does mean *to kill*, but it is never used in relation to animals and is always associated with murder. Furthermore, it is never used of killing an enemy in battle. Therefore, not all life-taking is murder."

[5] Boettner, Loraine. *The Christian Attitude Toward War.* Presbyterian and Reformed Publishing Company, New Jersey 1985. pp2-3.

[6] Stokka, Terry L. Lt Col., USAF (Retired). Interview by email, 7 February 2006.

courages it, whether it is the case of a "school-yard bully or Adolf Hitler."[7] As Augustine and Aquinas argued when they formulated what would become the Just War doctrine, there are righteous reasons for war: generally, the attainment of good or the elimination of evil. Augustine himself maintained that "war is waged to serve the peace."[8] While some deride war for wanton loss of life, in some cases war is necessary to *preserve* life; just as a medical professional may amputate to protect the body, a military professional may engage in combat to preserve the nation or even humanity itself.[9]

As for Peter's violent protection of Jesus at His betrayal, Jesus' response is immensely enlightening when He says that *if it was the will of God*, He could call down angels to rescue Him (Matthew 26:53). His reprimand to Peter was not that violence was wrong (after all, He told Peter to put his sword away, not get rid of it), but that Jesus' betrayal and sacrifice had to continue to *fulfill God's will*. Jesus did not die because He refused violent opposition, nor was He a 'victim;' He died because He *chose* to. Also, Jesus did have powers that man does not; when the crowds of Nazareth wanted to throw Him off a cliff, He calmly walked through the crowd and away (Luke 4:29-30). He did not fight back, but because it was not yet His time, He was able to supernaturally "resist" and simply walk away. There is also more to the argument of those that say Christians are to follow Jesus' sacrificial example: Jesus was innocent. Human beings are sinners and far from innocent. Jesus' death had an objective: the ultimate sacrifice for the sins of man. Even though He struggled with His divine mission, He *had* to die (Luke 22:42). Moreover, as Jesus prepared to leave His disciples on the earth, He told them to sell their clothes to buy a sword (Luke 22:35-38). Finally, the same Jesus that some would describe as "peaceful unto death" fashioned a whip of cords and drove the money changers out of the temple court, overturning their tables and running their animals out of His Father's house (John 2:15). While Jesus' indignation had a level of righteousness that a Christian could never attain, His example shows that His love for the Father exceeded His love for the actions of those that would profane Him, and that peace does not mean submission at any cost.

Biblical Militarism

Many men of old and renown have been soldiers and still been faithful men of God, and nowhere was their military service questioned. Abraham, whom God selected to bless as the father of His chosen nation, was one of God's first "commanders" (Genesis 14:14-15). Moses and Joshua both led

---

[7] Harrison, William K. Jr. Lt Gen, US Army (Retired). *May a Christian Serve in the Military?* OCF of the USA. The pamphlet is undated. Lt Gen Harrison passed away in 1987.

[8] Driver, John. *How Christians Made Peace with War.* Herald Press, Scottdale, PA, 1988. p81.

[9] *A Christian Perspective on War.* Grace Chapel, as published on the OCF website, 13 April 2003.

the Israelites in countless battles. God Himself ordered the Israelites to battle, and He commanded His own army, for that matter (2 Kings 6:17). To claim that all war is evil is to say not only that God enjoined Israel to sin but that He did so Himself, which is inconsistent with the character of God (James 1:13).[10] David, a "man after God's own heart" (1 Samuel 13:14), said that God "trained his hands for battle" (Psalm 18:34). David not only fought in war but also participated in some of the most brutal acts of slaughter recorded in the Bible (for example, when he arbitrarily killed every two lengths of the defeated Moabites (2 Samuel 8:2)). In the military tradition of "praise the Lord and pass the ammunition," Nehemiah "prayed to...God and posted a guard," and told the leaders of Jerusalem to "remember the Lord...and fight" (4:9, 14). There are countless other military references in the Bible. Some speak of military service neutrally, neither condemning it nor advocating it; others are full of praise for military conquest. Proverbs, hailed as the book of wisdom, contains advice for military preparation— "for waging war you need guidance, and for victory many advisers" (24:6). In Judges, a town was cursed for *not* participating in war in support of Israel (5:23). In the New Testament, the writer of Hebrews didn't have enough time to fully list the heroes of faith who "conquered kingdoms" and "became powerful in battle and routed foreign armies" (11:32-34). While trying to teach the crowds about counting the cost of following Him, Jesus used a warfare example without passing judgment on the subjects of His story:

> Or suppose a king is about to go to war against another king. Will he not first sit down and consider whether he is able with ten thousand men to oppose the one coming against him with twenty thousand? If he is not able, he will send a delegation while the other is still a long way off and will ask for terms of peace. (Luke 14:31, 32)

Three individual soldiers are specifically mentioned in the New Testament, all members of the Roman army; nowhere is their profession criticized, nor are they directed to leave the service. First, a soldier asked Jesus to heal his servant, and even told Jesus to simply "say the word," because he was unworthy to have Jesus come to his house (Matthew 8:5-13). Jesus was "astonished," and said He had not seen so great a faith in all of Israel— but He didn't direct the soldier to abandon the military (v10). Second, at the foot of the cross one soldier acknowledged the crucified Christ as God (27:54). The third and most famous New Testament soldier was Cornelius, a God-fearing Roman centurion (Acts 10). Not only did an angel of God appear to him and acknowledge his faithfulness, but he was also used as an object lesson for Peter that resulted in the expansion of Christ's message to

---

[10] Harrison, William K. Jr. Lt Gen, US Army (Retired). *May a Christian Serve in the Military?* OCF of the USA. The pamphlet is undated.

the Gentiles. Neither the angel nor Peter commanded Cornelius to leave the military, nor was it a part of the important lesson taught.

Paul was not judgmental when he used an example of military service (2 Timothy 2:4), and he also described his friends as "fellow soldiers" (Philemon 2). When John the Baptist told those who approached him to "bear fruit" or be thrown into the fire, soldiers asked what they should do; he told them not to extort money or falsely accuse people, but to be content with their pay—he didn't take the perfect opportunity to tell them to quit (Luke 3:14). Paul spent years with soldiers in his travels to and imprisonment in Rome. In none of these cases were the soldiers encouraged to leave their profession. On the contrary, in his first letter to the Corinthians, Paul says that "each one should remain in the situation which he was in when God called him" (7:20).[11]

The New Testament says the state is created to maintain justice and is thus granted the right of force (Romans 13:4, 1 Peter 2:13, 14). The state employs force with "the sword," represented in government by the military (Romans 13:4). Therefore the "one in authority"—who is given authority by God—uses the military as "God's servant" (Romans 13:1, 3-4). John Calvin, one of the most prolific contributors to the modern Protestant church, agreed that governments have been given the authority to use force to protect their national interests just as they can rightfully protect their citizens from criminals.[12] In order to wield that authority states require both a military and a police force to ensure the security of the nation. American police and the American military differ only in geography and lethality; to say that the military violates Christian ethics is to say the same for the police.[13] Governments require a military because of the existence of war; war does not exist because of the military. To assert the latter is equivalent to saying that crime exists because of the police.[14]

Finally, there are some that accept the need for a military but not the need for aggressive actions; instead, they believe that the military should only be used for defense. While that desire is admirable, it displays naivety about military strategy. There is no progress in defense; just as a football team needs its offensive line to march down the field and score, the military will need to execute offensively to end a conflict. "Defensive" military action may be best executed in offense. Once a conflict begins, a decisive defeat of the enemy may be required to bring a secure and lasting conclusion; offense will be required to achieve a peaceful end. This also means that war must be fought in the place that it presents itself; whether it is defending US

---

[11] It is interesting to note that while no one in the Bible directed soldiers to leave their profession, Jesus *did* tell one man to abandon his worldly possessions (Matthew 19:21); many people advocate following the former, which is not in the Bible, while few follow the latter that is.

[12] Boettner, Loraine. *The Christian Attitude Toward War*. Presbyterian and Reformed Publishing Company, New Jersey 1985. p46.

[13] Stokka, Terry L. Lt Col., USAF (Retired). Interview by email, 7 February 2006.

[14] Harrison, William K. Jr. Lt Gen, US Army (Retired). *May a Christian Serve in the Military?* OCF of the USA. The pamphlet is undated.

borders, protecting citizens abroad, or asserting justice to protect the innocent, the conflict must be joined where it occurs.

The military profession has actually helped spread the cause of Christ. Throughout history, members of faith within the military have been responsible for the transmission of Christianity around the globe. Paul's interaction with the Roman centurions undoubtedly led to the spread of faith throughout the Roman Empire, which at that time was the greater part of the known world. The US military itself has probably been one of the greatest missionary causes in history, from the earliest parts of the 1700s to the Korean and Vietnam wars.

For those trying to understand the relationship between God, the military, and war, there is one important fact to remember. God does not change—the God of the Old Testament and the God of the New Testament are one and the same (Malachi 3:6; James 1:17). Nowhere does God claim that He desires war, death, and destruction, but there are many places where He acknowledges the necessity of it. The same God who directed human armies and commanded a superhuman one spoke of loving mankind and desiring peace. Nowhere does God command that a Christian avoid or leave the military, nor does He demand that he allow himself to be walked upon. A Christian is to act in love and peace as much as possible, but when the opposition will not accept it, God does not say that a Christian must let evil, injustice, or brutality prevail.

Because this is a fallen world, wars will never cease. So long as wars are sure to come, there will be a need for a military. One day Jesus will return in glory and Christians will participate in the "war to end all wars" that will establish His kingdom and complete the victory He has already won. Until that day, Christians must live as best they can in this present world.

APPENDIX 2:
USING THIS BOOK

F IGHTER PILOTS FLY MODERN, complicated, and expensive aircraft. The procedures to operate the aircraft—which include everything from starting the engine(s) to responding to emergency malfunctions—cover thousands of pages in thick binders called Technical Orders (TOs). For fighter pilots in single-seat aircraft it would be impossible to carry every TO in the cockpit. For that reason a fighter pilot learns to rely on checklists—pocket-sized manuals of numbered bullet statements that can be quickly and easily referenced while continuing to fly the aircraft. For almost every conceivable emergency there is a checklist a fighter pilot can reference. These manuals and checklists are titled by numbers; for example, the basic TO for the F-16 is the "1F16-1" and is referred to as the *Dash 1*.

Because pilots use checklists so often they come to rely on them for other aspects of their lives as well; they'll create checklists for their office, they'll have a checklist to complete before they go on vacation, and Christian fighter pilots may even begin to have checklists in their spiritual lives. While checklists may be good, as they serve as a reminder of things that might otherwise be forgotten, overreliance on abbreviated checklists can result in forgetting the basic document. A pilot that relies exclusively on a checklist and never studies the full manual will soon forget the reason for the checklist steps. Worse, if a situation arises that is not covered in the checklist a pilot may flounder in indecision at a critical time. For that reason I have endeavored to not write this book in a checklist fashion. I did not want this to become a step-by-step self-help book of to-do lists and feel-good acronyms to which a Christian might refer for answers; instead, I wanted this book to point to the parent manual—a Christian's *Dash 1*, the Bible. Rather than a checklist of *40 Days and Nights to Finding Your Purpose* or *Six Weeks to a Thinner You*, the purpose of this book is to present enough information for a Christian to be prepared for the contingencies he might encounter in the fighter pilot world.

I must qualify this book and emphasize the distinction that fighter pilots make between *procedure* and *technique*. There are many regulations that pilots are required to follow, even if they don't agree with them—those are *procedures*. As a pilot continues to learn to fly the aircraft, he will also be taught the opinions of instructor pilots—experience has shown them that certain ways are better than others. These "good ideas" are not required, and if pilots ever have a better one they are free to use it (with the caveat that it had better work); these recommendations are *technique*. When pilots discuss accomplishing a particular action, if they are advocating an opinion they will qualify their arguments by saying that their idea is "technique only."

For a Christian, some Biblical commands are unambiguous. Other concepts may not have a Biblical basis but are simply "good ideas." Finally, some ideas may be Biblically-based but not explicitly stated; they rely on scriptural interpretation. I believe that explicit Biblically-based commands should be *procedure* for a Christian—there is no question that they should be followed. Scripturally sound "good ideas" are *technique* only, but as every pilot will say about his own opinion, I think that they are a very good technique. For those areas that rely on scriptural interpretation, Christians must decide whether they hold those same beliefs, or whether the teachings of their own pastors, Bible commentators, or other religious leaders differ. Ultimately, the responsibility for acting within God's commands lies with the individual.

I would suggest that things I have listed here as Biblical commands have been generally accepted as such by the Christian community. I have, of course, included my own techniques. Finally, for those areas that require scriptural interpretation, I have endeavored to list both the scriptural basis and the logic for my perspective. In those instances, it is up to the individual Christian to decide.

Finally, some may get the impression that I think the "perfect" Christian is a teetotaling, expletive-free, unexciting person who wears plaid shirts with khakis and white sneakers. I know that is not the case (I wear ties with khakis). The body of Christ is made up of all kinds of people, as it should be; each person will have different traits necessary to the success and spread of the church. I do not presume to judge the relationship that each person has with God; their individual relationship is known only between God and themselves. I only propose some considerations for how Christians should live in the fighter pilot world.

INDEX

AAA, 7, 9, 10, 11, 12, 113
Abu Ghraib, 106
academy, 15, 17, 64, 69, 70, 71, 72, 73,
    74, 75, 76, 81, 82, 91, 92, 96, 107,
    125, 126, 127, 134, 137, 139, 167
acceptable level of risk. *See* ALR
Acts, 59, 63, 79, 133, 144
aerial refueling. *See* air-to-air refueling
Ahab, 114
Air Force Instructions
    36-2706, 66
    36-2909, 143
Airborne Warning and Control System.
    See AWACS
air-to-air refueling, 6
alcohol, 24, 25, 28, 33, 43, 45, 48, 51, 53,
    54
Alliance Defense Fund, 78, 81
ALO, 148, 154, 155
ALR, 43
ambition, 35, 111, 112
anti-aircraft artillery. *See* AAA
assignment system, 147
    possible assignments, 148
    remote assignments, 154
atheists, 11
AU, 69, 71, 72, 78, 80
AWACS, 8, 9, 11
back-dating. *See* situation ethics
base X, 139
Basic Surface Attack. *See* BSA
B-course, 18, 27, 33, 37, 129
Becket Fund, 80, 81
Bible study, 137
    relationships, 142
    starting, 140
BSA, 49
buffoonery, 6, 24, 51
Bush, President, 74
cadets, 15, 17, 23, 69, 70, 71, 72, 75, 81,
    91, 92, 93, 96, 107, 125, 126, 134,
    137, 138, 139, 140, 141
callsign, 6, 27, 28, 39, 47, 167
    FNG, 47, 49
    naming, 28, 52, 53, 54, 55
centrifuge, 18
CGOC, 166
chapel, 81, 84, 129, 130, 131, 132, 135,
    137, 143, 152, 153
    advantages, 131
    attendance, 130
    disadvantages, 131

chaplain, 32, 69, 72, 73, 74, 77, 80, 81,
    84, 86, 130, 131, 132, 140, 153
    Buddhist, 131
    Jewish, 74
    Muslim, 74
cheating, 91, 92, 93
checkride, 64, 89
chemical (threat), 10
Christian conduct, 90
Chronicles, 98
church, local community, 132
    changing, 134
    personalities, 134
coin, 25, 26, 53
Colossians, 60
combat departures, 5
Company Grade Officers' Council. *See*
    CGOC
compromise, 32, 34, 46, 48, 80, 91, 96,
    97
conform, 32, 50, 102, 107, 169
Congress, 73, 75, 76, 77, 80, 82
Constitution, 73
cooperate and graduate, 92
Corinthians, 32, 50, 85, 152, 176
Cornelius, 175
credibility, 42, 48, 88, 95, 96, 97, 103,
    104, 112, 168
Daniel, 34, 35, 47, 48, 49, 102
Dash 1. *See* TO
David, 88, 97, 98, 140, 175
Demas, 44
deployment. *See* TDY
Deuteronomy, 61, 172
discrimination, 65, 66, 67, 69, 71, 74, 80
DoDD 1300.17, 66
dollar ride, 15, 16
Dos Gringos, 27, 38
Ebenezers, 117
Ecclesiastes, 121, 151
eject, 17, 28
Elijah, 102
Elisha, 47, 48
enlisted corps, 167
Ephesians, 40, 60, 63, 93, 111
Esther, 102
evangelism, 45, 65, 82, 83, 84, 134
    military restrictions, 69, 70, 75
    most powerful tool, 85
    peers, 83
    subordinates, 83
    superiors, 83
Excellence in all we do, 64

Index

CPSIA information can be obtained at www.ICGtesting.com
Printed in the USA
LVOW052032300513

336147LV00002B/509/A